ROUTLEDGE LIBRARY EDITIONS: PHONETICS AND PHONOLOGY

Volume 9

PROSODIC CONSTITUENCY IN THE LEXICON

PROSODIC CONSTITUENCY IN THE LEXICON

SHARON INKELAS

LONDON AND NEW YORK

First published in 1991 by Garland Publishing, Inc.

This edition first published in 2019
by Routledge
2 Park Square, Milton Park, Abingdon, Oxon OX14 4RN

and by Routledge
711 Third Avenue, New York, NY 10017

Routledge is an imprint of the Taylor & Francis Group, an informa business

© 1991 Sharon Inkelas

All rights reserved. No part of this book may be reprinted or reproduced or utilised in any form or by any electronic, mechanical, or other means, now known or hereafter invented, including photocopying and recording, or in any information storage or retrieval system, without permission in writing from the publishers.

Trademark notice: Product or corporate names may be trademarks or registered trademarks, and are used only for identification and explanation without intent to infringe.

British Library Cataloguing in Publication Data
A catalogue record for this book is available from the British Library

ISBN: 978-1-138-60364-6 (Set)
ISBN: 978-0-429-43708-3 (Set) (ebk)
ISBN: 978-1-138-31741-3 (Volume 9) (hbk)
ISBN: 978-1-138-31746-8 (Volume 9) (pbk)
ISBN: 978-0-429-45520-9 (Volume 9) (ebk)

Publisher's Note
The publisher has gone to great lengths to ensure the quality of this reprint but points out that some imperfections in the original copies may be apparent.

Disclaimer
The publisher has made every effort to trace copyright holders and would welcome correspondence from those they have been unable to trace.

Prosodic Constituency in the Lexicon

Sharon Inkelas

GARLAND PUBLISHING, INC.
New York • London
1990

Copyright © 1991 by Sharon Inkelas.
All rights reserved.

Library of Congress Cataloging-in-Publication Data

Inkelas, Sharon
Prosodic constituency in the lexicon / Sharon Inkelas.
p. cm. — (Outstanding dissertations in linguistics)
Revision of the author's thesis (Ph. D.)—Stanford University, 1989.
Includes bibliographical references.
ISBN 0-8153-0160-X (alk paper)
1. Prosodic analysis (Linguistics) 2. Lexical phonology. 3. Grammar, Comparative and general—
Morphology. I. Title. II. Series.
P224.I48 1991

414'.6—dc20   90-27274

Printed on acid-free 250-year-life paper

Manufactured in the United States of America

Preface

This is a very lightly revised version of my 1989 dissertation. Besides correcting certain more mundane errors in the original, I have refined the exposition of chapters 4 and 7 and rewritten the introduction (chapter 1) to clarify the main claims of the dissertation.

Much of the thesis would be different were I writing it today. To the extent that this is due to insights contributed in work not cited in the original thesis, I have tried to add footnotes and references directing the reader to that literature. Several works are of sufficiently general relevance to merit mention here; in particular, I would direct the reader to the 1985 dissertation of Richard Sproat, and to the papers from the 1990 Workshop on Lexical Phonology held at the University of Washington, Seattle.

The bibliography has been updated to reflect the publication of a number of works which previously existed only in manuscript form. In all other respects the work remains unaltered.

Abstract

The goal of this thesis is to argue for the existence in the lexicon of a hierarchy of prosodic constituents, coextensive with the domains of lexical phonological rules. These form the lexical half of the prosodic hierarchy of constituents whose postlexical members include the phonological word, phonological phrase and intonational phrase (Selkirk 1978). I argue in support of lexical prosodic structure, as distinct from the copresent morphological structure, by showing that mismatches occur between the two. Two cases of misalignment between rule domains and morphological structure are discussed: those compounds whose members form individual domains for rules, and invisibility effects (in which some member of the morphogical string is excluded from the corresponding rule domain). Construing these phenomena as mismatches between prosodic and morphological structure provides a much more explanatory account than is possible in a framework which posits only a single structure.

A further consequence of the introduction of prosodic structure into the lexicon is the ensuing possibility that morphemes might subcategorize for attachment to prosodic constituents. Lieber 1980 characterized dependent (bound) morphemes as subcategorizing for a morphological sister. I show that lexical dependence can actually be factored into two dimensions: prosodic and morphological. By crossing these two independent dimensions we derive a four-way typology of morphemes corresponding to the recognized categories of affix, bound root, free stem, and clitic. In particular, the assignment of a prosodic subcategorization frame to clitics yields a number of correct predictions about the distribution of clitics across categories and within sentences.

Three sources of prosodic structure are posited. The most general is a mapping algorithm which parses strings into prosodic constituents on the basis of their morphological constituency. A second, more specific source is a rule of compounding which imposes a particular prosodic constituent structure on its output. The third source is prosodic subcategorization frames. These not only constrain the distribution of prosodically bound morphemes but also contribute structure to the representation. Where these various sources of prosodic constituency make conflicting predictions, the Elsewhere Condition causes the most specific to take precedence. These three mechanisms not only generate correspondence between morphological and prosodic structure, but are also capable of deriving all and only the attested mismatches between them.

Acknowledgments

Linguists like to derive specific results from general principles. In that spirit, this thesis on the interactions between different components of grammar derives in large part from the general interactive nature of the diverse Stanford community, where new ideas and rigorous argumentation are not only encouraged but in general insisted upon. To that community, students and faculty alike, I am fondly grateful.

The members of my committee are inextricably involved in this work. Will Leben sparked my initial interest in phonology, and has fed the fire ever since with his unflagging support and challenging arguments. The contributions made by Bill Poser's clear, precise and compendious mind, and his ability to detect unnoticed assumptions, are equalled by his friendship in their importance to my progress. An invaluable source of different perspectives and argumentational rigor, Joan Bresnan has helped me to see phonology in a broader context. And it is hard to imagine a more aptly measured blend of creativity and constructive skepticism than Paul Kiparsky has provided. Although many bad ideas met their reluctant end in his office, a disproportionally larger number of good ones arose there. From him I learned both the importance of detail and the importance (and fun) of rising above it.

In some sense, of course, my committee is an arbitrary subset of the people who contributed to the content of this thesis. The ideas of Draga Zec, in particular, lurk in every corner. Her comments continued to flow even across the Continental Divide, and to the extent that I interpreted them correctly my thesis is the better for it. Cleo Condoravdi never failed to ask an unforseen, probing question at just the right juncture. Her contributions are appreciable and appreciated. Lawan Danladi Yalwa provided many of the insights behind the analysis of Hausa in chapter 8 — and, not a small point, all of the data. Over the years, Jeff Goldberg, Kristin Hanson, Kathryn Henniss and John Stonham have been the source of many specific ideas as well as core elements in the linguistics atmosphere in which this work arose. Finally, these words would be only a handwritten scrawl were it not for the good-humored efforts of Dikran Karagueuzian in reducing the logistical difficulties of finishing a dissertation from afar.

Contents

Preface	v
Abstract	vi
Acknowledgments	viii
1 Introduction	**1**
2 Theoretical Background	**7**
2.1 Postlexical Rule Domains	7
2.2 The Prosodic Hierarchy	8
2.2.1 Domain Clustering	9
2.2.2 Exhaustive Parsing	10
2.2.3 Strict Layering	12
2.3 Arguments for Prosodic Constituency	12
2.3.1 Constituency	13
2.3.2 A Distinct Hierarchy	19
3 Prosodic Structure in the Lexicon	**28**
3.1 Lexical Rule Domains	29
3.1.1 Metrical Constituents	30
3.1.2 New Sublexical Constituents	33
3.2 Morphological vs. Prosodic Structure	35
3.2.1 Compounds	36
3.2.2 Invisibility	36
3.3 Metrical vs. Prosodic Structure	37
3.3.1 Ordering Paradox	38

		3.3.2 Metrical and Prosodic Mismatches	40
	3.4	Constituent Formation	43
	3.5	Bound Roots vs. Stems	48
		3.5.1 Underlying Representations	48
		3.5.2 Spanish	49
		3.5.3 Warlpiri	50
		3.5.4 Malayalam	52
		3.5.5 Analysis	53
	3.6	Summary	54

4 Constructional Constraints on Prosodic Constituency — 55

	4.1	Two Types of Compounds	56
	4.2	Malayalam	60
		4.2.1 The Loop	61
		4.2.2 A Prosodic Solution	62
		4.2.3 Phonological Rules	67
	4.3	English	71
		4.3.1 The Loop	72
		4.3.2 A Prosodic Solution	73
		4.3.3 Phonological Rules	75
	4.4	Summary	77

5 Prosodic Subcategorization — 78

	5.1	Dependence in the Lexicon	79
	5.2	Prosodic Subcategorization	83
	5.3	Selectional Restrictions: the Inner Frame	85
		5.3.1 Active Subcategorization	87
		5.3.2 Affixation to Roots	88
	5.4	Cyclicity: the Outer Frame	91
		5.4.1 Malayalam	91
		5.4.2 English	94
	5.5	Stem Cycle on Nonterminal Constituents	98
		5.5.1 Postcyclic Rules	104
	5.6	Stem Cycle on α Constituents	104
		5.6.1 English	106
		5.6.2 Dakota	108
	5.7	Appendix: Underspecified Subcategorization Frames	112

6	**The Representation of Invisibility**	**115**
6.1	Representation of Invisibility	119
	6.1.1 The Domains Approach	119
6.2	Sources of Mismatched Constituency	121
	6.2.1 The Diacritic Feature Approach	123
6.3	Exhaustive Invisibility	125
	6.3.1 The Diacritic Feature Approach	125
	6.3.2 The Domains Approach	126
6.4	Scope of Invisibility	127
	6.4.1 Across-the-board Invisibility	128
	6.4.2 Inherited Invisibility	133
	6.4.3 The Diacritic Feature Approach	135
6.5	Phonological Content of Invisible Element	135
	6.5.1 Lexical Invisibility	137
	6.5.2 Rule-governed Invisibility	141
6.6	Partial Underlying Invisibility	147
6.7	Peripherality	152
	6.7.1 The Diacritic Feature Approach	155
	6.7.2 The Domains Approach	157
6.8	Multi-source Invisibility	160
	6.8.1 The Diacritic Feature Approach	164
6.9	Bracket Erasure: Cyclic Loss of Invisibility	166
	6.9.1 Persistent Invisibility I: Turkish	168
	6.9.2 Persistent Invisibility II: Japanese	172
	6.9.3 Persistent Invisibility III: Yawelmani	175
	6.9.4 Reappearance of Invisible Elements	177
6.10	Morphological Content of Invisibility	177
	6.10.1 Spanish	178
	6.10.2 Polish	188
6.11	Infixation	195
	6.11.1 Invisibility × Infixation	197
7	**Case Study: Carib**	**203**
7.1	Basic Stress Rule	203
7.2	Cyclicity	211
	7.2.1 Prefixation	214
7.3	Strong Suffixes	217

	7.4	Unaffixed Forms	224
	7.5	Prefixes and Strong Suffixes	226
	7.6	Multiple Suffixation	229
	7.7	Summary	231

8 Clitics   233

	8.1	Clitics vs. Nonclitics	234
	8.2	Clitics and Prosodic Subcategorization	238
	8.3	Prosodic Category of Clitic	241
		8.3.1 Phonological Word: Serbo-Croatian	242
		8.3.2 Phonological Word: English	244
		8.3.3 Phonological Phrase: Hausa	245
		8.3.4 Phonological Phrase: Kivunjo Chaga	255
	8.4	The Clitic Group	259
	8.5	Lexical 'Clitics'	263

9 Implications   266

	9.1	Strict Layering and Exhaustive Parsing	266
	9.2	Bracket Erasure and the Strict Cycle	274
	9.3	Metrical 'Domains'	282

Chapter 1

Introduction

This dissertation introduces Prosodic Lexical Phonology, a theory of the morphology-phonology interaction. The theory has two basic goals. The first is to unify the theoretical treatments of lexical and postlexical phonological rule application. The second is to provide an explanatory account of systematic discrepancies that have been observed between the parsing of strings for purposes of the morphology, and the parsing of those strings into domains of phonological rule application.

Prosodic Lexical Phonology addresses both of these basic challenges in the same fashion: by altering the accepted architecture of the lexicon. Past lexical theories have posited at most two levels of representation in whose terms each string is simultaneously described: the morphological, and the metrical, though theories have differed as to which of those levels phonological rules pay attention to in defining their domains of application within any given string. The Prosodic Hierarchy Theory (Selkirk 1978, 1980, Nespor and Vogel 1982, 1986) assumes that lexical phonological rules apply within the domains described by the various metrical constituents (such as the syllable and foot). Conversely, Lexical Phonology (Kiparsky 1982, Mohanan 1982) assigns that same role to the morphology. The domains of cyclic phonological rules are identified directly with the constituents within morphological structure, while the metrical level of representation is simply one of the many products of phonological rule application.

Prosodic Lexical Phonology departs from both of these views and introduces a third, distinct level of lexical representation. The constituents of this level are termed 'prosodic', and their principal function is to parse a given phonological string into domains for phonological rule application. Neither the morphological nor the metrical level of representation carries this particular burden.

A New Level of Representation

The concept of representing rule domains as constituents derives from the Prosodic Hierarchy Theory, originated by Selkirk (1978), in which abstract constituents such as the phonological word and the phonological phrase are proposed as the domains of postlexical rule application. Selkirk terms these units 'prosodic' and distinguishes them crucially from the syntactic constituents to which they are typically related. In a sense Prosodic Lexical Phonology just extends this existing level of representation into the lexicon.

But several conceptual issues distinguish Prosodic Lexical Phonology and the Prosodic Hierarchy Theory. First, Prosodic Lexical Phonology takes the relationship between morphological/syntactic structure on the one hand, and prosodic structure on the other, to be nontransformational. Both levels of representation are copresent throughout the derivation; both simultaneously describe any given string. By contrast, the Prosodic Hierarchy Theory assumes a unidirectional transformation converting one level into the other, such that co-existence between syntactic and prosodic structure is a definitional impossibility. As discussed in chapter 2, Zec and Inkelas 1990 have argued in favor of co-existence on the basis of evidence from English and Serbo-Croatian that syntax is subject to prosodic constraints, and vice versa. To state these constraints, both levels of representation must be simultaneously present. The claim of Prosodic Lexical Phonology is that similar dual constraints play an role in lexical phenomena as well. Copresence of morphological and prosodic structure is one of the themes pervading the work as a whole.

A second innovation of Prosodic Lexical Phonology lies in the nature of the proposed lexical prosodic constituents. In the past (e.g. Selkirk 1978, Nespor and Vogel 1986), work in the Prosodic Hierarchy Theory has taken the set of phonological rule domains to be coextensive with the set of constituents in phonological representation. Thus the lexical end of the prosodic hierarchy was assumed to consist of all known phonological constituents smaller than the word: namely the metrical units, including the syllable and the foot. Prosodic Lexical Phonology rejects this view. As outlined in chapter 3, the hypothesis of coextensiveness in general, and that of metrical constituents in the prosodic hierarchy in particular, is untenable due to the incompatibility of metrical structure with sublexical rule domains; empirical evidence incontrovertibly supports the prediction of Lexical Phonology (Kiparsky 1982, Mohanan 1982) that phonological rules apply within *morphologically* defined, as opposed to metrically defined, domains. Prosodic Lexical Phonology solves this empirical problem and unifies the treatment of lexical and postlexical rule domains by introducing a new set of sublexical prosodic constituents. These share many properties with postlexical prosodic constituents and virtually no properties with metrical constituents, which form their own distinct hierarchy.

By altering the theoretical underpinnings of lexical phonological rule application, Prosodic Lexical Phonology yields a number of empirical results not available to other theories. These arise primarily in the area of potential mismatches between morphological and prosodic structure, a logical consequence of Prosodic Lexical Phonology's move to separate the two formally in different levels of representation. The discussion of these cases forms a third unifying theme of the thesis. Prosodic Lexical Phonology makes possible exactly two types of mismatch. In chapters 4 and 6 it is argued that these correspond exactly to the two, formerly problematic misalignments actually attested in languages between rule domains and morphological constituents: compounds whose internal boundary is a barrier to rules, and invisibility, or extrametricality, effects. Prosodic Lexical Phonology provides a more explanatory account of these individual phenomena than has been available in the past. And instead of viewing them as peripheral, exceptional effects, it ties them together as complementary facets of the same fundamental process of prosodic constituent formation.

Prosodic Lexical Phonology also yields certain insights into the theory of morphology. Relying on a morpheme-based theory of morphology, along the lines of Lieber 1980 and Kiparsky 1983, Prosodic Lexical Phonology takes morpheme combination to be largely driven by the subcategorization frames of bound, or dependent, elements. In Lieber's framework, bound morphemes were assumed to subcategorize for a morphological sister. Prosodic Lexical Phonology extends this notion to prosodic structure as well. In so doing a number of puzzling discrepancies among the types of bound morphemes fall into place. In chapter 5 it is shown that crossing the independent dimensions of morphological and prosodic subcategorization yields a four-way typology of morphemes: stems, clitics, affixes, and roots. Stems are dependent along neither dimension, affixes are dependent along both, roots are only morphologically dependent, and clitics are only prosodically dependent. As argued in chapter 8, this characterization of clitics explains certain restrictions often observed to hold on the distribution and syntactic categories of clitics, and obviates the need for an additional prosodic category (the 'Clitic Group') which some have claimed is necessary to express the close connection between a clitic and its host (Hayes 1984/1989a, Nespor and Vogel 1986). Instead of forming a separate level in the prosodic hierarchy, clitics form a unit of the same type as the host they subcategorize for. These units are predicted to vary, and indeed clitic hosts are argued to include not only the familiar phonological word, as in Serbo-Croatian and English, but also the phonological phrase, as in Hausa and Kivunjo Chaga.

Thus the phenemona to which Prosodic Lexical Phonology extends are seemingly quite disparate, ranging from the purely phonological (invisibility) to the seemingly morphological (compounds, and bound morpheme types) to the possibly syntactic (cliticization). Instead of being viewed as unrelated blemishes on a theory which predicts a perfect match between morphological and prosodic structure, these phenomena are tied together in Prosodic Lexical Phonology by the common thread of structural mismatches.

Generating Prosodic Structure

A substantial portion of the work centers on the means for generating the prosodic structure which is invoked in the prosodic accounts of morpheme dependence, compounding, cyclicity, invisibility, and cliticization.

A fundamental assumption of Prosodic Lexical Phonology is that all prosodic structure arises in a strictly structure-building, nontransformational manner. This premise permits only a restricted number of sources for prosodic structure. Prosodic structure can be present underlyingly; it can be inserted by a specific morphological rule; or it can result from a general mapping algorithm which is sensitive to the geometry of morphological trees. All three of these sources are tapped in Prosodic Lexical Phonology. All are intrinsically ordered, and all have analogs in postlexical prosodic phonology.

The most general source is a mapping algorithm which will generate prosodic constituent structure for a string dominated by a morphological constituent. This algorithm has its postlexical counterpart in, for example, the phrasing algorithms of Selkirk 1978, Nespor and Vogel 1986, and many others. A second, more specific source of prosodic constituency lies in morphological rules — ie., in rules of compounding (the only morpheme combination performed by rule in the morphological theory being assumed here). Chapter 4 discusses the familiar case of compounds whose bipartite prosodic structure is not generable by the one-to-one mapping algorithm. Since the prosodic structure of these comopunds is construction-specific, Prosodic Lexical Phonology generates them by a rule of compounding which is special in that it imposes constraints on the prosodic constituency of its output: in particular, it maps each input morphological constituent into a separate prosodic constituent. This constructional source of prosodic structure has a counterpart outside of the lexicon as well. Zec and Inkelas 1987, 1990 describe a class of syntactic constructions in English and Serbo-Croatian whose prosodic requirements cannot be attributed to general phrasing algorithms. They analyze these constructions as imposing their own direct constraints on prosodic structure. In both the lexical and the postlexical components, construction-specific sources of prosodic structure take precedence over the more general mapping algorithms that build prosodic constituents in the default case.

The third and most specific source of prosodic structure is lexical: namely, prosodic subcategorization frames. Prosodic Lexical Phonology interprets such frames as partial prosodic trees, whose need for their missing element to be supplied drives morpheme combination in general. This 'active' view of subcategorization as actual prosodic structure provides a means for individual morphemes to influence the geometry of prosodic constituent trees, both in the lexicon (in the case of affixation) and postlexically (in the case of cliticization). In each case the morpheme-specific prosodic information will block the application of the more general mapping algorithms. As the only source of prosodic structure in underlying representation, prosodic subcategorization frames provide the sole means of capturing lexical exceptionality to generalizations about prosodic structure.

In the unmarked case the mapping algorithm and prosodic subcategorization frames generate prosodic constituency which closely matches the corresponding morphological structure. However, each of these sources is also potentially capable of joining the compounding rule in generating mismatches between morphological and prosodic constituency.

Though the norm is for prosodic and morphological subcategorization frames of affixes to match, specifying marked information lexically on prosodic frames can lead to the mismatches underlying invisibility effects, as is discussed extensively in chapter 6. Even the phrasing algorithm is subject to parametric variation that can produce mismatches in the default case, as argued in chapter 7. Chapters 5 and 6 confirm that independently motivated constraints on phonological rules and representations predict that all and only the attested mismatches are generated by the various sources the theory provides for prosodic constituency. Thus the prosodic theory, while more flexible than theories which posit only one structure in the lexicon, is at the same time appropriately constrained.

General Theoretical Assumptions

In addition to the main themes, discussed above, a number of subsidiary themes run underground throughout the thesis. One is the general attempt to construe phonological rules as strictly structure-building, assigning structure just in case none is already present. Though derivational, the generation of prosodic structure is crucially nontransformational. Relying on the existence of underspecified representations, this structure-building property holds exceptionlessly for the prosodic constituent formation algorithms invoked in the thesis and pervades the other phonological rules as well. Related closely to this theme is the Elsewhere Condition (Kiparsky 1972), which ensures a disjunctive ordering between a more specific and a more general source of phonological structure, in favor of the former. This in turn leads to another subsidiary theme, the treatment of lexical exceptionality. In this dissertation all exceptional behavior is encoded in a principled fashion by specifying exceptional forms in underlying representation with the structure that makes them exceptional. Underlyingly present, this independently needed phonological material overrides (by the Elsewhere Condition) the application of later, potentially neutralizing phonological rules. No diacritic exception features are needed. A fourth subtheme is a strict adherence to locality. Not only are the algorithms building prosodic structure subject to locality, but so are all the phonological rules invoked in the thesis. Finally, intrinsic ordering is sought as far as possible. In cases where extrinsic ordering is admitted, at least in cases of prosodic constituent formation, the entire range of possibilities is explored and shown to be attested.

Though referred to here as subsidiary, these themes are crucially important to Prosodic Lexical Phonology. They provide the constraints which counterbalance the increased descriptive power of the theory's additional level of representation. Such constraints are of especial importance given that the rearrangement of prosodic and morphological structure introduced by Prosodic Lexical Phonology leads necessarily to the abandonment or amendment of several principles, important to past theories, with which it is no longer compatible. These are discussed in chapter 9 and include the Strict Layer Hypothesis of Selkirk 1984; the Strict Cycle Condition of Mascaro 1978 (see also Kean 1974 and Kiparsky 1982); and Prosodic Licensing (Itô 1986).

To summarize, Prosodic Lexical Phonology provides a formal level of representation at which the seemingly distinct morphology-phonology and syntax-phonology interactions look identical. It draws together such varied phenomena as the typology of morpheme dependence; extrametricality; cyclicity; infixation; and cliticization as complementary exponents of a complex system of phonological rule domain generation. This unified prosodic treatment makes unnecessary a number of unproductive stipulations of previous theories, and results in greater generality.

Chapter 2

Theoretical Background

The prosodic hierarchy theory, as conceived by Selkirk 1978 and elaborated in Selkirk 1980, 1986, Nespor and Vogel 1982, 1986, Hayes 1984/1989a and others, has been motivated mainly by issues in postlexical phonology, phenomena relating to the word-sized and larger entities in the hierarchy. In what follows we will review the arguments and evidence for construing postlexical phonological rule domains as constituents in a single hierarchy which exists independently of syntactic structure — i.e., evidence for the postlexical prosodic hierarchy theory, with the ultimate goal of using similar arguments to motivate a lexical prosodic hierarchy as well.

2.1 Postlexical Rule Domains

A starting point for theories of postlexical rule domains has been the following set of cross-linguistic empirical observations:

(1)
  a. Domain Clustering: There are fewer postlexical rule domains than there are postlexical rules; that is, in each language, there is a small, fixed set of domains (D), and each postlexical rule in the language applies within at least one of these domains.
  b. Exhaustive Parsing: Every utterance is exhaustively parsed by each domain in D.

c. Strict Layering: Within each language, the domains in D are strictly ordered along a scale such that (except for the very largest domain) each domain is properly contained within a domain of the next higher level in the scale.

2.2 The Prosodic Hierarchy

The prosodic hierarchy theory has aimed to explain the facts in (1) by hypothesizing that phonological rule domains actually consist of a small, universally determined number of prosodic constituents, organized into a nonrecursive hierarchy which is distinct from syntactic structure. One such hierarchy, that proposed in Selkirk 1978, is given below:[1]

(2) utterance
  |
  intonation phrase
  |
  phonological phrase
  |
  phonological word
  |
  foot
  |
  syllable

Accompanying this postulated hierarchy is the Strict Layer Hypothesis (Selkirk 1984, 1986), enforcing well-formedness in the constituent tree. The following statement of this hypothesis is taken from from Nespor and Vogel 1986:7:

---

[1]This is the sparest of all the proposed hierarchies. Potential additional constitituents have been suggested in subsequent work. Hayes 1984/1989a and Nespor and Vogel 1986 propose to include the clitic group between the phonological word and the phonological phrase; Itô 1988, Hayes 1989b and Zec 1988b argue for adding the mora as the lowest constituent. Condoravdi 1990 presents evidence from Modern Greek for a constituent ('z') which intervenes between the clitic group and the phonological phrase. Kanerva 1989, 1990 argues that effects in Chicheŵa of focus on phonological rules can be accounted for by the addition to the hierarchy of the 'focal phrase', which he hypothesizes is higher than the phonological phrase and lower than the intonation phrase.

2.2. THE PROSODIC HIERARCHY

(3) Strict Layer Hypothesis:

   a. A given nonterminal unit of the prosodic hierarchy, X^p, is composed of one or more units of the immediately lower category, X^{p-1}.
   b. A unit of a given level of the hierarchy is exhaustively contained in the superordinate unit of which it is a part.

The prosodic hierarchy theory has typically been defended by comparing it favorably with a particular alternative hypothesis, characterized by Odden 1987 as the 'direct reference' model (p. 13). Assumed in the detailed study of Kaisse 1985, and argued for explicitly in Odden 1987, 1990 (see also Chen 1990), this latter approach essentially claims that phonological rule domains themselves have no formal representation in the grammar. Rather, they are merely interpreted by each phonological rule on the basis of the information present in labeled syntactic constituent structure, to which they directly refer.

Indeed, in terms of explaining the first three facts mentioned above, the prosodic hierarchy theory fares better than a direct reference model.

2.2.1 Domain Clustering

By positing a small, universal set of prosodic domains which is instantiated in each language,[2] the prosodic hierarchy theory is able to account for the clustering behavior of postlexical rules. This is achieved by imposing the additional claim that once prosodic domains are introduced as formal entities in the grammar, phonological rules then need to refer only to these domains, and never directly to the syntactic constituent structure constraining the original construction of the prosodic domains.

---

[2]The creation of these domains is sensitive to various parameters of X' structure. According to Selkirk 1986, the relevant information is location of edges of particular projections. Nespor and Vogel 1982, 1986, Hayes 1984/1989a and many others argue that the distinction between head and complement is also necessary. McHugh 1985 invokes the notion of c-command. Cowper and Rice 1987, Inkelas 1988, Bickmore 1990 and Zec and Inkelas 1987 propose that branchingess of nodes must be considered. Along with branching, Zec and Inkelas take sisterhood to be crucial as well. Some notion of focus is argued to be relevant in Selkirk 1984, Inkelas 1988, Cho 1990, Zec and Inkelas 1987, Selkirk and Shen 1990, Vogel and Kenesei 1990, and Kanerva 1989, 1990. Finally, the algorithms of Nespor and Vogel 1986 and Selkirk and Shen 1990 refer to the difference between content and function word (but see Zec and Inkelas 1987, and chapter 8, for arguments that this distinction is more appropriately captured prosodically). Bickmore 1990 and Cho 1990 discuss and compare of some of these various approaches to the parameterization of syntactically relevant information.

This hypothesis is tentatively suggested in Selkirk 1986 and assumed explicitly in later work (Zec and Inkelas 1987, Zec and Inkelas 1990). We may state it as follows:

(4) Indirect Reference Hypothesis: phonological rules refer to only prosodic constituent structure

When constrained by this important hypothesis, the prosodic hierarchy theory has an explanation for the clustering effect of postlexical rule domains.

In contrast, any similarity among the domains of different rules could only be viewed as an accident on a direct reference model, where each rule looks independently at syntactic structure to determine its domain of application. At best, one could stipulate a limited set of parameters for each language, which rules can use to set up their syntactic environments. For example, the parameters suggested by Selkirk 1986 for governing the algorithms which generate prosodic domains (level of projection in the syntax, and right vs. left end of a constituent) might be construed as actually regulating the kind of information phonological rules may refer to. However, the values of these parameters have to be repeated in the syntactic environment for each individual rule, entirely missing the generalization that domains cluster.

2.2.2 Exhaustive Parsing

'Exhaustive parsing' refers to the observation that for each postlexical rule, every segment in the utterance will be incorporated into some domain on which that rule applies. That is to say, no subpart of an utterance will automatically be invisible to the rule by virtue of its syntactic properties. We do not find cases, for example, where the first element of an utterance fails for syntactic reasons to undergo a rule applying to the initial element of a phonological phrase, or word. Instead, every utterance-initial element will also be a phrase-initial and a word-initial element.[3] Since allowing the grammar to incorporate only some, but not all, elements into rule domains would allow for unmotivated contrasts, we may safely hypothesize that a theory which can incorporate an exhaustive parsing constraint is to be preferred over one which cannot.

The exhaustive parsing generalization obtains a simple statement in the prosodic hierarchy model, where it takes the form of a well-formedness constraint on the parsing

---

[3]Of course, there will be cases where for *phonological* reasons a phrase-initial rule fails to apply to the initial element of an utterance; phonologically conditioned extrametricality would fall into this category. However, these cases are not relevant here.

2.2. THE PROSODIC HIERARCHY

of syntactically labeled strings into prosodic constituents.

A formal statement of this constraint is given below, amended slightly from that of Selkirk 1986:384:

(5) Exhaustive Parsing: For any domain in the set, the sentence (utterance) is exhaustively parsed into a sequence of such domains.

By contrast, in the direct reference model where each rule looks individually to syntactic structure to determine its own domain of application, there is no natural way of ruling out the hypothetical, unattested situation where only a subpart of a given string is selected to form a domain for some rule, leaving the remainder of the string ineligible even to be scanned by the rule.

Let us consider how one might incorporate the exhaustive parsing constraint into the direct reference model, where each rule will be listed with both a phonological and a syntactic environment. In order to force the domains which each rule finds to apply in to exhaustively cover each utterance, we will need to place an unusual, if not impossible, condition on the syntactic environment of the rule: the environment must be such that it is met by every utterance. Such a condition would prohibit a rule that applies only within PP's, or only within branching NP's, for example, since not every utterance contains these constituents.

But this is certainly a different interpretation of rule environment from the one given to phonological environments of rules. A rule which applies to a focus F in the environment of a determinant D does not require each string it scans to contain D.

And even if we could find a way to implement this condition, it would still not be sufficient to guarantee exhaustive parsing. Suppose, for example, that a phonological rule P applies only within the configuration described by Q. Ensuring that every utterance is divisible into substrings each of which contains the syntactic environment Q still does not guarantee that each substring will be exhaustively described by Q — but that is what it will take in order for the entire substring to form a domain for P.

Thus, we see that a constraint that is captured naturally in the prosodic hierarchy theory is difficult if not impossible to impose on a direct reference model, an imbalance which argues in favor of the prosodic hierarchy theory.

2.2.3 Strict Layering

By establishing an implicational, subset relationship holding among all prosodic domains, the prosodic hierarchy theory explains why there is no overlap among the domains of different rules; i.e., the fact that if a string a is (properly) contained within a prosodic unit p_i then it will also be properly contained by the prosodic unit p_{i+1}, one level up on the implicational scale shown in (2). By contrast, the direct reference model offers no explanation for this relationship among domains of different types, since the rules which select these different domains are independent of one another.

In fact, it is not clear how one could impose the constraint of strict layering on a direct reference model at all, even if one were willing to resort to stipulations. As we mentioned, strict layering is a relationship holding among domains at different levels. Yet under the direct reference model, where rule domains have no representation of their own, this constraint will have to be stated in terms of the rules which apply within the relevant domains. Thus to establish its own domain of application, each rule will need knowledge of the domains of all the other rules in the postlexical phonology. The attempt to state a formal constraint on rule domains falters in the absence of a formal characterization of rule domains.

2.3 Arguments for Prosodic Constituency

The prosodic hierarchy model is favored over the direct reference model because it offers a formal representation for rule domains and, therein, the necessary means for stating constraints and generalizations holding over those domains. Explaining domain clustering, strict layering and exhaustive parsing requires only that rule domains must be formal entities, organized into an implicational relationship along the lines in (6):

(6)   phonological word < phonological phrase < intonation phrase < utterance

But accepting that rule domains have some formal representation in the grammar still does not mean accepting the prosodic hierarchy theory, since this theory makes at least three further claims about the nature of these entities. First, it claims that all rule domains are constituents, and second, it claims that these constituents are all phonological, not syntactic. Its third claim, that all phonological constituents are

2.3. ARGUMENTS FOR PROSODIC CONSTITUENCY

rule domains, I will argue against later; for now, we may concern ourselves only with the statements in (7).

(7) Constituency Hypothesis:

  a. If a stretch of phonological material functions as a domain for phonological rules then it is a constituent in phonological representation
  b. The constituents corresponding to rule domains are phonological, as opposed to syntactic

In what follows I will address the issue of constituency, developing arguments that postlexical rule domains are in fact constituents in a prosodic hierarchy. I will also argue in support of the further claim, advanced in Zec and Inkelas 1990, that prosodic structure is autonomous, existing side-by-side with and independently of syntactic constituent structure.

(8) Copresence Hypothesis: Prosodic and syntactic structure are autonomous and copresent

2.3.1 Constituency

A plausible objection to the prosodic hierarchy theory is that if the units referred to as word, phrase, etc. function merely as domains for rules, there is no real motivation for construing them as constituents (Kaisse 1990).

The alternative would be to represent these domains simply as spans, the material contained between certain entities represented in the syntactic string. Under such an account, no higher structure would need to be referred to. And entities of this sort have, of course, been offered in the literature, most notably in the boundary symbol proposals of SPE. Early analyses of syntactic effects on phonology were formulated in terms of these boundary symbols (see e.g. Selkirk 1972, Selkirk 1974, and Rotenberg 1978, among others). In such a framework, domains are interpreted on the basis of some structural properties of the representation, but need not themselves correspond to any one structural node.

(9) No-Constituent Hypothesis: Rule domains are not constituents in any hierarchical representation, but are demarcated by boundary symbols residing among the terminal elements of syntactic constituent structure. There are as many different types of boundary symbols as there are postlexical rule domains; each domain D_i is defined as the span between boundary symbols of type b_i.

I believe it is true that the three generalizations discussed earlier, about the number of postlexical rule domains and about the relationships between them, could all actually be implemented as constraints on the number and distribution of boundary symbols; they do not require a prosodic constituent tree in order to be formalized.[4]

In order to argue crucially for the constituency of phonological rule domains, we will thus need to appeal to a rather different source of evidence, one which has not been paid much attention in the literature. In the next section I will draw on some recent work by Zec 1987 (also discussed in Zec and Inkelas 1990) which argues from the perspective of constituent weight for the constituency of phonological rule domains. In particular, Zec shows that size constraints on the topic construction in Serbo-Croatian and on the Heavy NP-shift construction in English are properly stated

---

[4]Mohanan 1982, 1986 presents a number of arguments to the effect that a theory which uses boundary symbols is more powerful than one that does not, and that this extra power is not warranted. Examples of this unwanted power include the predicted ability of rules to insert, delete, transpose, or refer to more than one different type of boundary symbol. Thus parsimony might present additional arguments against representing rule domains as stretches in between boundary symbols. However, at least some of the putatively unattested types of operations mentioned by Mohanan have actually been invoked in later work, though expressed in terms of the prosodic framework. Creation of prosodic structure by means of algorithms, a backbone of prosodic theory, corresponds in some sense to the insertion of boundary symbols, while rules restructuring prosodic constituent structure (see e.g. Nespor and Vogel 1986) would have the effect of deleting boundary symbols in a boundary symbol framework. In chapter 6 I invoke rules which change the location of the the edge of a prosodic constituent with respect to the phonological material that it dominates. This might alternatively be viewed as metathesizing a boundary symbol and some phonological material.

One possibility that Mohanan mentions is still, as far as I know, unattested. This is the hypothetical situation in which a rule might simultaneously refer to two different types of boundary symbols in its environment (Mohanan 1986:144). Actually, this hypothetical and unwelcome rule could be formulated just as easily in terms of constituents as in terms of boundary symbols. However, in both frameworks rules of this type can be ruled out on independent grounds anyway. Locality conditions on rule environments and principles of bracket erasure make the rules impossible to state. (Environments like # ___ + will be impossible to satisfy, assuming the bracket erasure convention adopted in this thesis and elsewhere; environments of the type # + ___ are prohibited by locality conditions (see Poser 1985b).)

Thus, while it would be nice to make use of the argument that a boundary approach is more powerful than the data warrant (and, to complete the argument, more powerful than a constituent-based approach), it is not clear that this is actually true.

2.3. ARGUMENTS FOR PROSODIC CONSTITUENCY

only in prosodic terms. In the framework of the prosodic hierarchy, the generalization is that Serbo-Croatian topics and heavy English NP's must correspond to branching prosodic constituents.

English

The proper characterization of heaviness has been a long-standing problem for syntacticians; syntactic branchingness alone is not sufficient to qualify an NP as heavy, as the following example shows:

(10) *Mary showed to John that letter

However, some degree of syntactic complexity is relevant. As Zec observes, NP's with material following the head tend to count as heavy:

(11) Mary showed to John that letter of resignation

Zec suggests that the explanation for the contrast in grammaticality between (10) and (11) lies in the prosodic structures of these two sentences. According to the phonological phrasing algorithm developed for English by Zec and Inkelas 1987, the NP in (10) will obtain the prosodic structure in (12), while that in (11) will obtain the structure in (13):

(12)

(13)

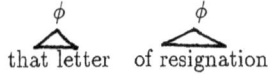

To prove that the syntactic criterion of having material following the head is not sufficient, and that the prosodic requirement is the relevant one, consider the following pair of sentences:

(14)
    a. Mary gave to Susan that report on Dukakis.
    b. *Mary gave to Susan that report on him.

In this pair of examples, the syntactic constituent structure is identical; where the two differ is in their prosodic structure. According to Zec and Inkelas, unemphasized object pronouns such as *him* in (14b) are always enclitics in English. That is, they do not constitute phonological words on their own. As a result, *on him* is a single phonological word, and by the phrasing algorithm developed for English in that same paper, will have to phrase with the material on the left. As a result, *that report on him* is a single phonological phrase. By contrast, *Dukakis* does form its own phonological word, and together with *on* constitutes a well-formed phonological phrase. As (15) shows, the direct object NP in (14a) differs from the NP in (14b) in that only the former is prosodically branching.

(15)

These facts strongly support Zec's hypothesis that prosodic branching is the proper characterization of heavy NP's in English.

Serbo-Croatian

In English, the subconstituents into which a heavy constituent must branch are phonological phrases. A similar effect is found in the Serbo-Croatian topic construction, with the crucial difference that in this case, the units into which topics must branch are phonological words.

Zec 1987 (see also Zec and Inkelas 1990) shows that to be grammatical, a left dislocated topic in Serbo-Croatian must qualify as heavy, a property which cannot be characterized in syntactic terms. Syntactic branching is neither necessary nor sufficient to make a topic heavy. However, prosodic branching is both necessary and sufficient. This can be shown by examining the four types of topics generated by the possible combinations of the binary property of branchingess along the two dimensions of prosodic and syntactic structure.

2.3. ARGUMENTS FOR PROSODIC CONSTITUENCY

The relevant level of prosodic structure is the phonological word. As argued in Zec and Inkelas 1990, these prosodic units are created lexically, where they form the domains for a number of phonological rules; that phonological words are also visible postlexically is demonstrated by the fact that clitics are crucially ordered with respect to them.

With this in mind, let us now turn to some examples. As mentioned, topics which branch both syntactically and prosodically will count as heavy, and such a case is given in (16). The syntactic and prosodic structures for the topic are presented in (17) (the following examples are from Zec and Inkelas 1990).

(16) Taj   čovek   voleo je   Mariju
      That(Nom)   man(Nom)   loved Aux-Cl Mary(Acc)
      'That man loved Mary'

(17)

By contrast, the topic in the ungrammatical sentence in (18) branches neither syntactically nor prosodically, as shown in (19):

(18) *Petar   voleo je   Mariju
       Peter(Nom) loved Aux-Cl Mary(Acc)
       'Peter loved Mary'

(19)

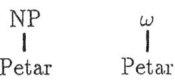

The examples which actually demonstrate that it is prosodic branching which is relevant are those where the syntactic and prosodic branchingness of the topic do not match.

The first such case is in (20), where the topic branches only syntactically. As a proclitic, the preposition does not constitute its own phonological word, and as we see in (21) the PP is thus prosodically nonbranching, rendering (19) ungrammatical.

(20) *Sa   Petrom   razgovarala je   samo Marija
     With Peter(Ins)   talked   Aux-Cl   only Mary(Nom)
     'To Peter, only Mary talked'

(21)

Finally, if a topic branches prosodically but not syntactically, it will still qualify as heavy, as shown by the sentence in (22).

(22) U   Rio de Žaneiru   ostali   su   dve godine
     In Rio de Janeiro(Nom)   stayed   Aux-Cl   two years
     'In Rio de Janeiro, they stayed two years'

The proper name *Rio de Žaneiro* counts as two phonological words in Serbo-Croatian; both *Rio* and *de Žaneiro* undergo word-bounded rules of tone insertion and stress assignment (Inkelas and Zec 1990). However, the name is a single unit for syntactic purposes, as shown in part by the inability of the first half (*Rio*) to inflect. Crucially, the proper name *Rio de Žaneiro* counts as heavy and can be used as a topic. It contrasts with *Petar* (18), which is prosodically nonbranching and hence ungrammatical in topic position.

(23)

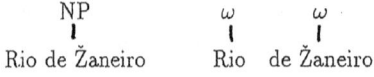

2.3. ARGUMENTS FOR PROSODIC CONSTITUENCY

Zec concludes that in Serbo-Croatian as in English, heaviness is characterized as the property of containing two prosodic domains. Heaviness is a prosodic phenomenon. The prosodic hierarchy theory offers a natural account of heaviness by providing the parameter of branchingness as a means of distinguishing prosodically heavy from non-heavy constituents. The appeal of this treatment lies not only in its descriptive adequacy but also in its explanatory power; as we know from other prosodic phenomena (e.g. syllable weight, and the difference between branching and unary feet), branchingess is the typical correlate of prosodic 'size' elsewhere in phonology. The branching constraints in Serbo-Croatian and English are just one instance of a more general phenomenon.

The ability of the prosodic hierarchy theory to handle heaviness constraints is not matched by that of the boundary symbol framework. Unlike the properties of hierarchical ordering and exhaustive parsing, prosodic branchingness can not be defined in the absence of prosodic constituents. The correlate of a prosodically branching NP in a boundary symbol approach to prosodic domains would be the requirement that an NP contain some arbitrary number of boundary symbols. For the Serbo-Croatian case, following an SPE-type algorithm for assigning word boundary symbols, the minimum number necessary to guarantee heaviness should be four ($[\# \: Rio \: \# \: \# \: de \: Žaneiro \: \#]_{NP}$ vs. $[\# \: sa \: \# \: Petrom \: \#]_{NP}$). That is, the heaviness 'parameter' will be many-valued instead of binary-valued. A prediction would then be that the different possible values of heaviness might be distinctive, but this possibility is unattested and certainly seems remote. Furthermore, it is not at all clear that the ability to count should be within the scope of syntactic constraints; it is certainly not needed in phonology, as argued in Poser 1985b. A final defect of the boundary symbol approach is its failure to capture any correlation between NP heaviness and syllable heaviness, even though both are structurally defined properties of weight (Zec 1988b).

We may thus conclude from these facts that one further claim of the prosodic hierarchy theory can be supported, namely that rule domains are constituents.

2.3.2 A Distinct Hierarchy

With this argument behind us, we may now address the second unresolved area mentioned above, namely the precise nature of the prosodic constituents corresponding to rule domains. That is, must these constituents occupy their own level of representation, as proposed in Selkirk 1978, 1980, or can we represent them simply by readjusting the entities already present in syntactic constituent structure so that they correspond to the 'prosodic' structure required by rule domains (the position taken in SPE)? Assuming that we do end up accepting a second, non-syntactic, prosodic level of representation, the additional question arises of the relationship between the prosodic hierarchy and the syntactic phrase-structure tree.

The approach to rule-domain constituents which is most representationally parsimonious is essentially that assumed in SPE, which I term the Single-Level Hypothesis. On this account, the entities input to the phonological rule component are the same as the entities manipulated in the syntactic component, merely rearranged a little.

(24) Single-Level Hypothesis: Rule domains are constituents, but belong to readjusted syntactic structure. That is, they do not constitute a distinct level of representation. The process which restructures surface syntactic constituents into those corresponding to rule domains respects the constraints of strict layering and exhaustive parsing.

No restructuring analyses of this kind have been worked out in detail,[5] but we can assume that such a process would take as input a tree whose geometry corresponds exactly to surface syntactic structure and produce as output a tree whose internal geometry has been adjusted to correspond exactly to the hierarchically arranged set of phonological rule domains for the sentence in question.

Under such an account, what were described in the preceding section as prosodic constraints on syntactic structure will have to be interpreted as filters constraining the output of restructuring. Non-heavy NP's in English and PP's in Serbo-Croatian may branch at the input to restructuring, but they will not branch in the output. Conversely, while a Serbo-Croatian topic need not branch at the input to restructuring, it must branch in the output. Thus the input structure can be geometrically distinct from the output: neither need subsume the other.

This raises some serious questions about what constraints, if any, will hold on the restructuring process. As the Serbo-Croatian case shows, restructuring cannot be regarded merely as a flattening process (the typical outcome in SPE restructuring effects). Instead, it must create constituents where none existed previously, as in the case of *Rio de Žaneiro*. Moreover, as this same example shows, the (postlexical) restructuring process must have access to the lexical identity of morphemes in order to know which proper names will map into one phonological word and which will not.

Thus, restructuring rules will have be quite powerful. Furthermore, their output will not obey many of the constraints which hold on its input; for example, due

---

[5] However, see Selkirk 1984 for a restructuring analysis of object pronoun encliticization in English.

2.3. ARGUMENTS FOR PROSODIC CONSTITUENCY

to flattening, constituents can be created which would not otherwise be licensed by phrase structure rules.

(25)

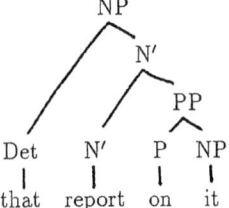

becomes

(26)

Because the string in (25) corresponds to only one phonological phrase (26), the output of restructuring must provide only one node of the type corresponding to the phrasal domain. But no syntactic constituent in English will ever have a determiner, noun and preposition as its daughters. In that the output can be of such a different nature than the input, syntactic restructuring thus differs from other restructuring processes known to occur; for example, in two familiar cases of restructuring in phonology, resyllabification and the Obligatory Contour Principle (Leben 1978, McCarthy 1979), the resulting structure obeys the same constraints as the input structure. (In fact, these cases of restructuring are repair strategies, triggered by the creation of a configuration in the input structure which violates some structural constraint.) But in the kind of restructuring assumed in hypothesis (24), whatever constraints (if any) hold on the output structure differ greatly from those holding on the input.

Thus, this particular kind of restructuring would appear to be an extremely powerful, unconstrained device. Its only apparent virtue is that it allows one to maintain what I will term the 'Transformation Hypothesis.' This is the idea that syntactically relevant constituent structure and phonologically relevant constituent structure are derivationally related and, concomitantly, that once the latter has been created, the former is no longer relevant.

(27) Transformation Hypothesis: syntactic and prosodic structure are transformationally related

As the work of Selkirk 1978, 1980 demonstrates, restructuring is not the only way to maintain this hypothesis: the ordering relationship between syntax and phonology is equally compatible with the idea that syntactic and prosodic structure are different levels of representation. Instead of assuming that the phonological phrase is a restructured maximal projection in syntactic phrase structure, the prosodic hierarchy theory takes this entity to be of a different kind altogether: a prosodic node. Selkirk proposes that prosodic entities are created from syntactic ones by a mapping, $\emptyset/s/p$ in (28):

(28) $\{S_1, ... S_i, ... S_k\} \emptyset/s/p \{P_1, ... P_n\}$

[Selkirk 1980:108]

The mapping in (28) has the same empirical effect as restructuring rules, and the model, with its two distinct levels of representation (S and P), circumvents the need to mold syntactic constituents into shapes and forms not licensed by syntactic constraints.

We may therefore discard the restructuring proposal, since its only apparent advantage also characterizes a proposal which shares fewer of its disadvantages. In fact, however, I will argue that maintaining the Transformation Hypothesis is itself not an advantage at all, as the hypothesis is wrong.

The idea that syntactic and prosodic structure are transformationally related persists, not because of empirical evidence in its favor or theoretical arguments from within work on rule domains, but because it accords with the commonly accepted T-model of grammar, in which all phonology is assumed to take place after all syntax.[6] However, a mounting body of evidence suggests that this hypothesis is not correct.

---

[6] As evidence that I am correctly characterizing the views of proponents of the T-model and the prosodic hierarchy theory, here is the position of Vogel and Kenesei 1990: "...the only way syntax interacts with phonology is through the application of a set of mapping rules which convert a syntactic surface structure into a phonological structure ... additional phonological rules, the so-called prosodic domains rules, may then apply to this structure." Although most authors are not as

2.3. ARGUMENTS FOR PROSODIC CONSTITUENCY

In what follows I will present two kinds of evidence showing that there must be a stage in the derivation of utterances at which syntactic and prosodic structure are copresent. This answers two of our questions at once. First, as was foreshadowed above, the constituents to which rule domains correspond occupy a prosodic level of representation, not the syntactic hierarchy. Second, the prosodic hierarchy and the syntactic hierarchy must exist side-by-side in the grammar. The syntax-phonology mapping expresses correspondences between the geometry of the two structures, but it does not transform one into the other. This is the position taken in Zec and Inkelas 1990, and I will argue for it in some detail below.[7]

The first of the two general arguments I will present comes from the set of algorithms proposed for deriving prosodic structure in the literature. Essentially any stepwise procedures in the generation of prosodic structure call into question the notion that there is only one structure present at a given time.

First, creating different prosodic constituents in the order in which they appear in the hierarchy, as is commonly assumed, leads to inconsistencies in other assumptions about the nature of tree structures. For example, phonological words are generally assumed to be formed before phrases are built. Yet in order to construct phrases syntactic information must be present. Thus it appears that there must be a stage in the derivation when both prosodic and syntactic constituents exist. Theories which disallow copresence of prosodic and syntactic hierarchies will have to posit hybrid structures in which syntactic constituents dominate phonological words.

A worse problem in this same class is presented by algorithms which themselves are stepwise. Consider the following example from a work whose authors take the position that the existence of prosodic structure logically follows and supplants syntactic structure. Nespor and Vogel 1982, 1986 propose that phonological phrasing is generated in two stages. First, a universal algorithm forms phonological phrases on the basis of syntactic information. Second, language-specific restructuring processes merge adjacent phrases under certain conditions. Crucially, these conditions are syntactic. The example phrasing process below is adapted from Nespor and Vogel 1982:

---

explicit, it is true that most work in prosodic hierarchy theory does implicitly accept the Indirect Reference Hypothesis, as well as the hypothesis that syntax cannot access phonological structure. Taken in tandem these positions are essentially equivalent to the Transformation Hypothesis.

[7]Zec and Inkelas restrict the possible interactions between the copresent syntactic and prosodic modules to reference to constituent structure.

(29)
   a. Phonological phrasing algorithm: Join into a phonological phrase any lexical head (X) with all items on its nonrecursive side within the maximal projection and with any other nonlexical items on the same side

   b. Restructuring clause: A nonbranching phonological phrase which is the first complement of X on its recursive side loses its label and is joined to the phonological phrase containing X.

Rules of the kind in (29b) must refer simultaneously to prosodic and to syntactic structure — again tacitly requiring the two kinds of structure to be copresent.[8] And in this case we cannot resort to the sorts of hybrid structures postulated just above in order to maintain the claim that only one constituent tree is present at any given stage in the syntax-phonology connection. For the phonological phrasing algorithm in (29) to work, the very syntactic constituent nodes which are input to clause (a) of the algorithm (i.e. maximal projections) must still be visible — as syntactic nodes — to clause (b). But this is impossible, given that clause (a) will already have mapped those syntactic nodes into prosodic ones.

Consider, for concreteness, the following example from French:

(30)

```
          AP
         /  \
       Adv   AP
        |    |
       trés  intelligent
```

The phrasing algorithm will map the adverb and lower AP into separate phonological phrases.

---

[8]If we wanted to beat this into the ground we could mention an embedded problem. Suppose, as is commonly assumed, that phonological words are built before phonological phrases exist. This means that the syntactic terminals which get converted into those phonological words will not, on a transformational account, be available to the subsequent phrasing algorithm. But with them goes the head/nonhead distinction taken to be crucial to many phrasing algorithms — wreaking havoc for the phrasing system.

2.3. ARGUMENTS FOR PROSODIC CONSTITUENCY

(31)

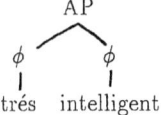

$$
\begin{array}{c}
\text{AP} \\
\phi \quad \phi \\
| \quad | \\
\text{trés} \quad \text{intelligent}
\end{array}
$$

On the assumption that prosodic structure supplants, instead of coexisting with, syntactic structure, we must assume that the result of the phrasing algorithm is to get rid of the lower AP node and insert a ϕ node in its stead. But given the representation in (31) it is impossible to apply the restructuring clause — which needs to know the syntactic identity of that final phonological phrase. As a result it should not be possible to collapse the adverb and adjective into a single phrase, though, as Nespor and Vogel show, this is the desired result.

(32) [très intelligent]$_\phi$

Restructuring rules and stepwise constituent formation are simply inconsistent with the idea that syntax and phonology are ordered components, that entering the latter entails exiting the former. But they present no problems for a theory like that of Zec and Inkelas 1990, which posits copresent, related structures, to which rules may make simultaneous reference.[9]

It is conceivable that ways could be found to generate prosodic structure in a non-stepwise manner, in which case this class of objections will no longer be relevant. However, recent work by Inkelas and Zec has introduced new and even less easily reanalyzed evidence that syntactic and prosodic constituent structures must be copresent. This second body of evidence cements the argument against any kind of transformational or restructuring analysis of the syntax-phonology connection. It

---

[9]It may well be that some people who work in the prosodic hierarchy theory assume for practical purposes a weaker version of the Transformation Hypothesis, and allow for a little overlap between the syntactic and prosodic components. During that overlap the mapping rules would apply. Only upon their completion will the syntactic component be considered officially terminated. However, I think it is incoherent to assume that coexistence comes in degrees. Either the syntactic and phonological components do not coexist, in which case the Transformation Hypothesis is an accurate characterization of the mapping algorithms assumed by proponents of the T-model version of prosodic hierarchy theory; or they do coexist, in which case we have a copresence model like that of Zec and Inkelas 1990.

supports the existence of an independent prosodic hierarchy.[10]

One piece of such evidence we have already discussed, namely the prosodic conditions on topicalization in Serbo-Croatian and on heavy NP-shift in English. In order to enforce these constraints, any framework will have to make simultaneous reference to syntactic and prosodic structure. There will have to be some stage at which both syntactic and prosodic structure are accessible. Zec and Inkelas assume that the two are always copresent; a theory which assumes a derivational relationship between syntactic and prosodic structure will have to posit some intermediate stage at which syntactic structure has not yet disappeared in order to state the prosodic constraints on these syntactic constituents.

A second class of examples involve clitics. As argued extensively in Inkelas and Zec 1988, Zec and Inkelas 1990, the position of second position clitics in Serbo-Croatian is regulated by the following constraint:

(33) Within the relevant domain, 2P clitics must follow the first syntactic word which is also a phonological word.

This constraint is best illustrated by the following sentences (taken from Zec and Inkelas 1990), which illustrate two allomorphs of the conjunction *ali*. Occurring in apparently free variation, these allomorphs differ in two ways: one allomorph (34) undergoes word-level rules of tone and stress insertion, and qualifies as the host of a second position clitic (in this case, the pronoun *nam*); the other allomorph (35) does not undergo word level rules, and cannot host clitics. As a result, the clitic *nam* in (35) follows not the conjunction *ali* but the following word, *niko*.[11]

(34) mi smo zvonili, ali =nam niko nije otvorio
    we Aux rang but us(Dat)-Cl nobody neg.Aux opened
    'We rang but nobody opened the door for us'

(35) mi smo zvonili, ali niko =nam nije otvorio
    we Aux rang but nobody us(Dat)-Cl neg.Aux opened
    'We rang but nobody opened the door for us'

---

[10]Booij 1984 also argues that the ellipsis of certain elements in coordinate structures in Dutch depends on both prosodic and morphological/syntactic information, and suggests that a model in which these two components are never copresent is too restrictive.

[11]The method of expressing clitic attachment with the '=' symbol is that of Klavans 1982.

2.3. ARGUMENTS FOR PROSODIC CONSTITUENCY

Zec and Inkelas explain this collection of facts by appealing to a lexically marked prosodic difference between the two forms of *ali*: the allomorph in (34) is a phonological word, and the one in (35) is not. On their analysis, where prosodic and syntactic constituency are copresent, the phonological word status of *ali* is visible and can be straightforwardly referred to by the constraint in (33).

The prosodic requirement is clear: clitics must follow a phonological word. But how can we state the syntactic requirement? If we say clitics must follow the first syntactic word in a domain, we will incorrectly generate clitics after the non-phonological word allomorph of *ali*. In order to allow for that allomorph, we will thus have to allow the syntax to place clitics after either the first *or* the second word. But this in turn causes us to overgenerate structures; in particular, we will incorrectly allow clitics to be generated after the second word in phrases beginning with the phonological word allomorph of *ali*.

Thus, unless we allow the syntactic and prosodic structures of an utterance to exist simultaneously, the grammar will either overgenerate or undergenerate possible clitic sites in Serbo-Croatian. But given copresent structures, the statement in (33) can be implemented as a simultaneous constraint on syntactic and prosodic structure. We may thus conclude that a restructuring analysis is untenable. The Constituency and Copresence hypotheses have been supported once again.

To sum up this chapter, we have concluded that postlexical rule domains are constituents, and further, that they belong to a hierarchy which coexists with, but does not necessarily match, syntactic constituent structure. In chapter 3 we turn to the question of whether a similar relationship holds between prosodic and morphological structure.

Chapter 3

Prosodic Structure in the Lexicon

According to the standard view (e.g. that advanced in Selkirk 1978), the prosodic hierarchy extends into the lexicon, where it consists of the units from the phonological word through the syllable. Recent accounts (Itô 1987, Zec 1988b)[1] have extended this hierarchy down one more level to include the mora.

(1)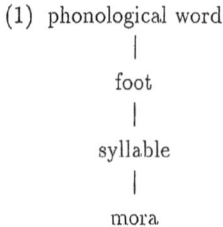

Although a great deal of substantiation exists for the status of the mora, syllable and foot as phonological entities, less work has been done in the area of establishing these entities as rule domains. In fact, I will suggest, the primary reason for considering them to be members of the hierarchy at all is the implicit assumption underlying work in the prosodic hierarchy theory that the Constituency Hypothesis is bidirectional. That is, the theory assumes not only the hypothesis in (2a), which

---

[1] For more general arguments that the mora is a constituent in phonological representation, see also Hyman 1985, McCarthy and Prince 1986, and Hayes 1989b.

we argued for in chapter 2, but also its converse, resulting in the claim that the set of phonological rule domains is coextensive with the set of phonological constituents.

(2)
  a. If a unit functions as a domain for phonological rules, then it is a constituent in phonological representation
  b. If a unit is a constituent in phonological representation, then it functions as a domain for phonological rules

In this chapter I will challenge the second of these implicational statements, arguing that phonological constituency is not a sufficient criterion for membership in the prosodic hierarchy. Specifically, I will propose to remove the foot, syllable and mora from the sublexical end of the prosodic hierarchy.[2]

This is not to suggest that the prosodic hierarchy does not play a role in the lexicon. On the contrary, I will argue that the Indirect Reference Hypothesis (repeated below) can and should be maintained in the lexical phonology as well as outside of it.

(3) Indirect Reference Hypothesis: for determining their domains of application, phonological rules refer only to prosodic constituent structure

To this end, I will propose a new set of sublexical prosodic constituents which serve as lexical rule domains; these replace the mora, syllable and foot (henceforth 'metrical constituents') as the sublexical end of the prosodic hierarchy. The claim is that only by separating prosodic and metrical constituents into two independent hierarchies can we obtain a natural account for the mismatches between metrical structure and phonological rule domains.

3.1 Lexical Rule Domains

In its standard formulations, the theory of Lexical Phonology (Pesetsky 1979, Kiparsky 1982, 1983, 1984, 1985, Mohanan 1982, 1986) is incompatible with the prosodic hierarchy theory. As part of its crucial claim that phonological rules can apply at each

---
[2] A number of rules have been described as having one of the metrical constituents as their domain. In chapter 9 I will argue that such rules can always be restated by locating the relevant metrical constituent in their environment. Their domain, the string within which they seek that environment, is a distinct prosodic constituent.

step of word formation, Lexical Phonology has assumed that these rules look directly at morphological structure, applying within strings of morphemes supplied to them by the morphology.[3] However, this latter assumption is clearly incompatible with the Indirect Reference Hypothesis.

There are two ways to resolve this conflict: either weaken the Indirect Reference Hypothesis so that it applies only to postlexical phonology, or alter our conception of Lexical Phonology so that it makes use of prosodic constituent structure.

Weakening the Indirect Reference Hypothesis would strip it of explanatory power; if lexical rules can look at and apply within non-prosodic constituents, then it becomes an arbitrary stipulation to say that postlexical rules are more constrained. A radical and unexplained asymmetry would be introduced into the application of phonological rules.

We thus turn to the alternative: an ultimately more restrictive theory which maintains the Indirect Reference Hypothesis at all levels by construing the domains of all lexical phonological rules as prosodic constituents. Mirroring the relationship between postlexical prosodic constituents and syntactic structure, lexical prosodic constituent structure coexists with but is crucially independent from morphological constituent structure.

3.1.1 Metrical Constituents

The prosodic hierarchy theory makes at most four sublexical constituents available for the potential use of lexical rules: the mora, the syllable, the foot and the phonological word.[4] In this section we will briefly examine and quickly reject the proposal that these units are sufficient to accommodate the domains of lexical phonological rules.[5] That is, the standard prosodic hierarchy theory fails on grounds of descriptive adequacy.

---

[3]Direct reference by phonological rules to some kind of internal morphological structure is, of course, not specific to Lexical Phonology per se, but common to all cyclic theories, including SPE and Mascaro 1976.

[4]This last domain is sometimes treated as lexical (Booij and Rubach 1984; Nespor and Vogel 1986, others) and sometimes as postlexical; I will take the position that it is visible both in and out of the lexicon (Booij and Rubach 1987, Inkelas and Zec 1990). This special status comes from the independent fact that the transition from lexical to postlexical phonology occurs at the point in the derivation when the phonological word is the largest available prosodic constituent. Thus it cuts across both modules.

[5]This problem has been raised before; see e.g. Nespor and Vogel 1986:18, who acknowledge the inability of the syllable and foot to handle cyclic lexical rules, Selkirk 1986:385, who questions whether these constituents belong to the prosodic hierarchy at all, and Zec 1988b.

3.1. LEXICAL RULE DOMAINS

We can demonstrate this point easily by looking at examples of morphologically complex words. Under the dual assumptions that phonological rules apply within prosodic constituents and that lexical rules apply cyclically, it will have to be the case that every word formation process results in a prosodic constituent of some sort.[6] The word *uncompromising*, which undergoes three phonological cycles during its derivation, will thus require three prosodic constituents (represented by generic p in (4)) to be built:

(4) [un [[compromis $]_p$ ing $]_p$ $]_p$

As is obvious from this example and many others like it, one cannot possibly claim that every affixation process results in a single mora, or syllable, or foot. (5) depicts the phonological constituents which (4) consists of; observe that in no case does any of the rule domains marked p contain exactly one stress (foot), or a single sonority peak (syllable or mora).

(5)
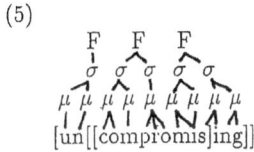

Given, then, that the mora, syllable and foot cannot be candidates for the instantiation of the p's in (4), our only other option within the standard theory is to turn to the phonological word. Because phonological words, unlike moras, syllables and feet, have no single phonetic or phonological correlate, we could plausibly draft an infinite number of these more abstract constituents to serve as the domains for all lexical rules.[7] That is, we might hypothesize that the result of every affixation process is a phonological word.

---

[6]The one exception is (derived and underived) bound roots; see chapter 5.

[7]In an analysis in the prosodic framework of bracketing paradoxes in Indonesian, Cohn 1989 suggests that in addition to the phonological word, lexical rules may make reference to another prosodic constituent, the clitic group. While I support in principle the proposal to add another prosodic constituent to the lexical end of the hierarchy, I assume that the clitic group is not actually the right choice, for two reasons. First, I take clitics to be separate syntactic terminals which, under the assumptions of Lexical Phonology, could never be combined with a host in the lexicon. Second, as argued in chapter 7 (see also Inkelas 1987, Zec 1988b), there are good arguments against considering the clitic group to be a separate level in the hierarchy. Instead, the phonological word

(6) [un [[compromis]_ω ing]_ω]_ω

But this approach, while it allows us to maintain both the standard prosodic hierarchy theory (1) and the Indirect Reference Hypothesis (3), has a significant drawback: it robs the theory of any prosodic means of distinguishing between cyclic and postcyclic rules, a distinction which in recent work has come to be attributed to the fact that only *post*cyclic lexical rules apply within phonological words (Booij and Rubach 1987).

A number of languages (e.g. Hungarian, Turkish, Serbo-Croatian, English) have postcyclic lexical rules of this type; their domain is co-extensive either with a single syntactic terminal element (e.g. Serbo-Croatian, Greek) or with each half of a compound (e.g. Hungarian, Turkish (Nespor and Vogel 1986)).

In Serbo-Croatian, for example, a rule assigns High tone to the initial syllable of a toneless word only postcyclically, at the last level of the lexical rules (Inkelas and Zec 1988). Inkelas and Zec argue that Initial High Insertion is bounded by the phonological word.[8] Evidence that the rule does not apply cyclically comes from words like that in (7), which contains a prefix and a stem. If Initial High Insertion applied on each cycle, as in (7), we would predict High tone on the second syllable, but this is incorrect. Instead, as shown in (8), the entire word undergoes the rule, surfacing with High only on its initial syllable.

(7) * [po [tonu]]
            |
            H
'perf.-*sink*3sg.Aorist'

(8) [po [tonu]]
       |
       H

To capture the fact that rules bounded by the phonological word apply only once,

---

in its postlexical capacity, or the phonological phrase, can serve as the unit containing a clitic and host. Cohn's proposals will work equally well if another prosodic constituent (e.g. of the type I propose in this chapter) is substituted for the clitic group.

[8]See also Booij and Rubach 1987 for analyses of phonological words as the domains for postcyclic lexical rules.

3.1. LEXICAL RULE DOMAINS

our theory will have to be forced to create the phonological word exactly once as well, in languages like Serbo-Croatian. But like English, Serbo-Croatian does have cyclic lexical rules (see Zec 1987, Inkelas and Zec 1988, Zec 1988b) whose domain cannot universally be characterized as forming a single foot, syllable or mora. We have already seen that the phonological word cannot be drafted to accommodate cyclic rules; the theory thus provides us with no constituent which could be matched with p in examples like that in (4), repeated in (9), or in the Serbo-Croatian example in (10):

(9) [[un [compromis]$_p$ ing]$_p$]$_p$]$_\omega$

(10) [[[ne [doosleed an]$_p$]$_p$ ost]$_p$]$_\omega$ '*inconsistency*'

To sum up, the standard prosodic hierarchy is not sufficiently rich to cover all of the domains needed by cyclic and noncyclic lexical rules across languages.

3.1.2 New Sublexical Constituents

To fill the gap just demonstrated in the prosodic hierarchy, I propose a new set of sublexical prosodic constituents which will fit into the prosodic hierarchy below the level of the phonological word and serve as domains for lexical rules. Like the phonological word and higher constituents — and unlike the syllable and foot — these proposed new constituents have no single phonological correlate. Instead, in keeping with the observed intimate connection between lexical rule domains and morphology, lexical prosodic constituents will be formed largely on the basis of morphological structure. I will call the new framework Prosodic Lexical Phonology.

The processes by which prosodic structure is generated I will postpone until section 3.5, and chapters 4 and 5. For now, however, let us simply anticipate the result of these varied processes: at each stage in the morphological derivation, a new prosodic constituent will be created which corresponds to the newly formed morphological constituent.[9] This new prosodic constituent then triggers the application of phonological rules. In the general case, morphological and prosodic constituency will correspond exactly:

---

[9]By morphological constituent I really mean saturated constituent — one with no unsatisfied subcategorization requirements. This point is not important here, but it does play an important role in the discussion of bound roots later in this chapter (3.5).

(11)

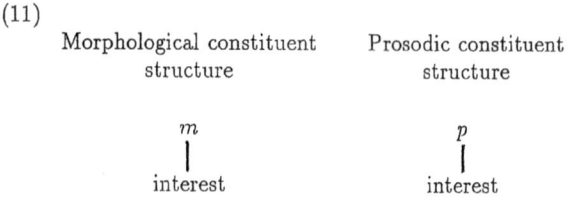

Because each process of affixation results in a prosodic constituent, it will be the case that multiple affixation will result in the construction of multiple, nested prosodic constituents. This corresponds to the fact that phonological rules apply more than once to such forms.

(12)

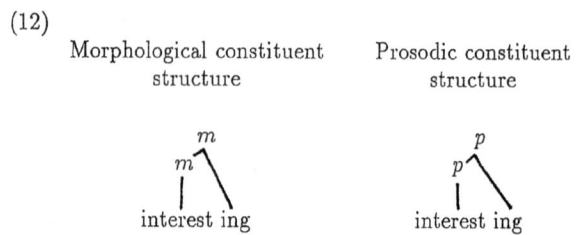

Besides cyclicity, a further component of the lexical phonology of many languages involves level ordering — that is, the division of the lexicon into an ordered sequence of levels, each corresponding to a set of phonological rules (see e.g. Pesetsky 1979, Kiparsky 1982, Mohanan 1982). The translation of principles of level ordering into the constituent terms of Prosodic Lexical Phonology is trivial: to each 'level' of level-ordered morphology there corresponds a unique constituent category in the morphological and prosodic hierarchies. That is to say, sublexical constituents come in more than one type; a three-level language like English (Kiparsky 1982) will thus have three lexical constituents, which I will call α, β and γ. The phonological rules applying within α, β and γ correspond to those rules applying within Levels 1, 2 and 3, respectively.

(13)

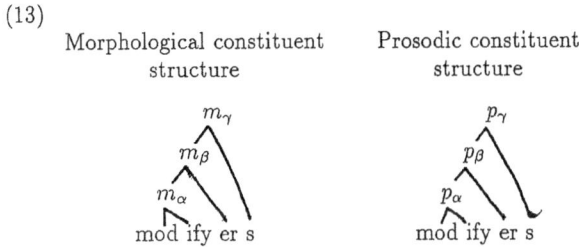

Morphological constituent structure   Prosodic constituent structure

Treating levels as constituent types allows us to characterize sublexical levels in just the same way that we characterize the relationship between postlexical constituents. Both the lexical and the postlexical phonology are contain constituents of different types, organized hierarchically. The difference between them lies only in the simplicity of the algorithms grouping constituents of a lower hierarchical rank into constituents of a higher rank. Lexically structures are very simple. Words, as they are being built, generally consist only of one constituent at a time, and so the the mapping algorithms between constituents at different 'levels' in the hierarchy are typically one-to-one. Postlexically, however, parsing algorithms have much more complex inputs.

Viewing lexical levels as constituent types also allows us to capture Kaisse's (1985) intuition that the division between kinds of postlexical phonological rules is akin to the division between the lexical levels of lexical phonology.

3.2 Morphological vs. Prosodic Structure

So far, our main motivation for construing lexical rule domains as prosodic constituents has been the desire to uphold the Indirect Reference Hypothesis. Morphological and prosodic constituency have coincided exactly in the examples we have seen, making the empirical case for two separate structures less than persuasive so far.

However, there is an abundance of empirical evidence in favor of copresent morphological and prosodic structures, and this comes from various mismatches obtaining between the two. In later chapters we will concentrate on deriving these mismatches; for now, I would just like to illustrate several different types of cases where phonological rule domains are not directly interpretable from morphological structure.

3.2.1 Compounds

It has been noted for a number of different languages that compounds, which form one single morphological constituent, behave as two constituents for the purposes of phonological rules. Italian, as described in Nespor and Vogel 1986:135-124, is one such case. The generalizations are as follows:

- While all other words in Italian contain at most one primary stress, compounds contain two.

- A word-bounded rule of nasal assimilation applies within each member of a compound but is blocked across the compound-internal boundary.

- Intervocalic voicing applies to *s* word-medially but not if its environment contains a compound boundary.

As Nespor and Vogel 1986 argue, following Selkirk 1980, facts of this kind point to a configuration in which compounds correspond to one morphological constituent, but two prosodic constituents. The mismatch in Italian is illustrated in (14) with respect to the compound noun *tóstapáne* 'bread toaster'.

(14)
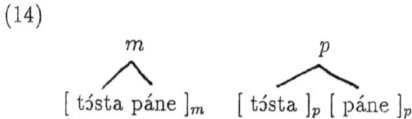

In chapter 4 I investigate cases of this kind in more detail, looking in particular at Malayalam and English.

3.2.2 Invisibility

A rather different type of mismatch between morphological and prosodic constituency involves the phenomenon characterized by Poser 1984 as 'invisibility'. Often referred to in individual cases as extrametricality (Harris 1983, Hayes 1981), extratonality (Pulleyblank 1983), or extraprosodicity (Kiparsky 1985), invisibility involves the exclusion of some part of the phonological string from the domain of phonological rules.

For example, the final syllable of nouns in English behaves as if it is invisible to stress rules, inducing the construction of a stress foot on the preceding syllable(s):

(15) Pame(la)

Although various alternative methods of handling invisibility have been proposed elsewhere, I will argue in chapter 6 that the proper characterization of invisibility is in fact prosodic: 'invisible' elements represent cases where certain elements of a morphological constituent are excluded from the corresponding prosodic constituent.

(16)
Morphological constituency   Prosodic constituency

[Pamela]$_m$ [Pame]$_p$ la

To sum up this section, our hypothesis that prosodic structure exists independently of morphological structure is supported by evidence that phonological rule domains — i.e. prosodic constituents — and morphological constituents do not always match.

3.3 Metrical vs. Prosodic Structure

Now that the existence of sublexical prosodic constituents has been more firmly established, we may turn to the question of whether the metrical constituents ought to remain in the prosodic hierarchy. That is to say, will the new prosodic constituents proposed in section 3.2 coexist with the mora, syllable and foot in the prosodic hierarchy, or will they supplant the latter three constituents? Given that the mora, syllable and foot are themselves hierarchically related, this latter option would force the postulation of a second, metrical hierarchy. The two alternatives are schematized below:

(17)

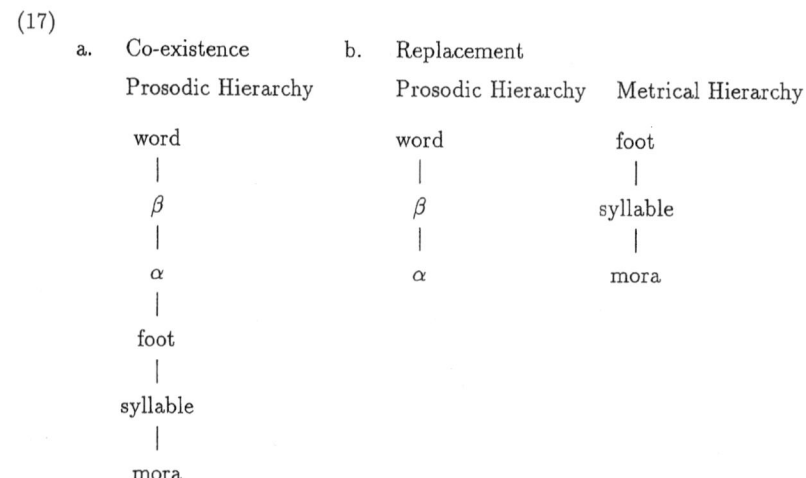

    a. Co-existence   b. Replacement

I will argue here in support of alternative (b), first suggested in Selkirk 1986,[10] in which the mora, syllable and foot are evicted from the prosodic hierarchy, on the grounds that including them would create an unresolvable ordering paradox with respect to the stage in the derivation at which prosodic units are introduced into the representation.[11]

3.3.1 Ordering Paradox

A well-known fact is that moras, syllables and feet are constructed by phonological rules; their content is regulated by phonological principles and their boundaries cannot, in most cases, be inferred from the morphological constituency of the strings they parse. If we are to maintain the Indirect Reference Hypothesis, the claim that morification et al. are accomplished by phonological rule thus entails a further claim:

---

[10]Selkirk notes various asymmetries between the higher and lower constituents in the standard hierarchy. For example, syllables are subject to phonotactic constraints while the larger constituents are not; related to this, syllables and feet (to the extent that Selkirk believes they exist) are built by purely phonological rules while construction of the larger constituents depends on the syntax (p. 385).

[11]Nespor and Vogel 1986 allude briefly to this paradox (p. 109) but do not discuss it in detail. Selkirk offers the fact that syllables and feet can be built by rules applying within a larger prosodic constituent as another difference between these and the larger constituents (p. 385).

3.3. METRICAL VS. PROSODIC STRUCTURE

that a prosodic domain already exists for these phonological rules to apply in. It is in this latter requirement that the paradox arises.

Recall that in the prosodic hierarchy theory, a prosodic constituent of type p_i consists of some nonnull number of constituents of type p_{i-1}, one level below in the hierarchy. That is, phrases consist of one or more words; words consist of one or more feet; syllables of one or more moras; and so on. But this assumption creates a paradox of mutual feeding: moras (or syllables, or feet) are built by phonological rules applying within some larger prosodic constituent whose own existence presupposes the existence of the mora (or syllable, or foot). The paradox is stated in (18) with reference to moras, but applies equally well to the syllable and foot:

(18) Paradox: morification feeds parsing into larger constituents, but the construction of larger constituents feeds morification

We will have to resolve the ordering paradox in (18) by eliminating at least one of the contradictory assumptions listed below:[12]

(19)

   a. Phonological rules apply only within prosodic constituents (Indirect Reference Hypothesis)
   b. Higher constituents are formed from (hence after) lower ones in the prosodic hierarchy
   c. Metrical constituents (mora, syllable, foot) belong to the prosodic hierarchy

Assumption (a) we can take as given, as it is our basic premise. Suppose, then, that we try to abandon assumption (b). This would mean allowing higher constituents to

---

[12]Note that this paradox rests on the assumption that constituents of different types are constructed sequentially. A conceivable way of avoiding the paradox would be to assume instead that moras, syllables, feet, and the larger domain(s) dominating them are all constructed simultaneously. However, this hypothesis would be falsified by any case in which any phonological rule can be shown to precede morification, syllabification or foot construction, thus presupposing the prior existence of a larger prosodic domain. One example of this kind is Tiberian Hebrew (McCarthy 1986), in which the rule-governed assimilation of a crucially unsyllabified suffix consonant to the preceding root consonant bleeds the following syllabification rule, which would otherwise have assigned a syllable to that consonant. Another case is Serbo-Croatian, where Zec 1988b argues that morification and syllabification must take place on different levels, with several phonological rules ordered in between. I will suggest in chapter 6 that in English, voicing assimilation applies before syllabification on level 1.

be formed before lower ones exist. But if phonological rules apply immediately upon creation of the prosodic constituents that form their domains,[13] such a move would result, for example, in the unattested situation where phrasal rules could precede phonological word level rules.

We would, in fact, lose all the ordering claims made by current versions of the prosodic hierarchy theory, a loss of predictive power which is entirely unwarranted by the empirical evidence. Aside from the interactions of moras, syllables and feet with prosodic constituents, virtually no violations of premise (19b) have been detected. Within each of the two hierarchies in (17b), a strict ordering relationship holds among the algorithms creating the constituents. Hypothesis (19b) is associated with important generalizations and should not be relinquished.

We are therefore left with only one option: to abandon the assumption stated in (19c) that moras, syllables and feet belong to the prosodic hierarchy. This means rejecting the idea in (2) that the implicational relationship between rule domains and phonological constituents is bidirectional. While (20 (=2a)) is true, its converse is not.

(20) If a unit functions as a domain for phonological rules, then it is a constituent in phonological representation

In the following section I will support the hypothesis that the metrical constituents belong to their own distinct hierarchy by presenting evidence of mismatches between the metrical and prosodic hierarchies. These phenomena could not be accounted for under the assumption that all constituents in phonological representation bear a strict hierarchical relationship to each other, but are precisely what we expect under the proposed account.

3.3.2 Metrical and Prosodic Mismatches

A few cases are all that is needed to ascertain that in fact, metrical constituents and rule domains bear no necessary hierarchical relation to one another. The syllable and foot frequently straddle the edges of the units known to function as domains for rules (this is mentioned as early as Liberman and Prince 1977:298), thus failing to satisfy strict layering. The mismatch occurs both lexically and postlexically.

---

[13]Immediate rule application of this kind is a crucial assumption in the proposed framework. It will be justified later in chapters 5 and 9, in conjunction with the discussion of bracket erasure.

3.3. METRICAL VS. PROSODIC STRUCTURE

An example of the latter case is found in Ossetic, where a postlexical rule of stress assignment produces a mismatch between metrical feet and phonological words. According to Hayes 1981 (see also Abaev 1964), a postlexical rule of stress assignment builds a binary, right-dominant, quantity-sensitive foot at the left edge of Ossetic phrases, regardless of the location of word boundaries in the phrase.

(21)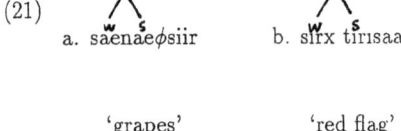
    a. saenaeφsiir   b. sɪrx tɪrɪsaa

    'grapes'   'red flag'

Ossetic has word-bounded rules as well[14] — confirming the existence of word-sized prosodic constituents in the language. Any feet which stretch across syntactic terminals, as in (21b), will thus also have to stretch across prosodic constituent boundaries, creating exactly the type of mismatch predicted to occur across hierarchies.

(22)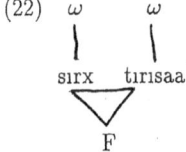

Note that these Ossetic feet could not be incorporated into the prosodic hierarchy even if we tried to exchange the positions of feet and words in a version of the hierarchy specific to Ossetic. As (22) shows, feet do not necessarily properly contain the phonological words whose edges they straddle.

Cases of mismatches between feet and sublexical rule domains present themselves frequently. Consider, for example, the derived words in (23).[15] In both cases, not only do the metrical feet and cyclic domains not match exactly — they also overlap in a way inconsistent with strict layering.

---

[14] Abaev notes, for example, that progressive voicing assimilation applies within words (p. 8), including compounds (p. 120), but not across word boundaries, and that word-final stops tend to be geminated (p. 9).

[15] See Rubach 1984:224 for similar examples from Polish.

(23)

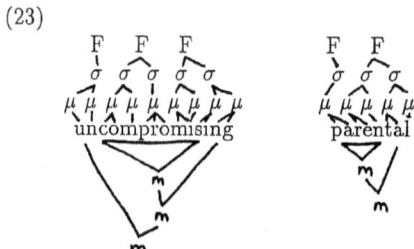

In English as in Ossetic, the partial overlap between feet and phonological rule domains is exactly what we expect in a framework which locates the two kinds of constituent in separate hierarchies. It could not be accounted for in any framework which tries to unify all constituents in phonological representation into a single hierarchy.[16]

Summary

To conclude this section, a theory in which all constituents are strictly layered in a single hierarchy is too restrictive, while a theory which abandons strict layering is overly permissive. By maintaining strict layering but separating constituents into three hierarchies, we correctly predict the cases where mismatches will occur among the metrical, prosodic and morphological constituents.

In the second half of the chapter we turn to the generation of sublexical constituency. I have nothing to add to the voluminous literature on metrical structure; thus, I will say no more about that particular hierarchy, focusing in what follows on the mechanisms for deriving prosodic and morphological structure.

---

[16]Although I have claimed here that no necessary relationship holds between metrical and prosodic constituency, that does not mean that there is never any correspondence. In fact, the edges of prosodic constituents typically do correspond roughly to the edges of metrical constituents, particularly in cases where metrical structure is built cyclically (e.g. English (Kiparsky 1979), Diyari (Poser 1986a), Chamorro (Kiparsky 1987a), Indonesian (Cohn 1989).) This is, of course, due to the fact that metrical constituents are constructed by phonological rules, which apply within prosodic constituents.

3.4 Constituent Formation

According to the Indirect Reference Hypothesis, each lexical phonological rule domain corresponds to a prosodic constituent. In this section we will take a first look at the mechanisms whereby the requisite prosodic constituency is generated in the lexicon, starting with the simplest case: unaffixed stems. We will see that the prosodic model not only captures the insights behind Lexical Phonology in a straightforward manner, but has some significant advantages to offer in addition.

The morphological and prosodic constituency of free, underived stems is entirely predictable: each free stem corresponds both to a well-formed morphological constituent and to a well-formed prosodic constituent. To capture this fact, I propose that the constituency of such stems is derived by general rules. These rules take the form of algorithms. They parse a string into constituents in the event such structure does not already exist.

The first such algorithm, Morphological Constituent Formation (MCF), takes a stem with no morphological constituency and groups it into a morphological constituent.

(24) Morphological Constituent Formation Algorithm

Morphological constituency		Morphological constituency
x	$\longrightarrow$	$[\,x\,]_m$

Next, to capture the one-to-one correspondence typically obtaining at each level between morphological stems and prosodic constituents, I propose a simple prosodic parsing algorithm (25). Prosodic Constituent Formation (PCF) takes as input information in the morphological constituent tree, gathering a string dominated by a morphological constituent into a prosodic constituent, as shown in the sample derivation in (26). As in the case of MCF, PCF applies only to material which is not already licensed by prosodic structure.

(25) Prosodic Constituent Formation Algorithm

Morphological constituency	Prosodic constituency		Morphological constituency	Prosodic constituency
$[\,x\,]_m$		$\longrightarrow$	$[\,x\,]_m$	$[\,x\,]_p$

The interaction of these intrinsically ordered algorithms is depicted below:

(26)
UR	stem
MCF	$[\,\text{stem}\,]_m$
PCF	$[\,\text{stem}\,]_m$
	$[\,\text{stem}\,]_p$

We may assume that phonological rules apply immediately upon creation of a new prosodic constituent, so that the culmination of the partial derivation in (27) is a cycle of phonological rules on the stem.

As we noted earlier, morphological and prosodic constituents come in different types. Specifically, to each level of level-ordered phonology and morphology there corresponds a constituent type, or level in the hierarchy.

A simple modification of the algorithms proposed above will accommodate this additional complexity. In particular, I propose that instead of applying just once at the beginning of the derivation, the Morphological Constituent Formation Algorithm applies as many times as there are sublexical levels, building constituents of type i out of those of type i-1. The revised algorithm is given in (27). Its instantiation in (26) merely represents the special case where $i = 1$.

(27) Morphological Constituent Formation Algorithm (Revised)

Morphological constituency		Morphological constituency
$[\,x\,]_{m_{i-1}}$	$\longrightarrow$	$[[\,x\,]_{m_{i-1}}]_{m_i}$

3.4. CONSTITUENT FORMATION

In the spirit of the 'level-connecting' rewrite rules of Selkirk 1982:95, this structure-building algorithm does not actually transform constituents of one type into those of another. Instead it expresses dominance relations between the two.

We observed earlier that MCF feeds PCF. This relationship between the two algorithms comes into play in capturing level ordering: each time MCF creates a new constituent of type i, the environment of PCF is met again, and a new prosodic constituent of type i is created. We must assume that PCF applies whenever the situation arises in which a morphological constituent does not correspond to a prosodic constituent of the same type.[17] Thus the PCF algorithm given in (25) is just the instantation where $i = 1$ of the more general PCF algorithm in (28):

(28) Prosodic Constituent Formation Algorithm (Revised)

Morphological constituency	Prosodic constituency		Morphological constituency	Prosodic constituency
$[\,x\,]_{m_i}$	$[\,x\,]_{p_{i-1}}$	$\longrightarrow$	$[\,x\,]_{m_i}$	$[[\,x\,]_{p_{i-1}}]_{p_i}$

The derivation in (29) takes a simple stem through α, β and γ levels:

(29)

	UR	stem
	α MCF	$[\,\text{stem}\,]_{m_\alpha}$
	α PCF	$[\,\text{stem}\,]_{m_\alpha}$
		$[\,\text{stem}\,]_{p_\alpha}$
	β MCF	$[[\,\text{stem}\,]_{m_\alpha}]_{m_\beta}$
		$[\,\text{stem}\,]_{p_\alpha}$
	β PCF	$[[\,\text{stem}\,]_{m_\alpha}]_{m_\beta}$
		$[[\,\text{stem}\,]_{p_\alpha}]_{p_\beta}$
	γ MCF	$[[[\,\text{stem}\,]_{m_\alpha}]_{m_\beta}]_{m_\gamma}$
		$[[\,\text{stem}\,]_{p_\alpha}]_{p_\beta}$
	γ PCF	$[[[\,\text{stem}\,]_{m_\alpha}]_{m_\beta}]_{m_\gamma}$
		$[[[\,\text{stem}\,]_{p_\alpha}]_{p_\beta}]_{p_\gamma}$

---

[17] I assume that morphological and prosodic structure codescribe a string. Thus the correspondence between morphological and prosodic constituents is indirect, mediated by that codescribed material.

By the time a stem has advanced to γ constituency, it is surrounded by a large number of brackets. These brackets in effect encode the derivational history of the stem. It has been observed in the literature (e.g. SPE, Pesetsky 1979, Kiparsky 1982, Mohanan 1982) that such information is not relevant to and should not be made available to phonology. We thus need to find a way to remove this information from the purview of phonological rules.

One way to do this is to implement a bracket erasure convention, the option taken in the references just cited. Such a condition is stated in (30). The claim is fairly strong, namely that internal brackets are erased as soon as additional brackets are constructed around them — except in the case that two sisters are incorporated into a constituent of a different type. That is, the convention imposes almost complete bracket erasure but allows for juncture rules. It may happen that in the future, all apparent cases of juncture rules can be reanalyzed along the lines proposed in Rice 1990;[18] however, as I am not in a position to make this particular claim here, I will weaken the bracketing erasure statement accordingly.[19]

(30) Prosodic Bracket Erasure:

    a. $]_{p_i} \ldots]_{p_n} \quad \longrightarrow \quad \ldots]_{p_n}$ where $n - i > 1$ (same for left brackets)
    b. $[[\quad]_{p_i}]_{p_{i+1}} \quad \longrightarrow \quad [\quad]_{p_{i+1}}$

Clause (a) imposes a type of subjacency condition; only one level of embedding is ever visible to phonological rules. Clause (b) further restricts the visible embeddings to juncture environments — i.e., to cases where the outer constituent is composed of more than one prosodic constituent.

---

[18]Rice suggests that the juncture environment may be characterizable in purely phonological terms. For instance, a phrasal resyllabification rule which seems to apply only at word junctures might alternatively be handled by 'turning off' word-final consonant extrametricality in the postlexical component. Assuming that only unsyllabified material is affected by postlexical syllabification rules, then only the previously extrametrical consonants will undergo the rule. Since these can only occur at word edges, there is no need for the resyllabification rule to expressly refer to internal brackets.

[19]Note that the brackets which this particular convention pertains are prosodic. I make no claims about morphological bracketing; there is some evidence from cases of semantic reanalysis (e.g. Kiparsky 1982) that morphological structure remains visible throughout a large stretch of the derivation. There is little if any such evidence for prosodic constituency, however; some apparent examples of the need for phonological rules to refer to internal bracketing will be discussed and reanalyzed in chapter 9.

3.4. CONSTITUENT FORMATION

The derivation seen earlier in (29) is presented again below, this time with Prosodic Bracket Erasure in effect:

(31)
	UR	stem
	α MCF	$[\text{ stem }]_{m_\alpha}$
	α PCF	$[\text{ stem }]_{m_\alpha}$
		$[\text{ stem }]_{p_\alpha}$
	β MCF	$[[\text{ stem }]_{m_\alpha}]_{m_\beta}$
		$[\text{ stem }]_{p_\alpha}$
	β PCF	$[[\text{ stem }]_{m_\alpha}]_{m_\beta}$
		$[\text{ stem }]_{p_\beta}$
	γ MCF	$[[[\text{ stem }]_{m_\alpha}]_{m_\beta}]_{m_\gamma}$
		$[\text{ stem }]_{p_\beta}$
	γ PCF	$[[[\text{ stem }]_{m_\alpha}]_{m_\beta}]_{m_\gamma}$
		$[\text{ stem }]_{p_\gamma}$

Though effective, crude erasure of internal bracketing is rather problematic; the rule in (30) would be the only apparently structure-changing operation on nodes in the prosodic hierarchy that the theory requires. I would like to put forth an alternative here (suggested to me by C. Condoravdi) and reinterpret the Prosodic Bracket Erasure convention in (30) as a constraint on what phonological rules may refer to. Instead of forcing internal structure to be erased, we need only impose the requirement on rules that they look only at the highest node in prosodic structure, with branching (into daughter constituents of a different type) as a relevant property. Recommending this aproach is the observation that while we may be able to make the claim that phonological rules appear not to need to refer to internal morphological structure, syntactic category is undeniably crucial in a number of cases (e.g. English Noun Extrametricality). We could account for this by restricting the reference of phonological rules to only the highest node in morphological structure, where category will be encoded. Thus the same restrictions will be imposed on what parts of prosodic and morphological structure phonological rules can access.

I will continue, however, to implement actual bracket erasure in derivations in the interest of notational simplicity. It should be understood that the structure is present in principle if not represented on paper.

To sum up, we now have a set of two simple rules and a convention which represent a good first approximation of a prosodic model of lexical phonology. The structure-building nature of the two constituent formation algorithms is reminiscent of their postlexical analogs, the algorithms building such prosodic constituents as the phonological phrase. Like Prosodic Constituent Formation, phrasing algorithms group into constituents elements which are not already licensed by (included in) a prosodic constituent of that level.

3.5 Bound Roots vs. Stems

An immediate advantage of the constituent formation algorithms presented above is that they allow us to capture an oft-noted generalization whose explanation has thus far eluded the nonprosodic theory of Lexical Phonology. This is the fact that bound roots do not form cyclic domains for rules, whereas free roots — what I am calling underived 'stems' — do.

3.5.1 Underlying Representations

I will assume here the underlying representation for bound roots proposed in Lieber 1980, who captures the distinction between bound roots and free stems by listing the former with morphological subcategorization frames. These frames encode the fact that bound morphemes cannot stand on their own: that is, in our terms, they will not form (saturated) morphological constituents in isolation.[20]

By contrast, stems are well-formed morphological constituents. Lieber marks them underlyingly as such; however, since it is predictable that any morpheme which does not subcategorize will be an independent constituent, I have proposed to omit any information about the morphological constituency of stems from UR. As we have seen, stems acquire their morphological constituency by the rule of Morphological Constituent Formation.

The lexical entries for roots and stems will thus contrast as in (32).[21]

---

[20] In the next chapter I will show that bound roots and free stems can be either underived, as in the examples here, or derived by affixation. Derived and underived forms of the same dependence category will obtain essentially the same representation, one of subcategorization.

[21] The subcategorization frame for the root -*ceive* is notationally slightly different from the kind developed by Lieber. Brackets are matched here, and extraneous information (category, diacritics) is omitted (for the present). Later we will see why the frame for the root is marked α; for now it

3.5. BOUND ROOTS VS. STEMS

(32)
```
              Bound root    Stem
     UR:   [ [   ]α ceive ]α   book
```

As is well-known, bound roots and stems differ not only morphologically but also phonologically. To be specific, stems may serve as the domains for phonological rules, while bound roots never may (Kiparsky 1982, 1983, 1988). This is attested by a growing body of cross-linguistic evidence (e.g. Sanskrit (Kiparsky 1982), Spanish (Harris 1983), Sekani (Hargus 1985), Malayalam (T. Mohanan 1988), Korean (Han 1988) and Warlpiri (Kiparsky 1988)). It is this phonological difference for which Prosodic Lexical Phonology offers a unique account. We will now look at several of these examples of the asymmetry between bound roots and stems; then I will show that the explanation follows naturally from Prosodic Lexical Phonology.

3.5.2 Spanish

In an oft-cited case from Spanish, Harris 1983 shows that the Spanish rule of depalatalization applies to the final -*n* of the derivational stem, which consists of a root plus derivational suffix(es). But the rule fails to apply to the final -*n* of a root properly contained in such a stem.

This alternation is illustrated by the minimal pair *desdeñes* 'disdain (pres.subj.2sg)',, *desdenes* 'disdains (n.)' (Harris 1983:54). Both are derived from a base of the phonological form /*desdeñ*/, with underlying palatality on the final nasal.

(33)
```
     desdeñ   -a    -e         -s       desdeñ   -es
     disdain  -TV   -pres.subj. -2sg.   disdain  -pl.

              desdeñes                   desdenes

         'disdain (pres.subj.2sg)'       'disdains (n.)'
```

Spanish has a general rule depalatalizing *ñ* in the coda. However, as Harris demonstrates, exactly when *ñ* is root-final and followed by a derivational suffix, depalatalization fails to apply. This situation is manifested in the verb in (33), which consists

---

does not matter.

of a verb root, a derivational suffix -a, and inflectional endings -e and -s.

We can account for these facts naturally by recognizing forms like the verb root *desdeñ*, which requires a suffix, as bound roots.[22] And precisely because they are bound, roots never serve as domains for phonological rules. Thus in the case of *desdeñ-*, syllabification is postponed until the suffix is added, at which time the root-final *ñ* is syllabified as an onset. The environment for depalatalization is never met.

By contrast, the form *desdeñ$_n$* is a free stem. As such, it undergoes phonological rules. These locate *ñ* in the coda, and palatality disappears as expected.

A similar palatalization alternation is exemplified by the words *donceλas* 'lass', *donceles* 'lads' (Harris 1983:52). These words are decomposed as in (34):

(34)

donceλ	-a	-s	donceλ	-es
lad	-TE(f.)	-pl.	lad	-pl.

$$donce\lambda as \qquad\qquad donceles$$
$$\text{'lass'} \qquad\qquad\quad \text{'lads'}$$

Like *ñ*, λ depalatalizes in the coda; however, it systematically fails to depalatalize root-finally when immediately followed by a derivational suffix. Just as in the case of Nasal Depalatalization, we may assume that Lateral Depalatalization applies cyclically, and that bound roots such as the feminine root *donceλ-* do not form cyclic domains.

3.5.3 Warlpiri

Kiparsky 1988 shows that vowel harmony in Warlpiri is composed of two processes: automatic linking of floating features to unspecified timing slots, and cyclic assignment of default feature values to those slots which remain unspecified after automatic linking has had a chance to apply.

An asymmetry exists in the language between the bases of nouns and verbs with respect to vowel harmony. In particular, verb bases acquire the roundness features of the suffix, while those of nouns exhibit progressive harmony.

---

[22] Harris has a slightly different account, which we will examine later in chapter 6.

3.5. BOUND ROOTS VS. STEMS

(35)

Verbs:			-rni (Nonpast)	-rnu (Past)
	/pangI/	'dig'	pangi-rni	pangu-rnu
	/kIjI/	'throw'	kiji-rni	kuju-rnu
	/nyunjI/	'kiss'	nyunji-rni	nyungu-rnu

Nouns:

    maliki-kirli-rli-lki-ji-li   'dog-Prop-Erg-then-me-they'

    kurdu-kurlu-rlu-lku-ju-lu   'child-Prop-Erg-then-me-they'

As a result, verbs, but not nouns, exhibit regressive vowel harmony. Kiparsky explains this asymmetry by noting that independent evidence (see Nash 1980) shows verbs to be bound roots, and nouns to be free stems. This difference is relevant to the application of phonological rules. As bound forms, verb roots do not undergo rules in isolation. They thus acquire no default feature values before suffixation. This explains why floating features introduced by a suffix will be able link to vowels in the verb root (p. 12).

(36)   kIpI- + -rnI ⟶ kIpIrnI   kupurnu   'winnow (past)'
                        +rd   +rd

By contrast, noun stems do undergo a cycle of rules before suffixation. Vowels unspecified for [rd] receive the default value, [-rd], as in the following example (p. 10):[23]

(37)   malIkI ⟶ malIkI   maliki   'dog'
                  -rd

Fully specified with feature values by the time the suffix is attached, noun roots do

---

[23] Certain additional segmental conditions obtain on the assignment of this value; see Kiparsky 1988.

not acquire the features of the suffix (p. 10). Rather, as in (38), those features delete and the default [-rd] feature is filled in on the suffix, creating the effect of progresive vowel harmony.

(38) malIkI + -kIrlI ⟶ malIkIkIrlI   malikikirli
       \| \| \| \|
       -rd   +rd   -rd -rd

Thus an otherwise puzzling asymmetry in the direction of vowel harmony in Warlpiri is traced to a more general asymmetry between bound roots and stems: only the latter form domains for phonological rules.

3.5.4 Malayalam

In a comprehensive analysis of syllable structure in Malayalam, T. Mohanan (1988) shows that a number of morpheme structure constraints hold of free stems in the language. In particular, both basic and derived stems must be exhaustively parsable into syllables which satisfy the well-formedness templates appropriate at the relevant stage of derivation.

However, T. Mohanan observes that certain nonderived forms fail to meet this requirement.[24]

For example, morphemes like the following are found, despite a well-motivated condition against non-geminate consonant clusters in coda position (p. 19):

(39) maarg-, wakṭr-, ašw-

T. Mohanan notes that these are precisely the roots which require a derivational suffix in order to be well-formed — that is, they are bound roots. We thus have an explanation for why they do not conform to morpheme structure constraints. Assuming, following Kiparsky 1982, that morpheme structure constraints are actually

---

[24]In the published version of this paper, which became available after this dissertation was completed, T. Mohanan adopts a different analysis of the Malayalam bound roots, according to which they are syllabified in underlying representation. The reader may want to evaluate the use to which the data are put here in the contexts of T. Mohanan's more recent arguments. See T. Mohanan 1989 for details.

3.5. BOUND ROOTS VS. STEMS

phonological rules, it will follow from the inability of bound roots to form phonological rule domains that morpheme structure constraints do not apply to them.

T. Mohanan offers support for the claim that bound roots do not undergo phonological rules by noting that while basic and derived obstruent-final stems will undergo a rule of final ə-epenthesis, obstruent-final bound roots will not (p. 18).

3.5.5 Analysis

To account for facts like these, Kiparsky 1982, 1983 proposed that cyclic rules apply only to those morphemes which are not bound — that is, only to stems (derived or underived). This stipulative constraint can now be shown to be a natural consequence of the prosodic treatment.

To prove this, we will call on both the representation proposed for bound roots in Lieber 1980, and the constituent formation algorithms proposed above. Under the assumption that Prosodic Constituent Formation applies only to well-formed (i.e. saturated) morphological constituents, the representations and rules already postulated will derive the fact that stems, but not bound roots, are mapped into prosodic constituents.

The logic is as follows. Bound roots like -*ceive* already possess information about morphological constituency, and as a consequence the Morphological Constituent Formation algorithm will not apply to them. Because they do not form morphological constituents of their own, bound roots will also never satisfy the environment for Prosodic Constituent Formation. They can thus never be mapped into a phonological rule domain. By contrast, stems do satisfy the environment for Morphological Constituent Formation. They are hence eligible to be mapped into prosodic structure, and as a result undergo phonological rules.

(40)

	Bound root	Stem
UR	$[\ [\quad]_\alpha$ ceive $]_\alpha$	stem
MCF	—	$[\text{ stem }]m_\alpha$
PCF	—	$[\text{ stem }]m_\alpha$
	—	$[\text{ stem }]p_\alpha$
phonological rules	(fail to apply)	(apply)

From subcategorization frames and our constituent formation algorithms, it thus follows without any stipulation that bound roots will not form domains for phonological rules.

3.6 Summary

To summarize, we have argued for the existence of nonmetrical prosodic structure in the lexicon, and proposed a set of structure-building constituent formation algorithms to build that structure. These algorithms encode the important predictions of Lexical Phonology into prosodic terms. Furthermore, we have seen that these algorithms make an additional prediction which Lexical Phonology does not: bound roots will not form domains for phonological rules.

The representations and rules we have developed thus far are assembled below:

(41) UR for bound roots: $[[\ \ ]_m \text{ --- }]_m$ (or $[\text{ --- } [\ \ ]_m]_m$)

(42) Morphological Constituent Formation Algorithm

Morphological constituency		Morphological constituency
$[\,x\,]_{m_{i-1}}$	$\longrightarrow$	$[[\,x\,]_{m_{i-1}}]_{m_i}$

(43) Prosodic Constituent Formation Algorithm

Morphological constituency	Prosodic constituency		Morphological constituency	Prosodic constituency
$[\,x\,]_{m_i}$	$[\,x\,]_{p_{i-1}}$	$\longrightarrow$	$[\,x\,]_{m_i}$	$[[\,x\,]_{p_{i-1}}]_{p_i}$

(44) Prosodic Bracket Erasure:

    a. $\,]_{p_i} \ldots]_{p_n} \ \longrightarrow \ \ldots]_{p_n}$ where $n - i > 1$ (same for left brackets)
    b. $[[\ ]_{p_i}\,]_{p_{i+1}} \ \longrightarrow \ [\ ]_{p_{i+1}}$

Chapter 4

Constructional Constraints on Prosodic Constituency

The Prosodic Constituent Formation algorithm accounts in Prosodic Lexical Phonology for what nonprosodic Lexical Phonology captures naturally: the case where prosodic and morphological structure exactly coincide.

However, as the hypothesis of autonomous structures predicts, one-to-one correspondence does not always obtain. In this chapter I examine a set of data which illustrate systematic mismatches between prosodic and morphological constituency. All the cases involve compounding. As has been noted in the literature, compounds come in two varieties: those which correspond to one rule domain, and those which correspond to two. This split is difficult for a nonprosodic theory of lexical phonology to handle, as it shows that phonological rule domains are not always directly interpretable from the geometry of the morphological constituent structure.

The prosodic hierarchy theory has made an important step towards the analysis of these forms. As suggested by Selkirk 1980, in an analysis of Sanskrit compounds, a straightforward representation for the two types of compounds follows from the assumption that some compounds correspond to one phonological word, and others to two. That is, certain compounds require a mismatch between morphological and prosodic constituency. This notion of a representational difference has inspired an outpouring of subsequent work on similar compounds in other languages, including Dutch (Booij 1985), Hungarian (Nespor and Vogel 1986), Indonesian (Cohn 1989),

Italian (Nespor and Vogel 1986), Malayalam (Sproat 1986), and Turkish (Nespor and Vogel 1986).

I will build on this important insight here, although in the cases we will examine, I will suggest that a sublexical prosodic constituent, rather than the phonological word per se, is implicated in the compounding processes. Furthermore, I will contribute a specific means, within the theory of Prosodic Lexical Phonology, of actually generating the requisite mismatched structures. The particular mechanism to be invoked is the imposition of prosodic constraints by morphological compounding rules. These specific constraints override the more general, default Prosodic Constituent Formation algorithm, producing as output prosodic and morphological constituent structures that do not match.

4.1 Two Types of Compounds

On the assumption that compounding, as a morphological process, is ordered before Prosodic Constituent Formation, the theory predicts that compounds will be mapped into a single prosodic constituent.

(1)
Compounding: $[\ x\ ]_m, [\ y\ ]_m \longrightarrow [\ xy\ ]_m$

PCF: $[\ xy\ ]_m \longrightarrow [\ xy\ ]_m, [\ xy\ ]_p$

Thus when compounding is the first morphological operation to take place on some level i, we expect the compound itself to be mapped into a prosodic constituent of type i before either of its member constituents has had an opportunity to become i prosodic constituents themselves. This will be true whether compounds are formed from α constituents, as in (2), or out of β constituents, as in (3).

4.1. TWO TYPES OF COMPOUNDS

(2)

input:	stem1	stem2
α MCF:	$[\text{stem1}]_{m_\alpha}$	$[\text{stem2}]_{m_\alpha}$
α compounding:	$[\text{stem1stem2}]_{m_\alpha}$	
α PCF	$[\text{stem1stem2}]_{m_\alpha}$ $[\text{stem1stem2}]_{p_\alpha}$	

(3)

output of α rules:	$[\text{stem1}]_{m_\beta}$ $[\text{stem1}]_{p_\alpha}$	$[\text{stem2}]_{m_\beta}$ $[\text{stem2}]_{p_\alpha}$
β MCF:	—	
β compounding:	$[\text{stem1stem2}]_{m_\beta}$ $[\text{stem1}]_{p_\alpha} [\text{stem2}]_{p_\alpha}$	
β PCF	$[\text{stem1stem2}]_{m_\beta}$ $[\text{stem1stem2}]_{p_\beta}$	

The situation illustrated schematically above corresponds exactly to a large class of compounds, including compounds in Greek (Nespor and Vogel 1986), subcompounds in Malayalam (Mohanan 1982, 1986), and reduced compounds in Japanese (Poser 1984). In each of these cases, compounds undergo phonological rules as a unit. For example, in Malayalam, simple subcompounds are formed by a β rule, and consist of two words which have crucially not undergone β rules prior to concatenation (Mohanan 1982, 1986). The subcompound itself forms a domain for β rules, including tone assignment and various segmental processes.

We may formalize the compounding rule required by these languages quite simply, as follows:

(4) Mcompounding:

$$
\begin{array}{ccc}
\text{Morphological} & & \text{Morphological} \\
\text{constituency} & & \text{constituency} \\
[\ x_i\ ]_m, \ldots [\ x_n\ ]_m & \longrightarrow & [\ x_i, \ldots x_n\ ]_m
\end{array}
$$

However, Mcompounding is not sufficient to describe another large class of compounds, exemplified here by Italian. As described in Nespor and Vogel 1986 (see also Nespor 1984), Italian compounds consist of two prosodic units. They differ crucially from Malayalam compounds in that both members of the compound undergo phonological rules individually; the compound does not behave as a phonological unit.

For example, although all other words in Italian may contain at most one primary stress, compounds contain two, supporting the hypothesis that they do not form a unit for purposes of word tree formation. In addition, a word-bounded rule of nasal assimilation applies within each member of a compound but is blocked across the compound-internal boundary. A third rule, intervocalic voicing, also voices s word-medially but not if its environment contains a compound boundary (Nespor and Vogel 1986).[1]

The Italian facts seem to require a different compounding rule, one which places constraints on the prosodic constituency of its output. This rule, which I will call Pcompounding, maps both of the input morphological constituents into their own prosodic constituents. In the case of Nespor and Vogel's analysis of Italian, the output prosodic constituents would be instantiated as ω, the phonological word.

---

[1] It also fails to apply to prefix-final consonants, which Nespor and Vogel account for by assigning phonological word status to the prefixes in question.

4.1. TWO TYPES OF COMPOUNDS

(5) Pcompounding:

Morphological constituency	Morphological constituency	Prosodic constituency
$[\, x_i\,]_m, ... [\, x_n\,]_m \longrightarrow$	$[\, x_i, ... x_n\,]_m$	$[\, x_i\,]_p, ... [\, x_n\,]_p$

Because Pcompounding is a more specific source of prosodic constituency, by the Elsewhere Condition it takes precedence over PCF, which applies only in the absence of prosodic structure. PCF is thus blocked in this case from mapping the newly formed morphological constituent into a single prosodic constituent. As a result, phonological rules apply within each member of the compound. They do not treat the compound as a whole.[2]

(6)
$$\begin{array}{ll}
\text{output of } \alpha \text{ rules:} & [\text{stem1}]_{m_\beta} \quad [\text{stem2}]_{m_\beta} \\
& [\text{stem1}]_{p_\alpha} \quad [\text{stem2}]_{p_\alpha} \\
\\
\beta \text{ MCF} & \text{---} \\
\\
\beta \text{ Pcompounding} & [\text{stem1stem2}]_{m_\beta} \\
& [\text{stem1}]_{p_\beta} [\text{stem2}]_{p_\beta} \\
\\
\beta \text{ PCF} & \text{---}
\end{array}$$

Nespor and Vogel distinguish Italian from Greek compounds by assigning different phonological word formation algorithms to the two languages. In Italian, each stem (and adjacent affixes) forms its own phonological word; in Greek, each syntactic terminal element is a single phonological word. In the following section I will argue in favor of ascribing the difference in compound structures to a difference in morphological compounding rules instead of to the nature of a given languages phonological

---

[2] Note that ordering the Mcompounding rule after PCF would produce the same result that Pcompounding achieves. It might thus seem simpler to posit only one compounding rule but order it before PCF for some languages and after PCF for others. However, for languages like Malayalam, which have both types of compounding (see below), this analysis would force us into the unacceptable position of allowing a single rule to apply twice on the same cycle: compounding would have to be ordered both before and after PCF.

word algorithm by arguing that both compounding rules are needed in the same language, Malayalam. Given that phonological word formation algorithms are stipulated only once per language, it would not be possible to accommodate Malayalam's two different compound types in the same way that the difference between Greek and Italian is handled by Nespor and Vogel.

In addition to providing a descriptive account of Malayalam's two types of compounds, the postulation of two different compounding rules in Malayalam permits the elimination of the loop (Mohanan 1982, 1986) from the theoretical devices needed to handle Malayalam phonology and morphology. The loop, whereby forms are allowed to re-enter an earlier stage of the derivation, was introduced into (nonprosodic) Lexical Phonology just in order to handle the difference between Malayalam's two types of compounds. But with its richer representations, Prosodic Lexical Phonology affords a simplification in the rule component and thereby greatly restricts the power of the theory.

4.2 Malayalam

Mohanan 1982, 1986 observes that the two morphological processes of sub(ordinate)-compounding and co(ordinate)compounding are associated with different bundles of phonological rules in Malayalam, concluding that they must therefore take place on different strata (2 and 3, respectively).

(7) Subcompounds (Stratum 2)

  Onset Fusion
  Sonorant Degemination
  Stem-initial Gemination
  Stem-final Gemination
  Nasal Deletion
  Vowel Lengthening
  Vowel Sandhi
  Stress Assignment
  Melody Assignment

4.2. MALAYALAM

(8) Cocompounds (Stratum 3)

    Nasal Deletion
    Vowel Lengthening
    Vowel Sandhi

4.2.1 The Loop

Because the two compounding processes can occur in either order, Mohanan proposes that the two strata to which they correspond are related by a special device termed the 'loop'. To be specific, it is claimed that after exiting stratum 3, a derived form may loop back and re-enter the lexical phonology and morphology at stratum 2.

(9)
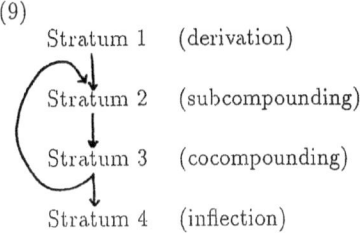
    Stratum 1   (derivation)
    Stratum 2   (subcompounding)
    Stratum 3   (cocompounding)
    Stratum 4   (inflection)

This relaxation of strict stratum ordering weakens the predictive power of Lexical Phonology, and is a priori undesirable for that reason. Furthermore, when the loop is translated into prosodic terms, it becomes a flagrant violation of the Strict Layering hypothesis (Selkirk 1984), as we will have to allow a constituent of the prosodic type corresponding to stratum 3 to both dominate and be dominated by a constituent of another prosodic type (that corresponding to stratum 2).

(10)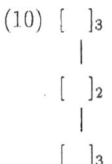
    [ ]$_3$
     |
    [ ]$_2$
     |
    [ ]$_3$

In the next section I will show that a prosodic treatment of these facts (as first suggested by Sproat 1986) eliminates the need for representations like that in (10), allowing us to maintain the claim of strict layering within the prosodic hierarchy. On this account, the asymmetries between subcompounds and cocompounds will be attributed not to differences in the levels at which each kind of compound is formed, but to asymmetries in their respective prosodic constituency.

4.2.2 A Prosodic Solution

In the prosodic account proposed here, both sucompounding and cocompounding will take place at the same morphological 'stratum', paring the total number of strata in the language down to three. Following the general program of Prosodic Lexical Phonology I will treat each 'stratum' as a different constituent type. As shown below, stratum 1 corresponds to constituent type α; stratum 2 to β and stratum 3 to γ:

(11)

	Mohanan 1986	Proposed account
Stratum 1	(derivation)	α
Stratum 2	(subcompounding)	β
Stratum 3	(cocompounding)	β
Stratum 4	(inflection)	γ

Building on the analysis of these facts in Sproat 1986 (and more generally, Selkirk 1980 and Nespor and Vogel 1982), I propose to capture the distinction between subcompounds and cocompounds prosodically. Noting that coordinate structures typically require some degree of prosodic weight of their component elements, Sproat 1986 proposed that the difference between subcompounds and cocompounds lies in their prosodic structure. To be precise, in the terms we have developed thus far, subcompounds will consist of one prosodic constituent of type β while cocompounds will consist of two.

4.2. MALAYALAM

(12)
        Subcompound   Cocompound

    [bhaaryasahoodari]$_\beta$ [bhaarya]$_\beta$ [sahoodari]$_\beta$

       'wife's sister'   'wife and sister'

This representational difference explains why most of the rules attributed in (7) to stratum 2 do not apply across the internal boundary of cocompounds; these rules are restricted to applying within the β domain.[3]

The theoretical apparatus just developed gives us the means of actually generating the structures that the phonology requires: Subcompounding and Cocompounding are simply the instantiations in Malayalam of Mcompounding and Pcompounding, respectively.

(13) Subcompounding: (=Mcompounding)

      Morphological   Morphological
      constituency   constituency

    [x$_1$]$_\beta$, ... [x$_n$]$_\beta$ $\longrightarrow$ [x$_i$, ... x$_n$]$_\beta$

(14) Cocompounding: (=Pcompounding)

      Morphological   Morphological   Prosodic
      constituency   constituency   constituency

    [x$_1$]$_\beta$, ... [x$_n$]$_\beta$ $\longrightarrow$ [x$_i$, ... x$_n$]$_\beta$ [x$_i$]$_\beta$, ... [x$_n$]$_\beta$

Example partial derivations of simple subcompounding and cocompounding are given below (examples amended from Mohanan 1986:117):

---

[3] I will argue presently that the three rules listed in (8) as applying within cocompounds actually apply to them at the γ level.

64   CHAPTER 4. CONSTRUCTIONAL CONSTRAINTS

(15) Subcompounding

    α output   [ṭii]$_{m_\alpha}$ [waṇṭi]$_{m_\alpha}$ [aappiis]$_{m_\alpha}$
                        [ṭii]$_{p_\alpha}$ [waṇṭi]$_{p_\alpha}$ [aappiis]$_{p_\alpha}$
    β rules
      MCF   [ṭii]$_{m_\beta}$ [waṇṭi]$_{m_\beta}$ [aappiis]$_{m_\beta}$
                      [ṭii]$_{p_\alpha}$ [waṇṭi]$_{p_\alpha}$ [aappiis]$_{p_\alpha}$
      Mcompounding [ṭiiwaṇṭiaappiis]$_{m_\beta}$
                      [ṭii]$_{p_\alpha}$ [waṇṭi]$_{p_\alpha}$ [aappiis]$_{p_\alpha}$
      PCF   [ṭiiwaṇṭiaappiis]$_{m_\beta}$
                      [ṭiiwaṇṭiaappiis]$_{p_\beta}$
      Rules $\left[\begin{array}{cc} \text{tíiwaṇṭiyàappìisə} \\ | \quad\quad\quad \searrow \\ \text{L} \quad\quad\quad \text{H} \end{array}\right]_{p_\beta}$

                      'fire of cart of office'

(16) Cocompounding

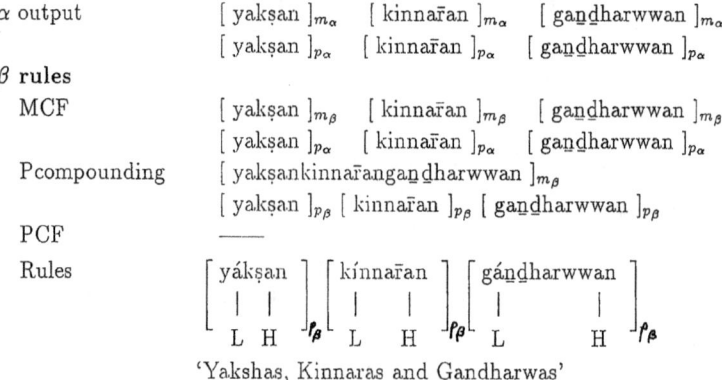

'Yakshas, Kinnaras and Gandharwas'

Besides condensing two strata into one, this analysis captures an additional generalization which a nonprosodic level-ordered analysis is forced to stipulate: the two halves of subcompounds do not undergo any β rules before compounding takes place. Mohanan 1986 was forced to specify stratum 2 as noncyclic in order to accommodate

4.2. MALAYALAM

this fact; by contrast, it follows naturally from the prosodic analysis.[4] Because Mcompounding feeds the Prosodic Constituent Formation Algorithm, those simple stems which are input to Mcompounding never have a chance to attain prosodic constituent status, and thus never themselves correspond to domains for β rules.

Now that we have accounted for the prosodic asymmetries between simple subcompounds and cocompounds, let us turn to the more complex case, where one kind of compound is nested within the other. These are the cases which Mohanan uses to argue for the loop.

Four kinds of structures need to be derived: those where a cocompound contains a subcompound, resulting in two prosodic constituents, as in (17a) and (17b); and those where a subcompound contains a cocompound, resulting in three prosodic constituents. These latter structures are depicted in (18a) and (18b).

(17)

(18)

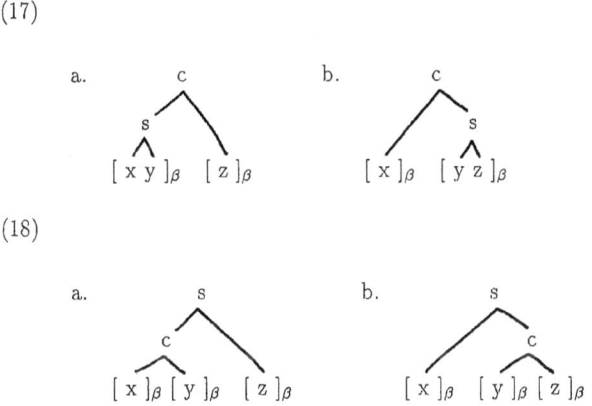

Under the assumption that stratum β is cyclic, the rules in (13) and (14) will derive the correct bracketing in all these cases. For example, consider (17b), a subcompound nested within a cocompound. As (19) illustrates, on the first cycle of β rules, the subcompound is formed by Mcompounding (13);[5] phonological rules apply within the single prosodic constituent containing the compound. On the next cycle, Pcompounding (14) combines the newly-formed subcompound with the remaining

---

[4]According to Mohanan and Mohanan 1984, all strata in Malayalam are noncyclic, although I believe noncyclicity is crucial only for stratum 2. I will argue later against the theoretical device of labeling levels as noncyclic.

[5]Mcompounding and Pcompounding are not ordered with respect to each other; the only constraint is that both are intrinsically ordered before Prosodic Constituent Formation.

word, producing two prosodic constituents. β phonological rules apply vacuously or not at all to the first constituent, and apply for the first time to the second word. The example in (19) is amended from Mohanan 1986:124:[6]

(19)

α output		[kaamuki]$_{m_\alpha}$	[bhaarya]$_{m_\alpha}$	[sahoodari]$_{m_\alpha}$
		[kaamuki]$_{p_\alpha}$	[bhaarya]$_{p_\alpha}$	[sahoodari]$_{p_\alpha}$
β cycle 1				
	MCF	[kaamuki]$_{m_\beta}$	[bhaarya]$_{m_\beta}$	[sahoodari]$_{m_\beta}$
		[kaamuki]$_{p_\alpha}$	[bhaarya]$_{p_\alpha}$	[sahoodari]$_{p_\alpha}$
	Mcompounding	[kaamuki]$_{m_\beta}$	[bhaaryasahoodari]$_{m_\beta}$	
		[kaamuki]$_{p_\alpha}$	[bhaarya]$_{p_\alpha}$	[sahoodari]$_{p_\alpha}$
	PCF	[kaamuki]$_{p_\beta}$	[bhaaryasahoodari]$_{m_\beta}$	
			[bhaaryasahoodari]$_{p_\beta}$	

Rules:

$$\begin{bmatrix} káamuki \\ | \quad | \\ L \quad H \end{bmatrix}_{p_\beta} \begin{bmatrix} bháaryàasahòodari \\ | \quad \vee \\ L \quad H \end{bmatrix}_{p_\beta}$$

β Cycle 2

MCF —

Pcompounding [kaamukibhaaryasahoodari]$_{m_\beta}$

$$\begin{bmatrix} káamuki \\ | \quad | \\ L \quad H \end{bmatrix}_{p_\beta} \begin{bmatrix} bháaryàasahòodari \\ | \quad \vee \\ L \quad H \end{bmatrix}_{p_\beta}$$

PCF —

Rules — —

---

[6]The final vowel of the first member of the cocompound (*kaamuki*) surfaces as long, by virtue of a lengthening rule assigned by Mohanan to the cocompounding level. See the following section for discussion of this rule in the proposed account.

4.2. MALAYALAM

In (20) we see the rules operating in a different order, to produce a cocompound within a subcompound, as in (18a):

(20)

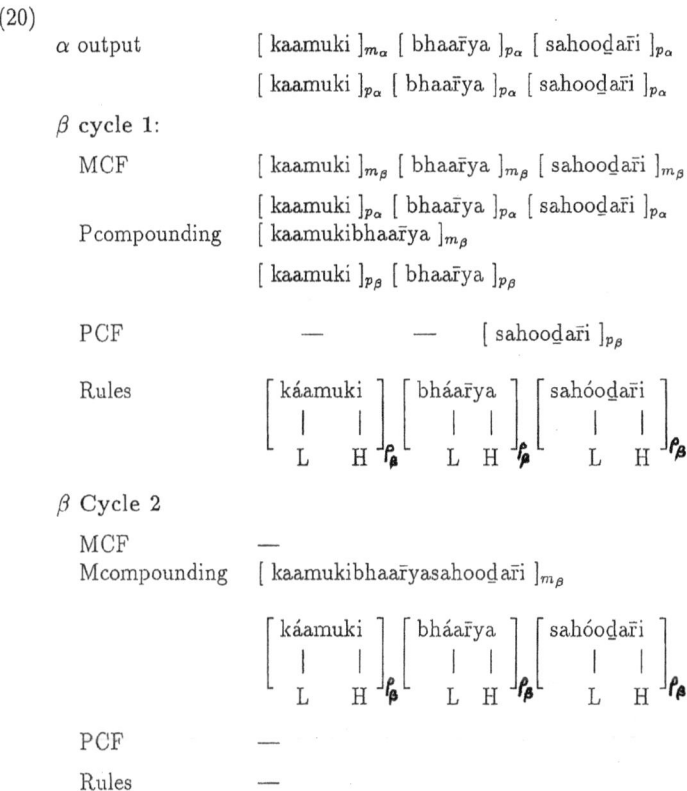

It can be verified that the remaining prosodic structures in (17)-(18) are generated by the rules given; we need not step through each example here.

4.2.3 Phonological Rules

Up to this point we have said little about the phonological rules applying within compounds. In fact, the prosodic analysis makes several strong predictions about the nature of these rules, all of which contrast sharply with the predictions of a loop analysis. First, the prosodic analysis outlined above predicts that no phonological rules will apply across the internal boundaries of cocompounds on the cycle on which they are formed. By contrast, in a loop analysis we would expect rules to apply within all cocompounds immediately upon formation on stratum 3. The loop account also predicts the possbility that some rules will designate stratum 3 as their exclusive, or at least their latest, domain of application, while the prosodic analysis makes the opposite prediction that all rules which apply within cocompounds apply within all γ constituents as well. This follows from the fact that cocompounds do not form a single β prosodic constituent when they are formed and become a single rule domain only with respect to γ rules.

The predictions of the prosodic account are largely confirmed by the data. Not only are there no rules applying solely to cocompounds; in fact, with the exceptions of Vowel Lengthening and Vowel Sandhi, no rules even appear to apply within cocompounds at all. We noted in an earlier section the gross asymmetry between the number of rules applying within subcompounds (nine) and within cocompounds (three). I will argue below that in fact, both the rules attributed to stratum 3 actually apply on stratum 4 (i.e. within the γ domain) and do not need to apply on stratum 3 at all. Thus what on Mohanan's analysis would be a striking and unexplained asymmetry between the number of rules applying on strata 2 and 3 is derived naturally on the prosodic account.

Vowel Sandhi

The problem posed by Vowel Sandhi, a rule assimilating two adjacent vowels into a single, long vowel,[7] is that it applies within subcompounds and cocompounds but not, according to Mohanan, on any following stratum.

(21) Vowel Sandhi (domain: strata 1-3, in [+Sanskrit] forms)

  a. If two nuclei in a sequence are separated by an empty onset, delete the first nucleus node and the onset node.
  b. If the remaining nucleus N is not branching, link the unsyllabified X on the left to the N on the right.

---

[7]If the first vowel is high and the second short, the result is a glide-short vowel sequence (Mohanan 1986:103.)

4.2. MALAYALAM

(22) shows the rule applying within a cocompound; in (23) the rule fails to apply across an inflectional suffix (data from Mohanan 1986).

(22) ṭaaṟa + iṉdṟan ⟶ ṭaaṟeeṉdṟan   'Tara and Indra'   [p. 121]

(23) ṭaaṟa + -aal ⟶ ṭaaṟayaal (*ṭaaṟaal)   'Tara(Inst)'   [p. 104]

Under the prosodic account outlined above, we have no way of stipulating that a rule will apply within cocompounds but not within the γ domain, since compounds do not constitute a prosodic domain of their own.

However, this problem obtains a simple solution if we follow a suggestion of Mohanan 1986. Noting that since Vowel Sandhi applies only to [+Sanskrit] stems, and since all inflectional (stratum 4) suffixes are [+Dravidian], Mohanan observes that there is no empirical evidence against assigning Vowel Sandhi to the inflectional stratum. In his account, indeed, it makes no difference, and it is only on grounds of parsimony that he decides against making Vowel Sandhi a stratum 4 rule. However, on the prosodic account, assigning Vowel Sandhi to the γ domain achieves exactly the right results. Since Vowel Sandhi can apply to only those γ forms without (Dravidian) suffixes, it will pick out exactly the forms we want: those which have immediately exited β rules, i.e. cocompounds. The following derivation shows only prosodic structure and the rules directly affecting it.

(24)
β rules	[ṭaaṟa]$_\alpha$	[iṉdṟan]$_\alpha$
Pcompounding	[ṭaaṟa]$_\beta$	[iṉdṟan]$_\beta$
Vowel Sandhi	—	—
γ rules		
PCF	[ṭaaṟaiṉdṟan]$_\gamma$	
Vowel Sandhi	[ṭaaṟeeṉdṟan]$_\gamma$	

In conclusion, if we take the option of allowing Vowel Sandhi to apply to cocompounds on the γ domain, this rule no longer presents an argument for treating cocompounds as a rule domain distinct from γ.

Vowel Lengthening

The reanalysis of Vowel Lengthening will be similar, namely that Vowel Lengthening indeed does apply on the inflectional level (the γ domain, or stratum 4), and that we do not require a special cocompounding domain for this rule.

As shown in Mohanan 1986, Vowel Lengthening applies to the final vowel of the first member of those co- and subcompounds whose second member is [+Sanskrit]. The rule is stated in (25) and shown applying to a cocompound in (26):

(25)
  Vowel Lengthening (domain: strata 2, 3)   [p. 100]

```
  N    →    N      / — ] [
  |         /\
  X        X  X         [+Sanskrit]
  |         \/
```

(26) ṭaaīa + kaaṇṭan ⟶ ṭaaīaakaaṇṭan   'Tara and Kantan'   [p. 99]

At first glance, the solution proposed above for the problem of Vowel Sandhi will work in the case of Vowel Lengthening as well: since the rule applies only to [+Sanskrit] forms, the fact that it fails to apply before inflectional endings is still compatible with assigning it to the γ domain (stratum 4).

However, Vowel Lengthening poses an additional complication which Vowel Sandhi does not, namely that Vowel Lengthening appears to make crucial reference to the internal bracketing of cocompounds. On all other theories of bracket erasure in the literature,[8] β internal brackets will be erased before γ rules have a chance to apply,

---

[8]Of those theories that have incorporated explicit statements of bracket erasure, even the weakest proposed version of that convention (Mohanan 1982, Kiparsky 1982) erases internal brackets after the end of each level. That would make the internal brackets of a co-compound invisible to stratum 4 rules.

placing a serious obstacle in the simple path taken above of assigning Vowel Lengthening to the γ domain. However, on the formulation of bracket erasure being assumed in Prosodic Lexical Phonology, internal brackets will be visible precisely when they belong to the immediate daughters of a branching node of a different constituent type. If a γ node branches into two β daughters, the juncture will be visible, exactly what is needed to state the rule of Vowel Lengthening.

To sum up, by locating both Vowel Lengthening and Vowel Sandhi on the domain of inflection (γ, or Mohanan's stratum 4), we obviate the need for a special domain within which phonological rules will apply only to cocompounds. As a consequence, we can collapse both subcompounding and cocompounding into one morphological 'level' and do away with the loop. Malayalam no longer presents a counterexample to strict layering and the prosodic hierarchy theory. On the contrary, the mismatch demonstrated in Malayalam between prosodic and morphological constituency provides important support for prosodic structure in the lexicon.

The analysis requires the introduction of another source of prosodic constituency into the theory, namely the ability of a morphological rule to impose prosodic constituency on its output.

4.3 English

As argued in Kiparsky 1982 and Borowsky 1986, compounding in English is a β morphological process, as evidenced by the fact that compounds can receive β but not α suffixes. English compounds resemble Malayalam cocompounds in that β phonological rules apply to each stem before it is compounded. In (27) are listed several rules which do not apply to α stems, but which do apply to each member of a compound (see Halle and Mohanan 1985).[9]

(27)

Rule	stem	compound	before α suffix
g deletion	sign	sign board	signature
n deletion	hymn	hymn book	hymnal
Voiced Obstruent Deletion	crumb	crumb cake	crumble
Stem-final Tensing	city	city hall	citify

---

[9]These and other β rules in English are discussed in more detail in chapter 5.

From what we have seen so far in this chapter, the facts in (27) strongly point to English having a β Pcompounding rule. Only Pcompounding will cause rules to apply to each member of a compound on the level at which compounding takes place.

(28) English noun-noun compounding (=Pcompounding)

Morphological constituency	Morphological constituency	Prosodic constituency
$[\,x_i\,]_\beta, \ldots [\,x_n\,]_\beta$ $\longrightarrow$	$[\,x_i, \ldots x_n\,]_\beta$	$[\,x_i\,, \ldots [\,x_n\,]_\beta$

4.3.1 The Loop

Halle and Mohanan 1985 propose a different analysis of English compounding, one which locates compounding on its own stratum (stratum 3). In order to account for the fact that compounds may acquire β (stratum 2) suffixes, their analysis, like that of Mohanan 1982 for Malayalam, requires the loop.

The basis for their decision to move compounding out of stratum 2 is the rule of stem-final vowel lengthening/tensing mentioned in (27). They claim that this rule distinguishes between those stems which precede level 2 suffixes and those which participate in compounding.

In certain dialects which Halle and Mohanan characterize as B and C, vowel lengthening/tensing applies at the end of each half of a compound, but not to the end of a stem which is followed by level 2 suffixes. The following example is from Halle and Mohanan 1985:59):

(29)

Environment	Example	UR	Dialect B	C
Word-final	baby, penny	ı	iy	i
Before inflection	babies, pennies	ı	iy	i
Stem-finally in compounds	baby sit, penny candy	ı	iy	i
Before -*ness*, -*hood*, etc.	babyhood, penniless	ı	i	ı

Halle and Mohanan take this as evidence that in dialects B and C, compounding takes place on stratum 3. The sole phonological rule to apply on that stratum is vowel lengthening/tensing.

While it accounts for the facts of lengthening/tensing, this proposal has a number of drawbacks. First, as mentioned, it requires the introduction into English of the loop, in order to accommodate the fact that the compounds in (29) can receive level 2 suffixes (e.g. *babysitting, pennilessness*). Especially since we were able to eliminate the loop in Malayalam, this addition of power to the theory is particularly undesirable. Second, as was the case in Malayalam, the fact that the proposed stratum 3 is the domain of only one phonological rule calls into question its legitimacy in the grammar.

4.3.2 A Prosodic Solution

Fortunately, an alternative account of the stem-final lengthening/tensing alternation is available within the proposed prosodic model. This solution relies crucially on the phonological properties of the members of compounds.

By concentrating on the morphological difference between compounds and level 2 derived words, Halle and Mohanan overlooked an equally significant *phonological* difference between them, a difference we may exploit to explain their asymmetric behavior with respect to stem-final lengthening/tensing. The relevant observation is the following: in forms with a β suffix, stem-final i is always followed by a metrically weak syllable within the same (β) constituent.

(30) [happiness]$_{p_\beta}$, [citihood]$_{p_\beta}$, [merriment]$_{p_\beta}$, [penniless]$_{p_\beta}$

By contrast, in β compounds, an i at the end of the first member is never followed by any material within the same β prosodic constituent.

(31) [city]$_{p_\beta}$ [hall]$_{p_\beta}$,   [baby]$_{p_\beta}$ [sit]$_{p_\beta}$

This asymmetry allows us to apply stem-final lengthening freely to all β stems, but appeal to another rule which will shorten the vowel in a metrically weak open syllable when another unstressed syllable follows. I propose to do this by invoking final extrametricality of final /iː/, and then applying a general rule shortening unstressed /iː/. Only when /iː/ is in final position will it (correctly) remain long.

CHAPTER 4. CONSTRUCTIONAL CONSTRAINTS

(32) Final /iː/ Extrametricality: make a word-final, unstressed /iː/ extrametrical

(33) /iː/ Shortening: shorten an unstressed /iː/ to /i/ if a metrically weak syllable follows

The rule of Final /iː/ Extrametricality is independently motivated in English: binary feet in word-final position do not count as branching for purposes of the word tree rule exactly when the second syllable which they dominate ends in /iː/.

(34)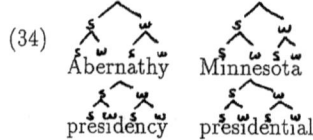

We may assume that Final /iː/ Extrametricality applies after Final *i* Lengthening and before word tree construction.

/iː/ Shortening applies only on level 1 in the dialect described by Hayes, but for Halle and Mohanan's dialects B and C it must apply on level 2 as well. Thus, the derivation for words like *happiness, citihood, merriment* and so forth will be parallel to that for the suffixed level 1 forms:

(35)
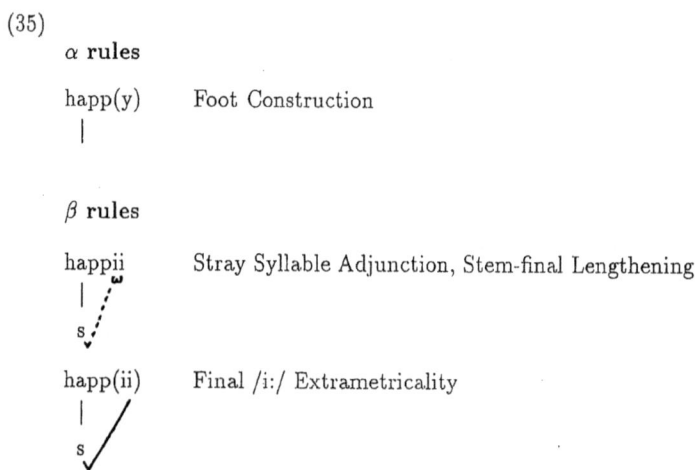

4.3. ENGLISH

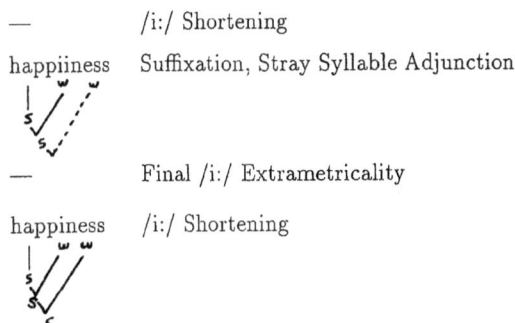

By contrast, an *i* at the end of a stem in a compound will be lengthened, become extrametrical, fail to satisfy the environment for Shortening, and persist.

(36) [city]$_\beta$ [hall]$_\beta$

By recognizing the phonological asymmetry between β suffixed forms and the first member of β compounds, and the parallel between β suffixed forms and α suffixed forms, we can account naturally for the alternations observed by Halle and Mohanan 1985 without requiring a special compounding stratum or the loop. Rather, the simple rule of Pcompounding is sufficient to capture the fact that members of compounds undergo β rules individually in English.

4.3.3 Phonological Rules

A prediction of the proposed prosodic analysis is that compounds will not form a unitary β domain on the compounding cycle. How, then, are we to account for the 'Compound Stress Rule' (SPE, Liberman and Prince 1977, Hayes 1981)?

(37) Compound Stress Rule: In a pair of sister nodes [N$_1$ N$_2$], N$_2$ is *s* iff it branches

Since this rule applies within compounds, it would seem to require that the compound form a single rule domain. However, the recognition that the Compound·Stress

Rule and the word stress assignment rule are one and the same (Liberman and Prince 1977) provides a very simple solution to the problem. Compounds do receive stress as a unit, but on the cycle *after* the one in which their members are concatenated. In the case of simple compounds, as in (38a), this will be the first cycle of γ rules. In the case of nested compounds, as in (38b), the embedded compound will be stressed on the second cycle of β rules by (37), which applies both to β and to γ constituents.[10]

(38)

β **rules**	a. simple compound	b. nested compound	
Pcompounding	[phone]$_{p_\beta}$ [book]$_{p_\beta}$	[phone]$_{p_\beta}$ [book]$_{p_\beta}$	
PCF	—	—	[listing]$_{p_\beta}$
Bracket Erasure	—	—	
Stress rule	—	—	
Pcompounding		[[phone]$_{p_\beta}$ [book]$_{p_\beta}$]$_{p_\beta}$ [listing]$_{p_\beta}$	
PCF		—	
Bracket Erasure		[phone book]$_{p_\beta}$ [listing]$_{p_\beta}$	
Stress rule		[phŏne bŏok]$_{p_\beta}$ [listing]$_{p_\beta}$ (s w)	
γ **rules**			
PCF	[[phone]$_{p_\beta}$ [book]$_{p_\beta}$]$_{p_\gamma}$	[[phŏne bŏok]$_{p_\beta}$ [listing]$_{p_\beta}$]$_{p_\gamma}$ (s w)	
Bracket Erasure	—	—	
Stress rule	[[phŏne bŏok]$_{p_\beta}$]$_{p_\gamma}$ (s w)	[[phŏne bŏok]$_{p_\beta}$ [listing]$_{p_\beta}$]$_{p_\gamma}$ (s w)	

---

[10] As in the original Liberman and Prince schema, branchingness is taken to be a property of metrical structure, not of prosodic constituency; bracket erasure does not interfere in its computation.

4.4 Summary

English compounding patterns with Malayalam cocompounding in support of the proposal that prosodic constituent structure co-exists with, and may differ geometrically from, morphological constituent structure. What under nonprosodic formulations of lexical phonology forces the overly powerful device of the loop obtains a natural characterization in the prosodic model, as a mismatch between morphological and prosodic constituency. The prosodic model is both more flexible and at the same time more constrained than the nonprosodic model.

To achieve the mismatch required by Pcompounds, it proved necessary to introduce into prosodic theory the ability for particular morphological constructions to impose specific prosodic requirements on the elements involved. Support for this added power comes from the fact that it is needed elsewhere in the grammar — in the phonology-syntax connection. The prosodic constraints associated with the morphological rule of Pcompounding are reminiscent of the discussion in Chapter 2 of English Heavy NP shift and Serbo-Croatian topicalization. In those cases, the claim was that particular syntactic constructions are associated with prosodic requirements. Pcompounding shows that this phenomenon occurs within the lexicon as well, and is therefore general.

Chapter 5

Prosodic Subcategorization

In this chapter I introduce the notion of prosodic subcategorization. This device is motivated, in combination with the orthogonal property of morphological subcategorization, as a means of crossclassifying morphemes and morphological strings in terms of their dependence properties. It also provides an important source of information about prosodic constituency. All affixes and clitics, it will be claimed, are lexically listed with prosodic subcategorization frames, formally encoding the fact that these morphemes are prosodically bound. Like morphological subcategorization frames, prosodic subcategorization frames convey information about the type of constituent that the morpheme attaches to and about the type of constituent that is formed.

Subcategorization frames play an active role in the derivation, contributing information to each representation they are part of. I supply a somewhat different interpretation for these frames than, for example, Lieber gives to morphological subcategorization frames. Instead of passively constraining the immediate context of the bound morpheme, subcategorization frames are construed on this account, as actual pieces of prosodic structure. Associating prosodically bound morphemes with prosodic structure ensures the formation of a new prosodic constituent each time such a morpheme is attached; and, together with the premise that rules apply each time a new prosodic constituent is built, produces the effect of cyclicity. Prosodic frames thus provide the theory with a third means of generating prosodic structure. Like the rule of Pcompounding introduced in Chapter 4, prosodic subcategorization frames introduce structure which blocks the application of the default Prosodic Constituent

Formation Algorithm. In some cases, the prosodic structure which is introduced corresponds exactly to its morphological counterpart, but this is not necessarily the case. Like Pcompounding, prosodic frames play a crucial role in generating mismatches between prosodic and morphological structure.

Although presenting a theory of morphology is far beyond the scope of this thesis, I should say a few words here about the nature of the morphological component that I am assuming. In general, I assume a morpheme-based theory of morphology (see e.g. Lieber 1980, Kiparsky 1982, 1984) in which morphemes combine freely, subject to various constraints which cause illicit combinations to be rejected. In this view I differ from Selkirk 1982, in which phrase structure rules license all and only the possible morpheme combinations. At the level of generality at which I will be discussing word formation, no formal distinction is drawn between inflection and derivation. Both, I assume, are lexical (Lieber 1980, Kiparsky 1982).

Morpheme combination is driven by two forces: compounding rules and subcategorization frames.[1] An example of the former is found in chapter 4. The latter is discussed in this chapter. Constraints on combination also find several sources. For example, certain nonproductive morphemes must be listed with the elements with which they may combine. In some cases, specific orderings among affixes must be indicated. The constraints I will focus on in this chapter are those which relate to constituency and which can be stated in the subcategorization frames of bound morphemes.

5.1 Dependence in the Lexicon

The presence of prosodic constituent structure in the lexicon enables us to capture important generalizations about the prosodic and morphological independence of morpheme types; in particular, the two dimensions of prosodic constituency and morphological constituency define a four-way typology which properly characterizes the different types of 'bound' morphemes.

It is a well-known cross-linguistic fact that, underlyingly, morphemes differ along the dimension of independence. Certain morphemes (the 'free') can stand on their own, and others (the 'bound') can not.[2]

---
[1] See Lieber 1980, Kiparsky 1983 for arguments in favor of subcategorization frames over insertion rules.

[2] Here and in the following pages, by 'morphologically free' I mean 'not requiring further derivational morphology'.

(1)

Free	Bound
stem	affix
	root
	clitic

The situation is, however, more complex than a simple binary distinction like that in (1) can handle. Consider affixes and bound roots, both of which must occur together with at least one other morpheme to form an independent word.

(2)

Affix:	*-ist	(cf. violinist)
	*dis-	(cf. distrust)
Root:	*-ceive	(cf. receive)
	*cran-	(cf. cranberry)

The two morpheme types differ substantially in their overall prosodic properties. While affixes automatically create phonological rule domains when they are introduced into the representation, roots never behave in this way. In fact, the failure to form prosodic domains is a characteristic property of bound roots, as we saw in chapter 3.

The classification in (1) also lumps clitics together with the other dependent morphemes. Clitics, which we may informally define for the present as 'bound' words, can be realized only in close conjunction with another word, as in the following example of English auxiliaries: ='s is the enclitic form of *is*, and =*l* the enclitic version of *will*.

(3)

Clitic:	*[z]	(is)	(cf. Mary='s eating)
	*[l]	(will)	(cf. Mary='ll eat that)

But unlike roots and affixes, clitics do not require the presence of a morphological sister in order to be morphologically well-formed. Clitics are in fact independent

5.1. DEPENDENCE IN THE LEXICON

syntactic terminals, while affixes and roots are not. Consider the illustrations in (4) of the English auxiliary clitic. ='s does not form a morphological unit with the preceding word, its 'host', from which it cannot be separated by pause, with which it is syllabified, and to whose final segment it assimilates in voice. In fact, the auxiliary and its host are not even part of the same syntactic constituent (the host is part of the subject NP, and the auxiliary is not).

(4)
    a. The [pilot's] in the cockpit [s]
    b. The pilot I [met's] in the cockpit [s]
    c. The pilot I talked [to's] in the cockpit [z]
    d. The pilot who knows [me's] in the cockpit [z]

If clitics are not morphologically attached to the preceding word, then how may we characterize their dependence on their host? I suggest that clitics are *prosodically* bound elements, which do not form independent prosodic units of their own but must be pronounced in conjunction with another word to produce a well-formed prosodic constituent.

Once we recognize prosodic dependence as a dimension separate from that of morphological dependence, we can properly factor apart the dependence properties of stems, roots, affixes and clitics. Clitics are dependent prosodically but not morphologically, while stems are not dependent along either dimension; affixes are dependent morphologically on another element and attached prosodically to that element as well, and bound roots are dependent only morphologically. [3]

(5)

	Morphologically dependent	Not morphologically dependent
Prosodically dependent	affix	clitic
Not prosodically dependent	root	stem

[3] The reasons why bound roots do not have prosodic subcategorization frames will be discussed in subsequent sections, as the arguments are somewhat intricate and depend on material presented later.

Given this intuitive typology of morpheme dependence, the next task is to come up with a formal representation of the relevant distinctions. An important step in this direction has already been taken by Lieber 1980. As we saw earlier, Lieber proposes to represent morphological dependence by means of morphological subcategorization frames. These frames are affiliated not only with bound roots, as we saw in chapter 3, but also with affixes — that is, with the set of morphemes characterized above as morphologically bound.[4]

(6)

    Affix: in- $[\underline{}[\ ]_{m_\alpha}]_{m_\alpha}$ (insane)
    Root: -mit $[[\ ]_{m_\alpha}\underline{}]_{m_\alpha}$ (admit)

Stems are morphologically independent. They do not subcategorize in this fashion, nor do clitics.[5]

We can incorporate the dimension of prosodic dependence into the framework by proposing a type of subcategorization exactly analogous to morphological subcategorization — but for prosodic constituency. Affixes and clitics will be listed with prosodic subcategorization frames; roots and stems will not.[6]

(7)

    Affix: in- $[\underline{}[\ ]_{p_\alpha}]_{p_\alpha}$ (insane)
    Clitic: ='s $[[\ ]_{p_\omega}\underline{}]_{p_\omega}$ (John's)

To summarize, we have exploited the independence of morphological and prosodic constituent structure to formulate generic representations of the underlying prosodic and morphological constituency of each of the four possible morpheme types: affixes, roots, clitics, and stems.

---

[4] Again, note that the frames presented in (6) differ notationally from those of Lieber (see e.g. Lieber 1980:65-66).

[5] I found no explicit mention of clitics in Lieber 1980, but it would be consistent with her overall program not to assign morphological subcategorization frames to clitics, which do not form morphological units with their hosts.

[6] Note that these frames share similarity only in name with the phonological subcategorization frames of Klavans 1985. These latter entities constrain only the syntactic context of an item, albeit for the purposes of phonological rules. Prosodic subcategorization frames also differ substantially from the phonological instantiation frames of Hayes's (1990) precompilation theory, which constrain the syntactic context of items which are not necessarily subcategorized. In a recent account of phrasally conditioned allomorphy in Modern Greek, however, Condoravdi 1990 has proposed to introduce prosodic constituency into Hayes's frames.

(8)

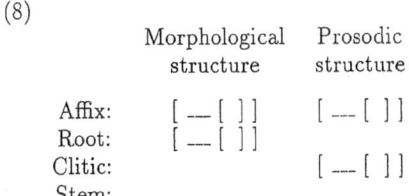

While the bound morphemes shown in (8) all subcategorize for a sister on the right, the opposite direction of dependence is also possible. In fact, in later sections (5.3.2, 6.11.1) we will make use of the third logical possibility, bidirectional dependence.

5.2 Prosodic Subcategorization

The immediate relevance of subcategorization frames to the proposal being outlined here is that prosodic frames represent, in addition to Prosodic Constituent Formation and Pcompounding, the third and most specific source of information about the prosodic constituency of affixed words. In the following sections we will see how both morphological and prosodic subcategorization frames contribute to the construction of fully specified morphological and prosodic hierarchies of the sort required in Prosodic Lexical Phonology.

We have already established that the presence of a subcategorization frame in the lexical entry for a morpheme tells us that this morpheme is dependent, for its realization, on some other constituent. In addition to encoding dependence, subcategorization frames include a number of properties which characterize bound morphemes. These properties, crucial to constituent formation, include the type of constituent attached to, the type produced, and the linear order of the combination. For a morphological subcategorization frame, therefore, the encoded information will be as follows:[7]

---

[7] I do not intend this information to exhaust the lexical entries of bound morphemes. Clearly, syntactic category, diacritic features such as [+/−Latinate], conjugation/declension class, and even the morphological identity of possible sisters (as in the case of nonproductive affixation) may also need to be mentioned in individual lexical entries. However, these properties are orthogonal to the distinction between bound and free morphemes, and thus not dependent on subcategorization. I am focusing here on those properties which are uniquely represented in subcategorization frames.

(9) Information encoded in morphological subcategorization frames

   a. Type of morphological constituent attached to (e.g. α or β)
   b. Type of morphological constituent produced
   c. Linear order in which the morpheme combines with its host

(10) provides examples of morphological subcategorization frames for a number of α morphemes.

(10)

	Affix:	in- :	$[\,\text{---}\,[\;]_\alpha\,]_\alpha$
		per-:	$[\,\text{---}\,[\;]_\alpha\,]_\alpha$
		-ity:	$[\,[\;]_\alpha\,\text{---}\,]_\alpha$
		-ous:	$[\,[\;]_\alpha\,\text{---}\,]_\alpha$
	Root:	mot-:	$[\,\text{---}\,[\;]_\alpha\,]_\alpha$
		-ceive:	$[\,[\;]_\alpha\,\text{---}\,]_\alpha$
		-fer:	$[\,[\;]_\alpha\,\text{---}\,]_\alpha$
		-mit:	$[\,[\;]_\alpha\,\text{---}\,]_\alpha$

Similar subcategorization frames accompany β morphemes in the lexicon:

(11)

	Affix:	un-:	$[\,\text{---}\,[\;]_\beta\,]_\beta$
		extra-:	$[\,\text{---}\,[\;]_\beta\,]_\beta$
		-less:	$[\,[\;]_\beta\,\text{---}\,]_\beta$
		-hood:	$[\,[\;]_\beta\,\text{---}\,]_\beta$

In a similar vein, those dominance and precedence relations relevant for prosodic structure are lexically encoded in the prosodic subcategorization frames of affixes and clitics.

(12) Information specified in prosodic subcategorization frames

   a. Type of prosodic constituent attached to (e.g. α or β)
   b. Type of prosodic constituent produced
   c. Linear order in which the morpheme combines with its host

5.3. SELECTIONAL RESTRICTIONS: THE INNER FRAME

Adopting the format of the morphological subcategorization frames presented above, we posit for the α affixes *in-* and *-ity*, the β affixes *un-* and *-less*, and the auxiliary clitic *='s* the prosodic subcategorization frames in (13):[8]

(13)

$$
\begin{array}{lll}
\text{Affix:} & \text{in- :} & [\,\text{---}\,[\ ]_\alpha\,]_\alpha \\
& \text{-ity:} & [\,[\ ]_\alpha\,\text{---}\,]_\alpha \\
& \text{un-:} & [\,\text{---}\,[\ ]_\beta\,]_\beta \\
& \text{-less:} & [\,[\ ]_\beta\,\text{---}\,]_\beta \\
\text{Clitic:} & \text{='s :} & [\,[\ ]_\omega\,\text{---}\,]_\omega
\end{array}
$$

(14) provides a summary of this section the relevant parts of actual lexical entries for four representative morphemes:

(14)

	Morphological frame	Prosodic frame
in-:	$[\,\text{---}\,[\ ]_\alpha\,]_\alpha$	$[\,\text{---}\,[\ ]_\alpha\,]_\alpha$
-ceive:	$[\,[\ ]_\alpha\,\text{---}\,]_\alpha$	
='s:		$[\,[\ ]_\omega\,\text{---}\,]_\omega$
talk:		

5.3 Selectional Restrictions: the Inner Frame

An important obligation of subcategorization frames is encoding selectional restrictions on the host of a dependent morpheme, and both morphological and prosodic frames perform this task. The mechanism by which the requirements of subcategorization frames are fulfilled is one of unification (see e.g. Shieber 1986). As a partial morphological or prosodic structure, a subcategorization frame is not in itself well-formed.

---

[8] Note that much of the information specified on these frames is redundant; in the Appendix to this chapter a set of redundancy rules is posited to take care of this problem. Also, in chapter 8 we will examine the reasons for assigning the value ω — i.e. phonological word — to the subcategorization frame for the clitic.

(15)

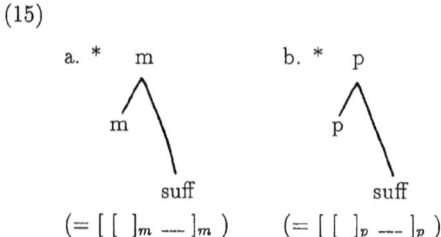

a. * m   (= [[ ]$_m$ ---]$_m$)

b. * p   (= [[ ]$_p$ ---]$_p$)

Every frame contains a node (the sister of the bound morpheme) which dominates no material. In order to force subcategorized elements to combine with a sister, we must impose a condition on the illformedness of empty nodes:

(16) Empty nodes in morphological or prosodic structure are ill-formed.

This constraint holds throughout the derivation, though not, of course, on lexical entries (which are generally exempt from configurational constraints). (17) thus ensures that the hypothetical suffix in (16) cannot stand alone, indirectly forcing it to combine with some other material so that the empty node will acquire content. However, the empty nodes in (16) perform another function as well: they impose selectional restrictions on the sister with which the suffix combines. In particular, the string must be nonnull, and its morphological or prosodic category must be compatible with the specifications on the subcategorization frame. In the examples in (18), the category of the stem is identical to the specification on the empty node in the subcategorization frame of the affix. Thus the two morphemes may combine.[9]

(17)

Stem	+	Affix	$\longrightarrow$	Stem
[conform]$_{m_\alpha}$		[[ ]$_{m_\alpha}$ ity]$_{m_\alpha}$		[[conform]$_{m_\alpha}$ ity]$_{m_\alpha}$
[conform]$_{p_\alpha}$		[[ ]$_{p_\alpha}$ ity]$_{p_\alpha}$		[[conform]$_{p_\alpha}$ ity]$_{p_\alpha}$
[historic]$_{m_\alpha}$		[[ ]$_{m_\alpha}$ al]$_{m_\alpha}$		[[historic]$_{m_\alpha}$ al]$_{m_\alpha}$
[historic]$_{p_\alpha}$		[[ ]$_{p_\alpha}$ al]$_{p_\alpha}$		[[historic]$_{p_\alpha}$ al]$_{p_\alpha}$

---

[9]In chapter 6 we will actually propose a slightly different prosodic frame for the extrametrical suffix -al, but this is not relevant here.

5.3. SELECTIONAL RESTRICTIONS: THE INNER FRAME

[childless]$_{m_\beta}$ [[ ]$_{m_\beta}$ ness]$_{m_\beta}$ [[childless]$_{m_\beta}$ ness]$_{m_\beta}$
[childless]$_{p_\beta}$ [[ ]$_{p_\beta}$ ness]$_{p_\beta}$ [[childless]$_{p_\beta}$ ness]$_{p_\beta}$

However, should there be any clash between the feature specifications of the host and those of the morpheme being added, unification will fail, and the combination will be rejected. Examples of this type of feature clash are given in (18), where an α suffix fails to attach to a β stem:

(18)

Stem	+	Affix	$\longrightarrow$	Stem
[sainthood]$_{m_\beta}$		[[ ]$_{m_\alpha}$ ify]$_{m_\alpha}$		*sainthoodify
[sainthood]$_{p_\beta}$		[[ ]$_{p_\alpha}$ ify]$_{p_\alpha}$		
[childlike]$_{m_\beta}$		[[ ]$_{m_\alpha}$ ity]$_{m_\alpha}$		*childlikity
[childlike]$_{p_\beta}$		[[ ]$_{p_\alpha}$ ity]$_{p_\alpha}$		
[helpless]$_{m_\beta}$		[[ ]$_{m_\alpha}$ ity]$_{m_\alpha}$		*helplessity
[helpless]$_{p_\beta}$		[[ ]$_{p_\alpha}$ ity]$_{p_\alpha}$		

5.3.1 Active Subcategorization

As noted above, the mechanism of subcategorization is given a different interpretation here from what is found elsewhere in the literature on morphology, e.g. Lieber 1980. In this latter view, which I term 'passive' subcategorization, subcategorizing elements check each potential host, failing to combine with that host if it does not satisfy the subcategorization requirements. By contrast, on the unification approach which I am assuming here, henceforth 'active' subcategorization, morphemes combine freely. Only the output of combination is checked. If the output is ill-formed then the derivation is halted.[10] We can think of subcategorization frames as pieces of

---

[10]The distinction between active and passive subcategorization is equivalent to the distinction drawn in Lexical Functional Grammar among functional annotations; some feature specifications are marked as constraining equations, and others are not. The former play a relatively minor role. A task for future study is to see whether passive subcategorization is really needed in morphology and syntax; although I do not attempt to resolve this here, in chapter 6 I do suggest that subcategorization for elements other than prosodic constituents might also be treated as active.

morphological or prosodic structure, which are ill-formed by themselves but become well-formed when they combine with an element which supplies the missing structure.

In the examples we have seen so far, active and passive subcategorization make exactly the same predictions. Where they diverge is with respect to the treatment of underspecified constituents. We turn now to one such case, which favors the active, unification approach.

5.3.2 Affixation to Roots

Given that affixes subcategorize for a prosodic host, and that bound roots have no prosodic constituency underlyingly, one might think that affixes will fail to attach to bound roots. In fact, however, the unification approach to subcategorization makes exactly the opposite prediction: because subcategorization is satisfied by unifying the feature specifications of the affix with those of the host, the prosodic feature specifications of the affix will never fail to unify with those of a root — as the latter is entirely unspecified for prosodic information. The prosodic subcategorization frame for the affix will itself contribute the necessary constituent structure to the representation. This process is demonstrated below, where several different affixes are shown attaching successfully to bound roots:[11]

(19)

Root	+ Affix	$\longrightarrow$ Stem
$[\,[\,]_{m_\alpha}$ fer $]_{m_\alpha}$	$[\,\text{in}\,[\,]_{m_\alpha}\,]_{m_\alpha}$	$[\,[\,\text{in}\,]_{m_\alpha}\,[\,\text{fer}\,]_{m_\alpha}\,]_{m_\alpha}$
	$[\,\text{in}\,[\,]_{p_\alpha}\,]_{p_\alpha}$	$[\,[\,\text{in}\,]_{p_\alpha}\,[\,\text{fer}]_{p_\alpha}\,]_{p_\alpha}$
$[\,[\,]_{m_\alpha}$ ceive $]_{m_\alpha}$	$[\,\text{de}\,[\,]_{m_\alpha}\,]_{m_\alpha}$	$[\,[\,\text{de}\,]_{m_\alpha}\,[\,\text{ceive}\,]_{m_\alpha}\,]_{m_\alpha}$
	$[\,\text{de}\,[\,]_{p_\alpha}\,]_{p_\alpha}$	$[\,[\,\text{de}\,]_{p_\alpha}\,[\,\text{ceive}\,]_{p_\alpha}\,]_{p_\alpha}$

---

[11]It should be noted that by the same mechanism, active subcategorization, that permits affixes and bound roots to satisfy each other's subcategorization requirements, the theory predicts the same of affixes. A prefix and suffix which subcategorize for units of the same type should be able to attach to each other, forming a constituent with the internal structure of a compound: $[[\ ]_p\ [\ ]_p]_p$. The same holds for clitics. This prediction seems counterintuitive for languages like English, where affixes are relatively devoid of semantic content. However, the hope is (though I have not been able to investigate this) that languages will be found where this sort of combination is allowed. In the event that such evidence is not forthcoming, the only way I can imagine of restricting the theory to rule out such cases is to impose the stipulative constraint that structures like $[[\ ]_{p_i}\ [\ ]_{p_i}\ ]_{p_i}$ are ill-formed. (We cannot impose the same constraint on morphological structure, as it is needed in the case of compounds.)

5.3. SELECTIONAL RESTRICTIONS: THE INNER FRAME

$$[\,[\,]_{m_\alpha} \text{ gress }]_{m_\alpha} \quad [\text{ pro }[\,]_{m_\alpha}]_{m_\alpha} \quad [\,[\text{ pro }]_{m_\alpha}[\text{ gress }]_{m_\alpha}]_{m_\alpha}$$
$$[\text{ pro }[\,]_{p_\alpha}]_{p_\alpha} \quad [\,[\text{ pro }]_{p_\alpha}[\text{ gress }]_{p_\alpha}]_{p_\alpha}$$

The principle of bracket erasure (chapter 3) applies automatically in all of the above cases, accounting for why the inner prosodic constituents created temporarily by affixation fail to trigger phonological rules on the root. Thus, as was the case with Mcompounding (chapter 4), only the *output* of this kind of affixation is input to phonological rules.

The combination possibilities of bound roots are by no means unrestricted, however. On the contrary, morphological subcategorization frames of bound roots constrain the kinds of affixes they may combine with. In English, most bound roots appear to subcategorize for an α morphological sister (Siegel 1974, Allen 1978, Mohanan 1986), a generalization which we can capture by applying a default fill-in rule to underspecified subcategorization frames. (See the Appendix to this chapter, where a set of such rules is developed.) The morphological specification of α on bound roots will prevent them from combining directly with a β affix.

(20)

$$[\,[\,]_{m_\alpha} \text{ mit }]_{m_\alpha} \;+\; [\text{ un }[\,]_{m_\beta}]_{m_\beta} \longrightarrow \;^{*}\text{unmit}$$
$$[\text{ un }[\,]_{p_\beta}]_{p_\beta}$$

A further property of bound roots which we have not discussed so far is that they can be derived as well as underlying. Up till now we have been comparing only isolated morphemes with respect to the parameter of dependence. In the cases we have seen so far, the result of morpheme combination has always been a free-standing form — a (derived) stem. But the morphological bound-free distinction extends to the result of morpheme combination as well. There are cases across languages where the result of combining two morphemes is a bound form — a (derived) root. An example of the latter, from Malayalam, is presented below (taken from T. Mohanan 1988; see also T. Mohanan 1989, fn. 50). Malayalam has a number of bound roots, which must combine with a derivational suffix in order to be part of a well-formed word. In most cases a single suffixation is sufficient to produce a stem which can then be inflected. However, there exist two suffixes (the verb-forming -*ikk*- and the noun/adjective-forming -*it*-) which, when they combine with a bound root, produce a form which is itself still bound. It must combine with yet another derivational suffix in order to form a stem. In the following example, forms followed by a hyphen are bound; others are free.

(21)
    a. ḏukk^h-
    b. ḏukk^h-ikk-
    c. ḏukk^h-ikk-uka   'to sorrow'
    d. ḏukk^h-ipp-ikk-
    e. ḏukk^h-ipp-ikk-aan   'in order to cause to be sorrowful'
    f. ḏukk^h-ipp-ikk-al   'the act of causing to be sorrowful (N)'
    g. ḏukk^h-am   'sorrow (N)'
    h. ḏukk^h-iṯ-
    i. ḏukk^h-iṯ-an   'sorrow-stricken person (m.)'
    j. ḏukk^h-iṯ-am   'affliction'

[T. Mohanan 1988]

We can account for such cases by treating the Malayalam suffixes as bi-dependent morphemes. That is, they subcategorize for a sister to either side.

(22) Bi-dependent suffix: [[ ]$_m$ ikk [ ]$_m$]$_m$

When a morpheme such as that in (22) combines with a bound root on the left, there still remains one subcategorized position to be filled. This accounts for the dependent behavior of the derived form.

(23) [ḏukk^h [ ]$_m$]$_m$ + [[ ]$_m$ ikk [ ]$_m$]$_m$ ⟶ [[ḏukk^h]$_m$ [ikk]$_m$ [ ]$_m$]$_m$

At the moment I do not know of any criteria for deciding whether morphemes of this type need a prosodic subcategorization frame as well. That is, it is unclear whether they belong to the cateogory of root or affix, in the typology in (5). Since the result of combining a bi-dependent morpheme with a single sister will not be a well-formed constituent, the presence of a corresponding bi-dependent prosodic frame will have no effect; phonological rules will be unable to apply in any case. I therefore assume that the presence of a prosodic frame would be unlearnable in these cases, and I treat morphemes such as Malayalam -*ikk*- as dependent only morphologically. But I consider this question very much open.[12]

One may wonder, now that we have introduced the option of subcategorizing for more than one sister, if there is any upper bound on the number of subcategorized elements. In chapter 6 I will suggest reasons for why the upper bound should be two. Another unaddressed question is whether or not morphemes can be bi-dependent only prosodically, and if so, how such a property would be manifested. This issue will also resurface in chapter 6 during the discussion of infixation. Let us place it on hold until then.

5.4 Cyclicity: the Outer Frame

A second consequence of the active interpretation of subcategorization is that an affix, which enters the representation with both inner and outer prosodic constituent frames, will always cause a new prosodic constituent to be formed around it and its host.[13] Since phonological rules automatically apply each time a new prosodic constituent is created, we thus predict that all affixation will trigger the cyclic application of phonological rules.

This prediction contradicts claims made in the literature to the effect that affixation on particular levels of the lexical phonology is noncyclic. In this section we will review a few of these cases, and conclude that in no case is noncyclicity necessary.

5.4.1 Malayalam

The argument that Malayalam strata are noncyclic (Mohanan and Mohanan 1984, Mohanan 1986) is twofold. First, Mohanan and Mohanan claim that Malayalam rules will be equally effective whether they apply cyclically or noncyclically, and Mohanan and Mohanan take the null hypothesis to be noncyclicity. They support this choice for Malayalam by pointing to a clearly lexical rule of nasal spreading which applies in nonderived environments, yet is structure-changing. This conflicts with the

---

[12]There is actually a possible test for whether or not the prosodic frame is there; it depends on the notion to be developed later in this chapter that affixation could take place before Prosodic Constituent Formation has had a chance to apply to a stem, and so I will discuss it at a later point.

[13]Actually, as we will see in chapter 6, while the presence of this outer frame is constant, its location may vary, resulting in invisibility effects.

assumption that structure-changing rules are subject to strict cyclicity (Mascaro 1976, Kiparsky 1982). Observing that other apparent lexical violations of strict cyclicity have been attributed to rules applying in noncyclic strata (see Halle and Mohanan 1985), Mohanan and Mohanan hypothesize that the Malayalam rule of nasal spreading also applies in a noncyclic stratum, thus explaining the ability of the rule to apply in a structure-changing fashion in nonderived environments.[14]

In a later section I will suggest that strict cyclicity is not actually a formal, inviolable constraint on grammars (see Kiparsky 1982, Rubach 1984, Borowsky 1986 for discussion), but rather an epiphenomenon, resulting from the interaction of underspecified underlying forms with the structure-building rules which cyclically add structure to those forms. However, even if we do maintain the version of strict cyclicity in Kiparsky 1982 (that assumed in Mohanan and Mohanan 1984), it appears that the rule of nasal spreading can actually be reformulated so as to be structure-preserving, in which case the argument for noncyclicity falls away.

As shown in Mohanan and Mohanan (see also Warrier 1976, Mohanan 1982), voiced stops in Malayalam become nasal when they follow a nasal (24).

(24) Anuṇaasikaaṭiprasaṟam (Nasal Spreading) [Mohanan and Mohanan p. 584]

$$\begin{array}{cc} [+\text{nasal}] & [-\text{son}, -\text{cont}, +\text{voice}] \\ \overline{} \\ C & C \end{array}$$

The examples in (25) are taken from Mohanan and Mohanan 1984:584.

(25)
paṇdi	>	paṇṇi	'pig'
waṇdu	>	waṇṇu	'came'
aṇdə	>	aṇṇə	'that day'

The lexical nature of Nasal Spreading is demonstrated by the fact that it applies obligatorily in [+Dravidian] words but only optionally in [+Sanskrit] words, and also by the fact that it fails to apply across word boundaries.

Anuṇaasikaaṭiprasaṟam is fed by Homorganic Nasal Assimilation, which guarantees that a nasal shares the place features of a following voiced stop.

---

[14]According to Mohanan 1986:70 the rule applies in stratum 1.

5.4. CYCLICITY: THE OUTER FRAME

(26) Homorganic Nasal Assimilation [Mohanan and Mohanan p. 583]

```
[+nasal]      [-son, -cont]
   |                |
   C                C
   ╪--------------┘
[PLACE]       [PLACE]
```

Mohanan and Mohanan's argument is that because the nasal spreading rule in (24) changes [-cont, -son, +voiced] (the voiced stop) to [-cont, +son, +nasal] (the nasal) in cases like (25),[15] it is therefore structure-changing (p. 593). This is the basis of the argument that the rule must be noncyclic.

However, if we cast the Malayalam facts in a framework of underspecification, the need for structure-changing rules diminishes dramatically. Because Malayalam has neither nasal stops nor voiceless sonorants, the features [+son], [-cont] and [+voice] are redundant on nasals; similarly, the feature [-son] is redundant on voiced stops. Removing these redundant features from underlying representations alters the nature of Nasal Spreading significantly. Instead of being a structure-changing rule, Nasal Spreading will simply spread the feature [+nasal] onto segments which lack it.[16]

(27) Nasal Spreading (revised):

```
[+nasal] [-cont, +voice]
   ┌---------┘
   C         C
```

We can reasonably conclude from this discussion that Malayalam does not present a compelling counterexample to the hypothesis that all levels are potentially cyclic.

---

[15]Mohanan and Mohanan do not include [+son] in the environment of the Nasal Spreading rule, but they make it clear in the text (p. 593) that they regard this feature as present on the nasal nonetheless.

[16]I am not sure what to say about the fate of [+voiced] and [-cont], which, though obligatorily present on the input to Nasal Spreading, become redundant once the voiced stop has become nasalized. Structure preservation ought to force them to delink. The question is, does the deletion of a redundant feature due to the structure preservation constraint count as a structure-changing rule? If so, we lose the otherwise appealing analysis of morpheme structure constraints as phonological clean-up rules (e.g. Kiparsky 1982).

In fact, there is some evidence in the language that actually argues in *favor* of cyclicity, namely an α rule which causes nasals to become dental in morpheme-initial position. From Mohanan and Mohanan 1984:583:

(28)
    [anu [ṉaasikam]]   'nasal sound'
    [[gr̄əha][ṉaayakan]]   'house leader'

Dental nasals do not occur morpheme-internally, except as they are derived by the independent rule of Homorganic Nasal Assimilation.

Thus even though it applies at the end of each noncyclic level on Mohanan and Mohanan's analysis, the rule of dentalization must make crucial reference to level-internal morpheme boundaries. This not only makes a noncyclic analysis rather unintuitive but also adds a lot of power to the theory (see Borowsky 1986), since it requires bracket erasure to be postponed until the end of the level (Kiparsky 1985, Mohanan 1986). By contrast, under a cyclic account (e.g. Mohanan 1982), both dentalization and bracket erasure can apply at the time each affix is added. The more rigorous version of bracket erasure permitted by this analysis results in more constrained representations and hence a more constrained theory.

5.4.2 English

Halle and Mohanan 1985 claim that stratum 2 in English (the stratum of class 2 derivation) is noncyclic. They base their argument on the familar rule of stem-final tensing/lengthening, which in certain dialects applies to lengthen stem-final *i*.

(29) beauty, city, country, dandy, gentry, happy, mummy, pretty

Halle and Mohanan's claim that the rule applies to stems on level 2, and not on level 1, is consistent with the rule's uniform failure to apply to those stems which are followed by the level 1 suffix *-ify*:

(30)
    beauty [ii]   beautify [ı]
    city [ii]   citify [ı]
    country [ii]   countrified [ı]

5.4. CYCLICITY: THE OUTER FRAME

gentry [ıi]   gentrified [ı]
dandy [ıi]   dandify [ı]
mummy [ıi]   mummify [ı]
ugly [ıi]   uglify [ı]

The crucial property of the version of stem-final tensing found in Halle and Mohanan's dialect 'A' (which I speak) is that it applies before some, but not before all, level 2 suffixes; in particular, the rule fails to apply before the suffixes *-ful* and *-ly*.[17]

(31)
	[iː]	[ı]
happy	happiness	happily
pretty	prettiness	prettily
scanty	scantiness	scantily
pity	pitiless	pitiful
merry	merriment	merrily
hardy	hardihood	hardily

Halle and Mohanan account for the alternation in (31) by means of the rule in (32). This rule must apply noncyclically on level 2 in order to produce the right results:

(32) $\begin{bmatrix} -\text{cons} \\ -\text{low} \end{bmatrix} \longrightarrow [\ +\text{tense}\ ]\ /\ \underset{R}{\_\_\_}\ ]]$ except before *-ly, -ful*.

If (32) were to apply cyclically, it would incorrectly tense all final *i*'s, including those before *-ly* or *-ful*.

As Borowsky 1986 observes (p. 255), there is an alternative, cyclic analysis of these same facts, one which Halle and Mohanan in fact propose but reject on the arguable grounds of complexity. This solution is to lengthen all final *i*'s on the stem cycle, and then, on a subsequent cycle, shorten those to which *-ly* and *-ful* are added. However, this analysis also presents problems for our model in that it appears to require reference by phonological rules to the identity of particular suffixes.

---
[17]See Allen 1978:121 and Borowsky 1986:250 for descriptions of slightly different dialects.

A simpler way out of the problem noted by Halle and Mohanan is to question the assumption that -ly and -ful actually belong to level 2. The strongest argument for locating them on level 2 instead of level 1 is their stress-neutral behavior. Affix ordering facts do not help out in this respect. While -ly can occur outside level 2 suffixes, as in (33a), it can also occur inside level 1 suffixes, as in (31b). As for -ful, it never occurs outside level 2 suffixes. The evidence for its occurring inside level 1 affixes is rather scanty as well, but a few forms do exist, as shown in (31c).

(33)
    a. tirelessly, helplessly
    b. friendlier, ghastlier, sicklier
    c. distasteful, disrespectful

Locating a suffix on level 2 is not the only possible means for explaining stress-neutral behavior. Another mechanism, familiar from the work of Hayes 1981 and others, is extrametricality. Suppose we treat -ly and -ful as level 1 suffixes (-ly will also have a level 2 variant), and make them extrametrical.

(34) happi(ly), beauti(ful)

On the assumption that level 1 extrametricality disappears on level 2, the /i/ preceding these suffixes will never appear in stem-final position for the purpose of level 2 rules. Since /i/ lengthening is a level 2 rule, it will thus not be able to apply to forms such as those in (34).

Some evidence in support of this proposal comes from stress patterns induced by -ly. -ly differs from all level 2 suffixes in that there is one context where it does affect stress. This context is words ending in the suffixes -ary and -ory. While -ary/-ory-final words do not normally exhibit primary stress on the suffix, when -ly is added primary stress shifts to the antepenultimate syllable — i.e. to the first syllable of -ary or -ory.

(35)
    prímary   prìmárily
    oblígatory oblìgatórily

The same phenomenon does not occur with clear cases of level 2 suffixes:

5.4. CYCLICITY: THE OUTER FRAME

(36)
    prímary   prímaryhood
    oblígatory   oblígatoriness

However, it does occur with clear cases of level 1 suffixes.

(37)
    térnary   ternárity
    cúrsory   cursórial
    sénsory   sensórium
    plánetary   planetárium
    mónetary   monetárial

We can explain why -ly patterns with level 1 suffixes instead of with level 2 suffixes by locating it on level 1. Although it is invisible, and hence stress-neutral in most cases, -ly does trigger stress-changing behavior in exactly the case where it attaches to a formerly invisible disyllabic suffix, such as -ary or -ory. When this happens, the invisible -ary and -ory regain their visibility. Because they are disyllabic and not monosyllabic, the English Stress Rule is not bled by stray syllable adjunction. Instead it builds a primary foot on these suffixes, subsequently triggering the assignment of word stress there.

(38) mŏnĕt(ary) + (ly) ⟶ mŏnĕtắrĭ(ly)

A second piece of evidence involves the degemination which takes place upon attaching -ly to a base ending in l. As Borowsky 1986 argues, consonant degemination applies on level 1 but not on level 2, as demonstrated by the following data:

(39)

Level 1	Level 2
in-numerable [n]	un-natural [nn]
en-noble [n]	non-native [nn]
dis-sonant [s]	dis-service [ss]
	fine-ness [nn]
	soul-less [ll]

Crucially, when -ly is added to a stem ending in l, the result is a single l — not the geminate which would be predicted if -ly attached on level 2.[18]

(40) civilly [l], awfully [l], naturally [l], ephemerally [l], fully [l]

These facts converge to support the location of -ly and -ful on level 1, thus allowing us to adopt an analysis of final i lengthening in English which does not require noncyclicity on level 2. This takes care of the last serious counterexample that I know of to the claim that all levels are cyclic.[19]

Summary

In conclusion, where the claim of noncyclicity has been made, it is almost always the case that although the data do not absolutely require cyclicity, they are nonetheless compatible with a cyclic analysis. The analysis of this kind of ambiguous data has depended in the past on the decisions of individual linguists as to whether cyclicity is the marked or the unmarked case. While Kiparsky 1982 and Mohanan 1982 took the default case to be cyclicity, Mohanan and Mohanan 1984, Halle and Mohanan 1985 and Mohanan 1986 made the opposite assumption.

In the prosodic framework we are operating in here, however, our theory provides us with a principled reason for choosing between cyclicity and noncyclicity as the default option. From the hypothesis that affixes are distinguished from other morphemes by the property of subcategorizing for a prosodic host, it follows that all affixation must set up cyclic domains for phonological rules.

5.5 Stem Cycle on Nonterminal Constituents

A unique property of the constituent formation rules posited thus far is that they produce asymmetries in the morphological and prosodic constituent type of stems at transitions between different constituent types (levels).

---

[18]Degemination appears to be sensitive to the preceding vowel; it does not apply in words *wholly, solely, cruelly, coolly*.

[19]Halle and Mohanan claim that Vedic Sanskrit has a level of noncyclic affixation (level 2, that containing the recessive suffixes). However, Kiparsky 1987 has reanalyzed these facts in a cyclic model. Also, Mohanan and Mohanan 1984 cite an unpublished paper, which I have not seen, in which Hammond argues for noncyclic rules in Tunica.

5.5. STEM CYCLE ON NONTERMINAL CONSTITUENTS

After Morphological Constituent Formation has applied to start off the component of rules of a new constituent type, but before Prosodic Constituent Formation has applied on the first cycle of the next level, the morphological constituency of a stem will be one level higher than that of the corresponding prosodic constituent.

(41)
    UR   stem

    α rules

        MCF   [stem $]_{m_\alpha}$
        PCF   [stem $]_{m_\alpha}$
                   [stem $]_{p_\alpha}$

    β rules

        MCF   [stem $]_{m_\beta}$ ⟵⟶ mismatch
                   [stem $]_{p_\alpha}$
        PCF   [stem $]_{p_\beta}$

I will argue here that this lag between the increase in morphological and prosodic constituent type is not a defect of the proposal; in fact, it is an asset, because it correctly predicts that every stem will undergo a cycle of phonological rules upon entrance to a new level, before any affixation has had a chance to take place on that level.

(42) Prediction: The first type k ($k > \alpha$) affixation in the derivation will necessarily follow a cycle of type k phonological rules.

This prediction follows from the fact that it will never be the case that both subcategorization frames for any given affix can be satisfied by a stem whose morphological and prosodic constituency are of different types. (This in turn is due to the fact that the morphological and prosodical sisters for which an affix subcategorizes will always be of the same type.) Therefore, PCF will have to apply to such a stem — triggering a cycle of phonological rules — before affixes can be attached to it.[20]

---

[20]Pcompounding could technically also perform the function of bleeding PCF. However, Pcompounding and PCF would have exactly the same empirical effect no matter which order they applied

Let us see how this works by taking an example from β suffixation in English: we will attempt to derive the word *happiness*, the product of a stem and a β suffix.

(43) UR: happy, $[\ [\ ]_{p_\beta}$ ness $]_{p_\beta}$

At the output of α rules, the stem *happy* will correspond to morphological and prosodic constituents of type α.

(44)
$$\text{Output of } \alpha \text{ rules:} \quad \begin{array}{l}[\text{ happy }]_{m_\alpha} \\ [\text{ happy }]_{p_\alpha}\end{array}$$

At this point β morphological rules begin to apply. The first rule, Morphological Constituent Formation, constructs a morphological consituent of type β out of the α morphological constituent which is its input. The next possible morphological process is morpheme combination. However, attachment of the β suffix *-ness* is blocked because the prosodic frame of the suffix clashes with that of the base. One is marked α and the other β, and they fail to unify.

(45)
$$\begin{array}{ll}\text{Output of } \alpha \text{ rules:} & [\text{ happy }]_{m_\alpha} \\ & [\text{ happy }]_{p_\alpha} \\ \\ \beta \text{ rules} & \\ \text{MCF} & [\text{ happy }]_{m_\beta} \\ & [\text{ happy }]_{p_\alpha} \\ \text{Affixation} & —\end{array}$$

Affixation being unable to apply to *happy*, the default rule of Prosodic Constituent Formation takes charge of assigning to *happy* a prosodic constituency of type β. Only now do its morphological and prosodic constituent types finally match.

---

in, namely that prosodic constituency would be assigned to each member of the compound formed on that cycle. In the absence of any test I have assumed that as the more specific operation, Pcompounding preempts PCF, but this assumption is not crucial.

5.5. STEM CYCLE ON NONTERMINAL CONSTITUENTS

(46)

Output of α rules:	[happy]$_{m_\alpha}$
	[happy]$_{p_\alpha}$
β rules	
MCF	[happy]$_{m_\beta}$
	[happy]$_{p_\alpha}$
Affixation	—
PCF	[happy]$_{m_\beta}$
	[happy]$_{p_\beta}$

Upon construction of the new β constituent, β phonological rules apply to *happy*. In addition, *happy* is now eligible for attachment to the β suffix *-ness*, which takes place on the following cycle.

(47)

Output of α rules:	[happy]$_{m_\alpha}$
	[happy]$_{p_\alpha}$
β rules	
MCF	[happy]$_{m_\beta}$
	[happy]$_{p_\alpha}$
Affixation	—
PCF	[happy]$_{m_\beta}$
	[happy]$_{p_\beta}$
MCF	—
Affixation	[happiness]$_{m_\beta}$
	[happiness]$_{p_\beta}$

The prediction that a stem cycle of β phonological rules precedes β affixation is supported for English by the work of Borowsky 1986, who shows that all stems in English undergo level 2 (β) phonological rules *before* acquiring level 2 (β) suffixes. For details, see Borowsky 1986, e.g. 236-7; here, I will illustrate one such rule, *n* deletion.

The rule of *n* deletion is responsible for deleting *n* word-finally when *m* precedes. It applies to monomorphemic forms such as those in (48):

(48)
    autumn   [m]
    column
    condemn
    damn
    hymn
    limn
    solemn

Because of final consonant extrametricality, n deletion never has the opportunity to apply to α constituents. The n of a stem-final mn cluster is never visible to α phonological rules. As a consequence, n shows up before α suffixes, with which it syllabifies:

(49)
    autumnal   [mn]
    columnar, columnist
    condemnation
    damnation, damnable, damnify, damnatory
    hymnal, hymnary, hymnology
    limnic
    solemnity, solemnize

By contrast, the n of an underlying mn sequence never surfaces when it immediately precedes a β suffix.

(50)
    condemner, condemning   [m]
    damning
    limning

Forms like a[mn]esty, hy[mn]al show that mn is not reduced to m when it occurs internal to a β constituent. Only in constituent-final position will n ever disappear. Because those stems which take β suffixes still act as domains for n deletion, we must conclude that the stems themselves form β constituents before suffixation. The prediction of our theory that the application of β phonological rules to stems precedes suffixation is borne out.

5.5. STEM CYCLE ON NONTERMINAL CONSTITUENTS

The intrinsic ordering of β PCF before β affixation thus correctly predicts an important contrast between β affixation to stems, which always follows a β stem cycle, and β Mcompounding of stems, which precludes a β stem cycle. Recall that compounding differs from affixation in that only the former places no restrictions on the prosodic constituency of its input. Thus it is exactly in the case of compounding that morphemes can be combined whose morphological and prosodic constituency do not match. The example in (51) of Malayalam subcompounding is presented below as a reminder of the behavior of Mcompounding. Note the labels on the morphological and prosodic constituents at the time Mcompounding applies:

(51) Subcompounding (β rules)

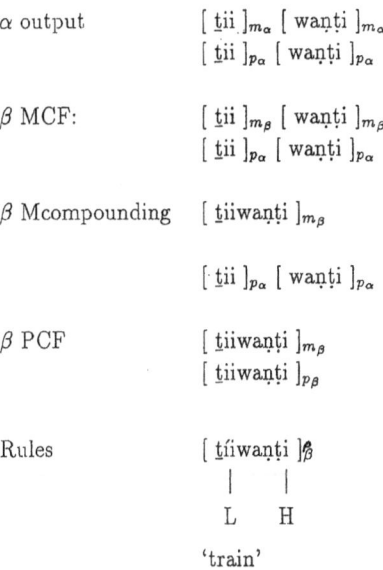

'train'

A stem cycle on β-affixed stems is not a necessary consequence of those conceptions of nonprosodic Lexical Phonology which permit arbitrary levels to be marked as noncyclic (Mohanan and Mohanan 1984, Halle and Mohanan 1985, Mohanan 1986). On noncyclic levels, a stem cycle could actually be avoided altogether — and, in fact, this added power is exactly what such theories have invoked in order to capture the facts of Mcompounding in Malayalam. However, in chapter 4 we saw a more constrained alternative account of these facts.

5.5.1 Postcyclic Rules

The claim that all affixation triggers the cyclic application of rules is compatible with the growing evidence for a postcyclic rule domain in the lexicon. Often referred to as word-level rules, postcyclic lexical rules apply exactly once — hence, by definition noncyclically — on the very last stage of the lexical phonology. I will adopt here the analysis of Booij and Rubach 1984, Booij and Rubach 1987, Inkelas and Zec 1988, and others that this domain corresponds to the phonological word.

To capture the fact that the phonological word does not appear to admit cyclic rule application, we may impose a constraint on underlying representations that no affix may subcategorize for the phonological word.[21] I will state this constraint on morphological subcategorization frames:

(52) *[[ ]m_ω __]m_ω (and mirror-image)

From this prohibition on encoding ω in morphological subcategorization frames, we derive its absence in the prosodic frames of affixes (recall that redundancy rules require morphological and prosodic subcategorization frames to match in constituent type). In fact, we have good reason not to state the prohibition in (52) in terms of prosodic frames: as we will see in chapter 8, the phonological word does appear underlyingly in prosodic subcategorization frames. But it is reserved for clitics, which have no morphological subcategorization frames, and which differ from affixes in that they attach only outside of the lexical component.

5.6 Stem Cycle on α Constituents

As we have seen, the prosodic domain model advocated here factors apart the sources of phonological rule domains into three: Pcompounding rules, which imposes prosodic structure on its output; affixation, which introduces new prosodic domains in a cyclic manner during word formation; and Prosodic Constituent Formation, a separate mapping algorithm which applies at most once per constituent type and provides prosodic constituency to stems which lack it.

---

[21]The term 'phonological word' might make the idea of morphological subcategorization for this constituent seem a little strange, but recall that the phonological word is just a lexical constituent type like any other, despite its name. It could equally well be called Q.

5.6. STEM CYCLE ON α CONSTITUENTS

My aim in this section is to validate the hypothesis that affixation and PCF are distinct sources of prosodic constituency by demonstrating that the order in which these two sources are tapped is parameterized across languages. I argue that there are two types of languages: one, type A, which orders Prosodic Constituent Formation before affixation and another, type B, where the order is reversed.[22]

(53)
	Type A		Type B
UR:	stem		stem
PCF:	[stem]	Affixation:	[stem-aff]
Affixation:	[stem-aff]	PCF:	—

PCF and affixation are the only two crucially ordered constituent formation rules whose order is extrinsic, and we hence expect their order to vary parametrically across languages. We now turn to evidence for this claim.

Languages of type A and type B diverge empirically in exactly one respect, namely the point at which affixed stems acquire α prosodic constituency. In type A languages, all stems will become α prosodic constituents before any affixes have a chance to attach. As a consequence, a 'stem cycle' of phonological rules will precede all cycles on α affixes. But this stem cycle is not a property of type B languages, where affixation bleeds PCF; those stems which are destined to acquire α affixes will do before PCF has had a chance to apply — and will not undergo any α rules prior to affixation. Of course, if no α affixes are available to attach to the stem, PCF will apply and create an α cycle of rules for the stem. In sum, while unaffixed stems are treated the same in both types of language, the behavior of affixed stems is predicted to differ.[23]

This prediction is unavailable to nonprosodic versions of Lexical Phonology, which have no means of differentiating the two types of languages shown in (53). Thus, any evidence for the dichotomy in (53) has dual importance: it not only supports one particular proposal within the prosodic domain model, but it also supports that model in general over nonprosodic models of Lexical Phonology.

---

[22]This distinction would be difficult to capture straightforwardly in a declarative, nonprocedural model of grammar.

[23]One of the predictions of not assigning prosodic frames to bound roots emerges here. In a language which lacks a preaffixal stem cycle (a type B language), if two bound roots were to combine, satisfying each other's subcategorization requirements, the resulting morphological constituent ([[ ]$_m$ [ ]$_m$]$_m$) would not undergo a preaffixal stem cycle. By contrast, if bound roots did possess prosodic frames underlyingly, a preaffixal stem cycle would be obligatory — triggered by the prosodic structure produced upon affixation: [[ ]$_p$ [ ]$_p$]$_p$. Admittedly, this prediction is a bit esoteric.

With this in mind, let us now turn to the evidence. It has already been shown in the literature that languages of type A exist. Diyari (Poser 1986a, 1989) presents a clear case in which the construction of metrical structure on monomorphemic stems crucially precedes any affixation. Pulleyblank 1986 makes similar arguments for Margi and Tiv, where rules of tone assignment (and in the case of Margi, tone spreading) must crucially apply to stems before the first suffix is attached (see e.g. pp. 68, 74). The reader is referred to these works for more details. In this section I will concentrate instead on proving the existence of type B languages.[24] The cases I will mention here are Dakota and English; in chapter 7 I advance the same claim in more detail for Carib.

5.6.1 English

Though I can present only a small portion of the complex stress system of English, a number of phenomena obtain a much simpler analysis when the preaffixal stem cycle is abandoned. The crucial alternations I will account for here are shown in (54):

(54)
	a. párent	paréntal	b. nátion	nátional
	órigin	oríginal	féderal	féderalist
	míracle	miráculize	nátional	nátionalize
	díplomat	diplómacy	íntimate	íntimacy

Each set of data consists of a stem paired with its counterpart after combination with a level 1 suffix. The sets of data differ in two ways. Phonologically, they are distinct in that in (52a) attaching the level 1 suffix induces a stress shift on the stem, while in (52b), attaching the same (or a similar) suffix does not induce a stress shift.

I will attribute this stress difference to the second (and only other) difference between the data sets: morphological structure. The stems in (52a) are nonderived, while those in (52b) have already undergone a cycle of derivation prior to the affixation depicted above.

In the case of the (a) words, both the nonderived and the affixed form exhibit the stress which would characterize a nonderived monomorphemic word with the same

---

[24] Note that I have been assuming that English is a type B language in the foregoing sections, where PCF is always shown applying after word formation on the cycle. It was not a crucial assumption in any of those analyses.

5.6. STEM CYCLE ON α CONSTITUENTS

syllable structure and extrametricality properties. This is just what we predict on the assumption that the words in the second column undergo stress rules for the first time only *after* the first level 1 suffix, if any, is attached.

(55)

	UR	diplomat	$[\ [\ ]_{m_\alpha}\ y\ ]_{m_\alpha}$
			$[\ [\ ]_{p_\alpha}\ y\ ]_{p_\alpha}$
	α MCF	$[\ \text{diplomat}\ ]_{m_\alpha}$	
	Affixation	$[\ \text{diplomacy}\ ]_{m_\alpha}$	
		$[\ \text{diplomacy}]_{p_\alpha}$	
	PCF	—	

Under this same account, the (b) stems — which have already undergone one cycle of level 1 suffixation — will already possess metrical structure when the outermost suffix shown in (54) is added.

We may exploit this difference between (a) and (b) stems to our advantage. In order to account for why (b) stems preserve the stress assigned on an earlier cycle, we are forced into the nice constrained claim that the English Stress Rule is structure-preserving. It will be blocked from assigning a binary stress foot when any one of the two syllables to which it would apply is already incorporated into metrical structure. Unlicensed syllables to which the ESR is unable to apply will simply be stray-adjoined to the preceding preexisting foot, as shown below:[25]

(56) féde(ral) + ist ⟶ féderà(list) (*federá(list))

The result of interpreting the ESR as structure-preserving is to simplify and tighten the theory. In the past it has been necessary to attribute structure-changing properties to the ESR exactly in the case of level 1 suffixation to underived (a) stems. But under the analysis proposed here we can explain why the stems appear to retain their stress in some cases but not in others, without having to allow phonological rules access to the internal morphological structure of the strings to which they apply.[26]

---

[25] For discussion of the extrametricality exhibited in these examples, see chapter 6.

[26] Further evidence in favor of treating the ESR as structure-preserving is that idiosyncratic, underlying stress is preserved even in derived environments. Consider the difference between *Tibetan*

This account is merely a suggestive demonstration of the benefits that can accrue when the preaffixal stem cycle is eliminated. We turn next to a slightly more detailed case, that of Dakota.

5.6.2 Dakota

In this section I show that by adopting for Dakota the hypothesis that affixation bleeds Prosodic Constituent Formation, we can improve on an analysis formulated by Kiparsky 1986 in standard Lexical Phonology. Building on earlier work by Shaw (1976, 1980), Kiparsky analyzes certain stress and epenthesis facts in Dakota in a cyclic model. A crucial component of his analysis is the need to block most rules from applying on the stem cycle before affixation.

As observed by Kiparsky, Dakota has a cyclic rule of stress assignment (Accent) which locates stress on the second (or only) syllable. Roots are underlined in the following illustrative examples:

(57)

wa + kté	'I kill him'
ni + kté + pi	'they kill you'
u + yá + kte+ pi	'you kill us'
wi + čhá + wa + kte	'I kill them'

A plausible analysis is that Accent builds a unary foot on the second syllable,[27]

---

and *pelican*, words with identical syllable structure but different stress patterns. The former has penultimate stress since its base, *Tibet* also bears stress on that syllable. By contrast, the underived *pelican* exhibits the stress which the ESR would predict.

Favorable evidence of this kind is, however, counterbalanced by exceptions; all the ones known to me are listed below. The first problem involves the class of *-ic/-icity* alternations exemplified by *cyclic, cyclicity*. If we assume that *-icity* is complex, then the analysis tendered above fails to account for why the stress of *cyclic* is not preserved upon suffixation of *-ity*. Similarly, on the assumption that *-ious* is composed of the two suffixes *-i, -ous* we cannot account for alternations of the form *ignonimy, ignominious*. Third, if *-ific* is properly broken down into *-ify* + *-ic* the forms *acidify, acidific* pose a problem. A last, single additional counterexample is *medicine, medicinal*. These exhaust the counterexamples I have found so far. And should the proposal prove worth pursuing further, it appears that these problems will yield to reanalysis; the assumption that the sequences *-icity ,-ious* and *-ific* have been fossilized into single suffixes will be sufficient. Evidence for this is that these sequences can attach to forms which do not take the suffix forming the first half of the putatively complex form, e.g. *multiplicity* but *multiplic; *laborious* but *labory; *honorific* but *honorify. As for *medicine*, either treating it as monomorphemic or simply listing *medicinal* as an exception will work.

[27] Positing initial extrametricality would make this a straightforward operation.

5.6. STEM CYCLE ON α CONSTITUENTS

and that a principle of leftmost wins guarantees that only the leftmost foot in the word will surface.

The Accent rule interacts with a rule of epenthesis which supplies consonant-final stems with a final vowel, /a/. While regular disyllabic roots exhibit stress on their second syllable, as expected, monosyllabic roots which acquire a second vowel via Epenthesis surface instead with initial stress.

(58)

Epenthetic V2	Underlying V2
sápa	čoká
púza	ixpé
čhápa	mašté

Kiparsky accounts for these alternations by assuming that both Accent and Epenthesis apply cyclically; but, because the Strict Cycle Condition permits only those rules assigning metrical structure to apply on the first cycle, only Accent will apply there. It is thus guaranteed to precede Epenthesis, which applies on the next cycle (the word cycle if no further word formation takes place). Evidence for the failure of Epenthesis to apply on the stem cycle is that when a monosyllabic stem is reduplicated, only the second half acquires an epenthetic vowel:

(59) leš ⟶ lešléša (*lešaleša)

Similarly, when a monosyllabic stem is suffixed or incorporated it also fails to undergo Epenthesis:

(60)

/čhap/	čhápa	'beaver'
	čhap-khúwa	'he is beaver hunting'
	čhap-síte	'beaver tail'
/pus/	púza	'be dry'
	pus-yá	'cause to dry'

As Kiparsky shows, underlying stem-final vowels do appear in these contexts, showing that what is going on is failure of Epenthesis, not deletion of the epenthesized vowel (p. 120).

This account works elegantly within the nonprosodic theory of Lexical Phonology, maintaining the Strong Domain Hypothesis (Kiparsky 1985) and making crucial use of the Strict Cycle Condition (Mascaro 1976, Kiparsky 1982).[28] However, it appears to suffer from two problems. First, it is not clear what to do with the stress which Accent assigns on the stem cycle to monosyllabic forms, given that stress does not appear on those forms when they are suffixed, reduplicated or incorporated.

(61) pús + -ya ⟶ pusyá (*púsya)

Kiparsky's solution is to allow Accent to override preexisting stress in derived environments. (The restriction to derived environments is necessary to account for why idiosyncratic stress is preserved on underived forms such as *núni* 'to stray', *háska* 'to be tall' (p. 123).) However, rampant deletion seems to be an excessively powerful means of capturing the generalization that stress assigned on the first cycle is essentially ignored.

It is also not clear how to force the Strict Cycle Condition to block Epenthesis on the stem cycle. The spirit of the Strict Cycle Condition (Mascaro 1976, Kiparsky 1982) is to prevent structure-changing rules from applying to underived forms. But Epenthesis is essentially nothing but addition of structure. Moreover, it is presumably triggered by syllabification, which provides a phonologically derived environment and should license even structure-changing rules (see the references just cited). Thus the failure of Epenthesis to apply on the stem cycle appears to have to be achieved by the stipulation that only metrical structure can be assigned there. But the whole motivation for assigning metrical structure on cycle 1 in Dakota is suspect anyway — as in almost every case it is simply deleted again on the very next cycle (as in the case of *pús, pus-yá*). And even in the nonderived cases where cycle 1 stress is presumably preserved, its presence is not crucial, since rules applying on the next (word) cycle would assign it in the same place anyway (e.g. *čoká*).

One possible way of accommodating these observations is to assume that what we have been calling stems in Dakota are actually bound roots, and that the seeming failure of rules to apply to them can be attributed to their lack of morphological constituency. But this cannot be true, as the morphemes in question are able to stand alone as words.

---

[28]I will actually argue in a later chapter that the present theory provides no systematic means of characterizing morphologically derived environments in the first place, since internal morphological structure is not available to phonological rules; thus accounts which rely crucially on the Strict Cycle Condition are potentially problematic.

5.6. STEM CYCLE ON α CONSTITUENTS

I therefore turn to the alternative option, and propose that the failure of Dakota stems to undergo rules before word formation is due to their lack of prosodic constituency. That is, like English, Dakota is most naturally characterized as a type B language. Prosodic Constituent Formation is bled by affixation, reduplication and incorporation, and does not assign prosodic constituency to those stems which have the opportunity of acquiring it by other means.

On the assumption that derivation preempts a stem cycle of phonological rules, we explain why the stress borne by monosyllabic stems in isolation does not appear on those same stems when they are combined with other morphemes. Further, we explain — without having to invoke the Strict Cycle Condition (or any other constraint) — why Epenthesis fails to apply on the first cycle: there is no first 'cycle' of rules prior to the first stage of word-formation. The only statement needed is that Accent precedes Epenthesis on the cycle. Sample derivations are provided below.

(62)

UR	pus	pus	čoka	čoka
MCF	[pus]$_m$	[pus]$_m$	[čoka]$_m$	[čoka]$_m$
Affixation	—	[pusya]$_m$	—	[čokaka]$_m$
	—	[pusya]$_p$	—	[čokaka]$_p$
Accent	—	[pusyá]$_p$	—	[čokáka]$_p$
Epenthesis	—	—	—	—
PCF	[pus]$_m$	—	[čoka]$_m$	
	[pus]$_p$	—	[čoka]$_p$	
Accent	[pús]$_p$	—	[čoká]$_p$	—
Epenthesis	[púsa]$_p$	—	—	—

Making our standard assumption that rules apply immediately upon the creation of the prosodic constituent which is their domain, the relative order of PCF with respect to word formation process correctly predicts the application of Accent and Epenthesis; no further conditions are required.

5.7 Appendix: Underspecified Subcategorization Frames

Much of the information represented in fully specified morphological and prosodic subcategorization frames is predictable. For instance, consider the generalization below:

(63) If an affix attaches to a type x morphological constituent, it will also attach to a type x prosodic constituent

To give a concrete example, we know from the fact that the prefix *in-* attaches to and forms an α morphological constituent that it will also attach to and form an α prosodic constituent.

Or consider the following:

(64) Bound roots in English usually attach to an α morpheme

As pointed out (though in slightly different terms) by Siegel 1974 (see also Allen 1978:53, Mohanan 1986), the subcategorization requirements for most bound roots in English are satisfied only by α morphemes, not by β ones. (The first four examples are from Allen 1978:18).

(65)

*-ert	inert	*unert
*-placable	implacable	*unplacable
*-maculate	immaculate	*unmaculate
*-ept	inept	*unept
*-mit	admit	*countermit
*-effable	ineffable	*uneffable
*-graphy, *tele-	telegraphy	*undergraphy, *telehood

This generalization does have a few exceptions, e.g. the bound root *-couth* in *uncouth* and the famous *cran-* of *cranapple, cranberry, cranmorph*.

Encoding generalizations like those in (61) and (62) in the underlying representation of each individual bound morpheme would be redundant at best. I will thus

5.7. APPENDIX: UNDERSPECIFIED SUBCATEGORIZATION FRAMES

propose a set of parameters which supply default values to underspecified underlying representations, capturing generalizations like those in (63) and (64) and reducing the amount of information that must be lexically listed.

A set of such parameters, and what I imagine to be the universal unmarked value for them, is given in (66). They permit the removal of redundant underlying information in the lexical entries for bound morphemes. Note that clause (a) encodes α as the unmarked values for the subcategorization frame of roots and affixes. This is the value I am assuming to be unmarked for English, but it may well be determined on a language-specific basis.

(66)
- a. <u>Type of morphological host</u>. Default value: any morphological subcategorization frame unspecified for type becomes α.
- b. <u>Range of prosodic host</u>. Default value: A prosodically bound morpheme will form a prosodic constituent with the base. (I.e. construct the outermost bracketing in the prosodic subcategorization frame such that it includes the bound morpheme and the host.)
- c. <u>Type of prosodic host</u>. Default value: for an affix of morphological type x, label the brackets in the corresponding prosodic subcategorization frame x as well. If no corresponding morphological frame exists, the default value is ω.

(65) illustrates the effect of imposing the parameters in (64) to some normal, unmarked morphemes. We start by removing all the redundant information from underlying subcategorization frames for some of the morphemes we have already seen, leaving the following set of underspecified underlying representations:

(67)

Morpheme type		Morphological frame	Prosodic frame
Affix	in-	--- [ ]	--- [ ]
	-less	[ ]$_\beta$ ---	[ ] ---
Clitic	='s	∅	[ ] ---
Root	-ceive	[ ] ---	∅
Stem		∅	∅

The output of the default rules in (66) yields the following fully specified lexical representations:

(68)

Morpheme type		Morphological frame	Prosodic frame
Affix	in-	$[\,\text{---}\,[\ ]_\alpha\,]_\alpha$	$[\,\text{---}\,[\ ]_\alpha\,]_\alpha$
	-less	$[\,[\ ]_\beta\,\text{---}\,]_\beta$	$[\,[\ ]_\beta\,\text{---}\,]_\beta$
Clitic	='s	$\emptyset$	$[\,[\ ]_\omega\,\text{---}\,]_\omega$
Root	-ceive	$[\,[\ ]_\alpha\,\text{---}\,]_\alpha$	$\emptyset$
Stem	stem	$\emptyset$	$\emptyset$

As true default processes, the rules in (66) apply only in the absence of specifications for the features which they manipulate, and this is what allows us to explain the exceptions to the generalization in (62). The bound roots *-couth* and *cran-* are underlyingly marked to combine with a β morphological sister, and thereby avoid the α marking which would be assigned to them by default.

(69)
-couth: $[\,[\ ]_{m_\beta}\,\text{---}\,]_{m_\beta}$
cran-: $[\,\text{---}\,[\ ]_{m_\beta}\,]_{m_\beta}$

Our system thus handles exceptional morphemes using only independently motivated features which those morphemes exhibit in the course of the derivation; the marked status of exceptional forms is captured by the fact that they are represented underlyingly with more information than is present on the unmarked cases.

Chapter 6

The Represention of Invisibility

'Invisibility' is the term coined by Poser 1984 to cover those phenomena known variously in the literature as 'extrametricality' (Liberman and Prince 1977, Hayes 1981), 'extratonality' (Pulleyblank 1983), and (most generally) 'extraprosodicity' (Kiparsky 1985). All of the phenomena referred to by these terms involve the functional invisibility of some part of a phonological string to rules applying on that string.

The first invisibility device, extrametricality, was proposed pretheoretically in Liberman and Prince 1977, and given formal status in Hayes 1979, Hayes 1981 and Harris 1983. Its purpose has been to identify a small set of elements which are systematically ignored by the stress rules of various languages.

For example, the final syllables (according to Hayes 1981, rimes) of nouns in English act as though they are not there for purposes of the English Stress Rule (Hayes 1981). Evidence from verbs and unsuffixed adjectives shows that this rule builds a maximally binary, quantity-sensitive foot at the right edge of the word. The same is true in nouns, with the special proviso that the syllable (or rime) adjacent to the right edge is simply skipped over.[1] Some relevant forms are listed in (1). Extrametrical syllables are indicated by the theory-neutral notational device of parentheses:

(1)
$$\overset{\wedge}{\underset{s\ w}{Páme}}(la) \quad (\text{not } ^{*}\overset{\wedge}{\underset{s\ w}{Pamela}})$$

---

[1]Selkirk 1984 departs from the analysis in Hayes 1981, treating noun syllable extrametricality as lexicalized instead of rule-governed.

$\overset{\wedge}{\underset{\text{ori}}{\overset{\text{s w}}{}}}$(gin)   (not *$\overset{\wedge}{\underset{\text{origin}}{\overset{\text{s w}}{}}}$)

$\overset{\wedge}{\underset{\text{ele}}{\overset{\text{s w}}{}}}$(phant) (not *$\overset{\wedge}{\underset{\text{elephant}}{\overset{\text{s w}}{}}}$)

As first argued in detail in Pulleyblank 1983 (and developed in Poser 1984), invisibility is not limited to stress rules. For example, it plays a role in tonal phenomena as well. One such case is presented by verbs in Japanese where, as shown by McCawley 1968, the location of High tone in accented verb stems is predictable:

(2) High tone is linked to the head of the syllable containing the penultimate mora.

The examples in (3) are from Poser 1984:51,61 (dots represent syllable boundaries):

(3) Accented verbs:

```
ka.ke.ru      su.kuu       too.ru
   |             |            |
   H             H            H
 'hang'    'build a nest'  'pass by'
```

McCawley's generalization is difficult to formalize as it appears to require the tone linking rule to count (to two), a power which we would like not to accord to phonological rules. However, Poser 1984 points out that the tone patterns of accented Japanese verbs can be generated quite simply using the crucial property of invisibility. Once the final mora of accented verbs is designated as invisible, then all — and only — the tone patterns in (3) can be generated by a single rule linking High tone to the head of the rightmost syllable.

(4)
```
     kakeru  ⟶  kake(ru)
       |            ⋮
       H            H
```

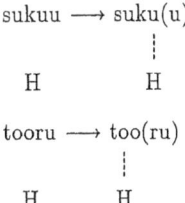

```
sukuu ⟶ suku(u)
          ⋮
  H      H

tooru ⟶ too(ru)
          ⋮
  H      H
```

In addition to tone and stress, vowel harmony has also been shown to exhibit invisibility effects. Kiparsky 1985, in an analysis of ATR harmony in Vata, proposes that final syllables in that language are 'extraprosodic'. This property is manifested in the failure of final syllables to undergo a lexical rule assigning [–ATR] (p. 118). This is shown in the following example, where [–ATR] is added to the first but not the second of the two vowels unspecified for that feature.[2]

(5)
    (input)   sAkA
    Invisibility   sAk(A)

    [–ATR] insertion: sAk(A)
                             ⋮
                            [–ATR]

In the cases of invisibility illustrated thus far, the invisible element has been characterizable phonologically, and its location is quite predictable. The assumption is that such cases of invisibility are governed by rule,[3] although the precise nature of the rule depends on the particular representation of invisibility one subscribes to.

In addition to rule-governed invisibility, lexical effects occur as well. Inherent morpheme invisibility has been demonstrated for various morphemes in English (Hayes 1981), Japanese (Poser 1984), Margi (Pulleyblank 1986), Serbo-Croatian (Zec 1988b), Spanish (Harris 1983), and many others. In English, for example, the adjectival suffixes -al and -ive are invisible, while -ic is not (Hayes 1981). This asymmetry is revealed by the stress patterns of the words containing them:

---

[2]Because, by virtue of its invisibility, the second A leaves the lexicon unspecified for [–ATR], it is subject to a postlexical, feature-filling rule spreading [+ATR]; by contrast, the first A is not.

[3]For an explicit discussion of the nature of extrametricality rules, see Hayes 1982. For early rules of this kind, see Hayes 1979, Dogil 1979, Hayes 1981, Hayes 1982, Harris 1983.

(6)

    Invisible suffix   Visible suffix

        pérsonal   prophétic
        rádical   nomádic
        négative   monástic
        frícative   histόric

To cite an analogous case in Japanese, Poser 1984 shows that certain monomoraic nominal suffixes induce the same tone pattern on nouns that is found among accented verbs: tone surfaces on the syllable containing the penultimate mora (p. 61). This is because the nominal suffix itself is skipped over by the tone assignment rule, which then links a High to the head of the rightmost visible syllable. These suffixes must be considered inherently invisible. As (7) shows, they behave differently from visible nominal suffixes, which do acquire High tone in the same environment.

(7)

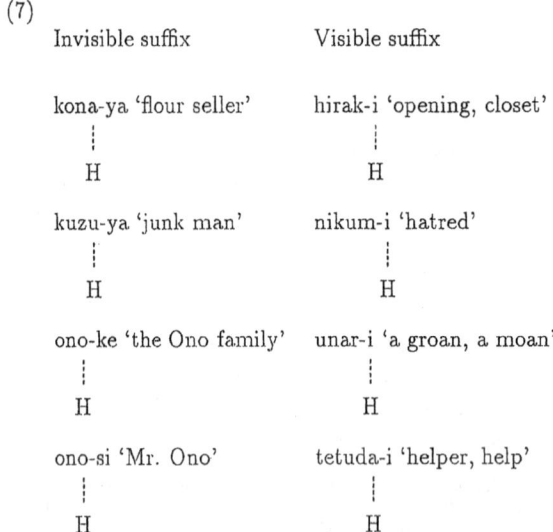

6.1 Representation of Invisibility

An intuitive statement of these invisibility phenomena is that invisible elements are not part of the domain of phonological rules. As Poser 1984 mentions, "an invisible element is not present in the representation at which the rule looks" (p. 88); according to Selkirk 1984, "the function of extrametricality is in essence to redefine the limits of a cyclic domain" (p. 89).

(8) Intuition: 'invisible' elements are outside the phonological rule domain

In morphological theories of rule domains, such as Lexical Phonology (or SPE, or cyclic phonology), this intuition is impossible to capture directly without creating a logical contradiction. Since morphological and phonological domains are one and the same, the intuitive approach to invisibility requires the same element e to be simultaneously present in the domain D (for morphological purposes) and absent from the domain D (for phonological purposes).

(9)
   Morphological evidence: $e \in D$
   Phonological evidence: $e \notin D$

Invisibility behavior thus presents quite a serious paradox for this class of theories, which can by definition capture only perfect correspondence between morphological units and phonological rule domains.

By contrast, what appears to be happening in the case of invisibility is a mismatch in the domains of particular phonological rules and the morphological structure that corresponds to those domains. While *Pamela* is a single unit for purposes of morphology, it must be separated into two parts for purposes of the English stress rule. One part, *Pame*, forms a domain for the rule, but the other part, *la*, does not.

6.1.1 The Domains Approach

The paradox in (9) finds a natural resolution in Prosodic Lexical Phonology. With its formal distinction between morphological and prosodic domains, this framework is perfectly suited to formalize the intuition in (8). As a consequence of its crucial claim that prosodic constituency exists independently of morphological constituency,

Prosodic Lexical Phonology is able to do what morphological theories cannot: represent invisibility as a mismatch between morphological and prosodic constituency.[4]

(10)

      Morphological constituency   Prosodic constituency

$$[\text{Pamela}]_{m_\alpha} \quad\quad [\text{Pame}]_{p_\alpha} \text{ la}$$
$$[\text{origin}]_{m_\alpha} \quad\quad [\text{ori}]_{p_\alpha} \text{ gin}$$
$$[\text{elephant}]_{m_\alpha} \quad\quad [\text{ele}]_{p_\alpha} \text{ phant}$$

$$[\text{kakeru}]_m \quad\quad [\text{kake}]_p \text{ ru}$$
$$[\text{sukuu}]_m \quad\quad [\text{suku}]_p \text{ u}$$
$$[\text{tooru}]_m \quad\quad [\text{too}]_p \text{ ru}$$

Invisible elements are precisely those which do not belong to a prosodic constituent, thus capturing the intuition expressed in the remarks of Poser and Selkirk. The reason invisible elements fail to undergo phonological rules is that they are excluded from the domain within which those rules apply.

(11) Definition: An element e of a morphological constituent m_i is defined as 'invisible' if it is not included in any corresponding prosodic constituent p_i.

This treatment of invisibility formalizes the intuition in (8) without creating the paradox in (9).

Invisibility thus joins Pcompounding in completing the typology of mismatches predicted to occur between morphological and prosodic structure at any given stage in the derivation. Put formally, a mismatch occurs when for some x, y belonging to a single morphological constituent m_i, the prosodic constituent p_i contains x but does not contain y. There are two possible ways for this to occur. Either y belongs to another prosodic constituent, p_j, or y does not belong to any prosodic constituent at all. The former case is instantiated by Pcompounding, and the latter by invisibility.[5]

---

[4]In an unpublished 1986 analysis of Chicheŵa tone, Kanerva proposes to represent extratonal (invisible) elements as outside the phonological rule domain. Though rule domains do not appear to have the status of (prosodic) constituents in his proposal, his insight that phonological rule domains and morphological structure are represented separately is exactly the idea I am developing here.

[5]I am assuming here that all lexical elements will belong to morphological structure at every stage in the derivation (not counting UR). If we did not make this assumption, the typology would

(12)

$x, y \in p_i$ $\qquad$ $x \in p_i, y \in p_j$ $\qquad$ $x \in p_i, y \notin p$

$[\text{ xy }]_{p_i}$ $\qquad$ $[\text{ x }]_{p_i} [\text{ y }]_{p_j}$ $\qquad$ $[\text{ x }]_{p_i}\text{ y}$

No mismatch $\qquad$ Pcompounding $\qquad$ Invisibility

6.2 Sources of Mismatched Constituency

The bracketing misalignments manifested by invisibility phenomena have two independent sources. One is the rule component. In the case of rule-governed invisibility, we may assume that a rule applies to prosodic constituent edges, moving them inward across the to-be-invisible element. English Noun Extrametricality (Hayes 1981) is one such rule. Its implementation in the prosodic domains framework is given in (13),[6] and (14) shows it applying to the word *Pamela*:

(13) English Noun Invisibility: $\quad [\ldots \sigma]_p \longrightarrow [\ldots]_p \sigma$

(14) $[\text{ Pamela }]_p \longrightarrow [\text{ Pame }]_p\text{ la}$

In Japanese, a rule similar to that in (13) can be motivated for accented verbs, as shown in (15) and (16):[7]

(15) Japanese Accented Verb Invisibility: $\quad [\ldots \mu]_p \longrightarrow [\ldots]_p \mu$

(16) $[\text{ kakeru }]_p \longrightarrow [\text{ kake }]_p\text{ ru}$

---

have two more slots. There could be some x which is part of a prosodic constituent but not part of a morphological one; or, some y which belonged to neither structure. The former possibility might arguably be instantiated by phenomena such as semantically null reduplication motivated by the need to satisfy minimal size constraints; the latter possibility strikes me as unlearnable.

[6]Note that I have followed Myers 1987 in assuming that this rule applies to syllables, not to rimes. For the sake of saving space I omitted from the statement of the rule the crucial information that the morphological constituent corresponding to the input prosodic constituent must be a noun.

[7]This is not the analysis given in Poser 1984; Poser assumes, as we shall see later, that invisibility is built into the environment of the rule instead of being represented in the string. But in very general terms the intuition is the same.

In the case of lexically invisible affixes, I propose, responsibility for the mismatch lies not in rules but in underlying representation. Specifically, it derives from the prosodic subcategorization frame of the invisible affix. We have seen that for 'normal', visible affixes, the outermost prosodic brackets in the subcategorization frame include both the affix and the host, while the innermost brackets contain the host. Of course, the very fact that both sets of brackets are available underlyingly allows for the possibility that some affix may idiosyncratically stipulate a different location for its constituent brackets. And this is exactly what happens in the case of invisible affixes. These affixes, though they attach to a host just like visible affixes do, are special in that both their inner *and* the outer prosodic domain brackets contain only the subcategorized host: even in UR, the invisible affix is outside of the constituent which its prosodic subcategorization frame creates. The representation of an invisible English suffix is given in (17), alongside that of a visible suffix.

(17)

	Morphological frame	Prosodic frame
Visible suffix:	$[[\ ]_{m_\alpha}$ ic $]_{m_\alpha}$	$[[\ ]_{p_\alpha}$ ic $]_{p_\alpha}$
Invisible suffix:	$[[\ ]_{m_\alpha}$ ive $]_{m_\alpha}$	$[[\ ]_{p_\alpha}\ ]_{p_\alpha}$ ive

While both affixes say: "Combine me with a prosodic host of type α", the invisible affix goes a step further in saying "and leave me out of the resulting prosodic constituent."

The outcome of combining an invisible suffix with a host is depicted below:

(18)
$[\text{dissertate}]_{m_\alpha}$ + $[[\ ]_{m_\alpha}$ ive $]_{m_\alpha}$ ⟶ $[\text{dissertative}]_{m_\alpha}$
$[\text{dissertate}]_{p_\alpha}$ + $[[\ ]_{p_\alpha}\ ]_{p_\alpha}$ ive ⟶ $[\text{dissertat}]_{p_\alpha}$ ive

The specific nature of the prosodic frames of the invisible affixes overrides the default parameter settings discussed at the end of chapter 5, which would locate the outer prosodic bracket outside the affix in the subcategorization frame.

As mentioned earlier, representating invisibility in terms of mismatched domains (henceforth the 'domains approach') straightforwardly captures the insight that invisible elements are excluded from the domain of phonological rules. It also makes a number of strong, testable predictions about the behavior of invisibility:

(19) a. Invisibility can never be **exhaustive** (i.e. some part of each morphological constituent must be prosodically visible)

b. Invisibility must be **across-the-board**

c. Any element of phonological representation can be invisible (**generalized invisibility**)

d. It is possible for part but not all of an affix to be lexically invisible (**partial invisibility**)

e. Invisible elements must be peripheral (the **edge condition**)

f. Invisibility is lost cyclically (**cyclic loss**)

g. Multiple sources can contribute invisibility on a cycle (**cumulative invisibility**)

h. Only those phonological elements belonging to affixes and clitics can be lexically invisible (**morphological invisibility**)

In the following sections I will discuss these predictions, comparing, when relevant, the prosodic domain representation of invisibility to the other main approach which has been taken in the literature. This is what I will call the 'diacritic feature approach,' first formalized in Hayes 1981.

6.2.1 The Diacritic Feature Approach

Virtually from its first treatment in the literature, invisibility has obtained formal representation as an entity located within the phonological string.[8] In Hayes 1981:72 and subsequent work (e.g. Harris 1983, Pulleyblank 1983, Selkirk 1984, and many others), invisibility is explicitly assumed to be a diacritic feature, e.g. [+ex], which lodges directly on the invisible element.

---

[8]The exception is the view of Poser (1984, 1986a) that invisibility is a property of rules instead of representations. Poser proposes that each phonological rule has the potential to overlook some constituent in the domain in which it applies. Thus, invisibility is encoded only in the environment of the rule, in the form of a variable. I will argue later that though an intuitively appealing and nicely constrained account of a subpart of the data, this approach is not sufficiently flexible to handle the wider range of invisibility phenomena. Furthermore, it is less constrained than the proposed model with respect to the scope of invisibility, and misses several generalizations which the domains approach captures.

(20)   Pamela
        |
        [+ex]

[+ex] causes its host element to be overlooked by the rules which scan the string containing it.

(21)
    input   [Pamela]
    Noun Extrametricality: [Pamela]
                                             [+ex]

    English Stress Rule: [Pámela]
                                             [+ex]

In some cases [+ex] links directly to syllables, and in other cases to segments. It thus enjoys special status among phonological features in having more than one possible linking site.

A further unique property of [+ex] is that, at least on some accounts, it has transmodular linking properties, showing up on nodes in morphological structure as well as on nodes in phonological structure. For example, Hayes 1981 proposes the following rule for adjective suffix extrametricality (Hayes 1981:154):[9]

(22) Adjective Extrametricality: $[X]_{Suffix} \longrightarrow [+\text{ex}] \;/\; \text{\_\_\_}\,]_{Adj}$

Hayes applies this rule to suffixes regardless of their phonological content; the fact that -atory, which he considers extrametrical (p. 196), does not constitute a single phonological constituent seems to require that its associated [+ex] feature be linked to a morphological node, as no phonological node dominates the entire affix.[10]

---

[9] Selkirk 1984 and Myers 1987 assume that [+ex] cannot link to morphemes, but they lack a graceful account of invisible disyllabic suffixes in English.

[10] A possible alternative in the diacritic model is to assume that the [+ex] feature admits multiple linking, i.e. that it could be directly associated to each segment of an affix. This would permit one to link [+ex] only to phonological material as opposed to morphological nodes. However, Hayes 1981 argues against this type of approach, interpreting it as a violation of the Peripherality Condition (Harris 1983) which says that every extrametrical element must be at the edge of the rule domain. We will return to the Peripherality Condition in a subsequent section.

6.3. EXHAUSTIVE INVISIBILITY

In the remainder of this chapter I will discuss and compare the general consequences of the diacritic and domain treatments of invisibility. My aim is to show that the treatment of invisibility available within Prosodic Lexical Phonology theory has greater descriptive and explanatory power than the diacritic feature approach. While more flexible, it is also more constrained.

6.3 Exhaustive Invisibility

A generalization widely assumed to hold about invisibility is that it may not be exhaustive. No free-standing form (simple or derived) is ever entirely invisible to phonological rules.

(23) Unattested: (x)

However, as pointed out in Hayes 1981:74, some languages appear to have the power to generate totally invisible forms. For example, English, Latin and Winnebago contain both monosyllabic words and a productive syllable extrametricality rule. The naive expectation is that monosyllabic forms would lack stress in these languages. But this does not occur. Rather, the syllable extrametricality rule is somehow blocked from applying in just the cases where an entire word would become extrametrical. It is the duty of an adequate theory of extrametricality to explain why.

6.3.1 The Diacritic Feature Approach

The diacritic approach is not in a good position to do so. It is unclear why — or how — a phonological or diacritic feature should be banned from linking to a node exactly in the case that the node exhaustively dominates a morphological string. Particularly problematic is the fact that this configuration actually seems ideal for the extrametricality feature, which prefers peripheral locations (see section 6). After all, exhaustive dominance is as peripheral as one could possibly want.

(24)

The diacritic approach has thus had to capture the distributional generalization in (23) by fiat, invoking statements like the following: "... we must assume that extrametricality rules are blocked if their application would mark the entire stress domain ... as [+ex]. This condition is apparently universal, and thus should not add any cost to the grammars of particular languages." (Hayes 1981:74). Though descriptively accurate, such accounts lack explanatory power.

6.3.2 The Domains Approach

By contrast, the prohibition against exhaustive invisibility follows directly from the representation accorded to invisibility in the domains approach. From the assumption that invisible elements are excluded from membership in a prosodic constituent, it follows that a totally invisible morphological string will correspond to an empty prosodic constituent.

(25) Totally invisible form:

$$\begin{array}{ll} \text{Morphological structure} & \text{Prosodic structure} \\ [\,\text{x}\,]_m & [\;]_p \text{ x} \\ [\,\text{x}\,]_m & \text{x} [\;]_p \end{array}$$

But these representations are ill-formed: as we know independently, empty constituents cannot be condoned in prosodic phonology.

(26) *[ ]$_p$

The prohibition is best understood in the context of subcategorization, a theoretical device whose effectiveness relies crucially on the unacceptability of empty constituents. The very reason bound forms are forced to combine with other elements is that their own representations, which contain empty constituents, are ill-formed. Prohibiting the existence of empty constituents at any stage in the derivation is also necessary in order to maintain the explanation for why affixes and bound roots do not constitute rule domains.[11]

(27) *[x [ ]], *[[ ] y]

As (28) shows, it is precisely the distinction between empty and filled constituents that licenses the representations in (28) but rejects those in (27).

(28) [x [y]], [[x] y]

Thus, the independently motivated constraint against empty constituents combines with the proposed representation for invisibility to yield a natural explanation for why no morphological constituent may be made entirely invisible.

P. Kiparsky points out that, on this account, minimal size constraints (see McCarthy and Prince 1986) should also constrain the assignment of invisibility. That is, we expect to find cases where an invisibility-assigning rule is blocked from applying just in case the output prosodic constituent would dip below the minimal size requirement — or cases where, in order to save the derivation, a repair strategy is invoked to restore the form to complicity with the minimal size constraint. Future study may unearth examples of this kind.

6.4 Scope of Invisibility

A second area where the domains account derives important conditions which must be stipulated on the diacritic account involves the scope of invisibility. Because it locates invisible elements outside of the reigning prosodic constituent, the domains approach makes the strong prediction that such elements will be invisible to all rules applying on the corresponding cycle. That is, invisibility will be across-the-board.

(29) Across-the-board Invisibility: if an element *e* is invisible to one rule on the cycle, it will be invisible to all subsequent rules on the cycle.

---

[11]Although they mention empty constituents, subcategorization frames are not ill-formed in underlying representation. Morpheme structure constraints, of which the prohibition on empty constituents (26) is just one, apply only in the process of derivation (Kiparsky 1982). They do not apply to lexical entries.

As a corollary of this prediction, we also expect invisibility to percolate downward. If a given node is invisible, then its daughters should be invisible as well.[12]

(30) Inherited Invisibility: the daughters of an invisible node will also be invisible.

I will address these two predictions in order in the following subsections.

6.4.1 Across-the-board Invisibility

The prediction that invisibility takes wide scope over all phonological rules is borne out by English, in which not just one but all four of the lexical segmental rules which refer to final consonants in their environment fail to apply to α-final consonants.[13]

(31)
      n-deletion (takes final mn to m)
      Syllabification
      g-deletion (takes final gn to n)
      Voiced Obstruent Deletion (takes final mb, ng to m, $ŋ$, respectively)

The Strong Domain Hypothesis (Kiparsky 1984) dictates that these rules must apply within α constituents; their systematic failure to apply to α-final consonants has been taken as evidence that these consonants are invisible when the four relevant α rules apply (Borowsky 1986). That is to say, the following invisibility rule precedes all four rules in (31):

(32) C Invisibility: $[\ldots C]_{p_\alpha} \longrightarrow [\ldots]_{p_\alpha} C$

---

[12]The Inherited Invisibility hypothesis appears to contradict a statement made by Hayes about the nature of [+ex] percolation; Hayes argues that [+ex] must *not* percolate down to daughters of the node to which it is linked, as this would violate the constraint that each element linked to [+ex] must be peripheral (more on this later). However, Hayes's concerns pertain only to the actual geometrical linking of [+ex], and not to its extent of its effect; it is the latter issue which (30) addresses.

[13]The temptation is to try and formulate all of these rules in terms of syllable structure, so that failure to syllabify will predict failure to undergo the other three rules. However, failure to syllabify at level 1 is not sufficient explanation for why n deletion et al. are blocked there. The final consonants to which these rules refer are not syllabifiable at level 2 either, yet there they do undergo the rules in (31). So syllable structure is held constant across levels (for these purposes); consonant invisibility has to be the relevant variable.

6.4. SCOPE OF INVISIBILITY

n deletion

We have already seen, in chapter 4, the relevance of final consonant invisibility to the α rule of n deletion. I will repeat only the gist of that discussion here, which is that α-final mn sequences are not simplified to m by n deletion, although those sequences are simplified when final in a β constituent. Thus, we follow Borowsky 1986 in concluding that α-final consonants must be invisible for purposes of n deletion.

(33)

Prosodic structure required by n deletion: [condem]$_{p_\alpha}$ n
Prosodic structure provided by C Invisibility: [condem]$_{p_\alpha}$ n

As (33) shows, C Invisibility produces exactly the prosodic structure needed in order to prevent n deletion from overapplying to α-final consonants.

Syllabification

Evidence that syllabification ignores α-final consonants as well comes from the rule of Closed-Syllable Shortening (Myers 1987). Best construed as part of the process of syllabification, Closed Syllable Shortening is the result of syllabifying a consonant together with a long vowel to its left.[14] In conformity to a two-mora-per-syllable constraint operative within α domains, that linking process causes the simultaneous deletion of the second mora of the long vowel.

(34)

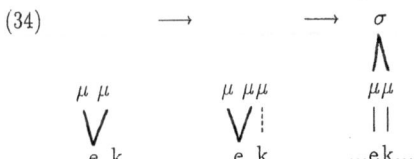

As Myers shows, this simple leftward syllabification process correctly accounts for Trisyllabic shortening in derived forms such as *conic, opacity, divinity*.

But, as Myers again shows, the process must be blocked from applying when the relevant consonant is final in an α domain. If the final consonant of words like

---

[14]This happens both to an unsyllabified consonant and to one which begins an unstressed syllable.

provoke, insane, concede, revise were visible to the syllabification algorithm, the preceding long vowel would be shortened. That the result of such a process is incorrect (*prov[ɔ]ke, *ins[æ]ne, *conc[ɛ]de, *rev[I]se) shows that final consonants cannot be visible to α syllabification rules. Again, the prosodic structure needed to produce the right syllabification coincides exactly with that produced by C Invisibility:

(35)
    Prosodic structure required by Syllabification: [conce]$_{p_\alpha}$ de
    Prosodic structure provided by C Invisibility: [conce]$_{p_\alpha}$ de

From the failure of syllabification to apply to final consonants, it follows that a domain-final CVC sequence will not constitute a heavy syllable for purposes of stress assignment. And, of course, this is true in English. As is well known, syllables with a short vowel which end in a single consonant pattern like light (CV) syllables, while those syllables ending in two or more consonants pattern as heavy (i.e. like syllables containing long vowels) with respect to the quantity-sensitive stress rules of English.

(36)

Light final	Light final	Heavy final	Heavy final
happy	hover	agree	select
wanna	interpret	intervene	intersect

As pointed out in Hayes 1981, these facts follow naturally from the assumption that final consonants are extrametrical in English.[15]

g-deletion

A third rule directly affected by C invisibility is *g*-deletion. Responsible for the departure of *g* when a stem-final nasal follows, this rule would normally be expected to delete the penultimate consonant of α words like *consign, design, resign, malign, paradigm*.[16] Yet it does not: the *g* shows up before α suffixes, as in *designation*,

---

[15] Hayes happens to attribute the extrametricality to a rule applying to fully syllabified structure, but the evidence from Closed Syllable Shortening shows that actually final consonants are invisible at an even earlier point in the cycle. Thus, the English Stress Rule itself refers not directly to consonants, but rather to syllable weight, and is affected only indirectly by final consonant invisibility.

[16] I have deliberately included morphologically complex words here, to make sure this argument is independent of the suggestion made in Chapter 4 that English has no preaffixal α stem cycle.

6.4. SCOPE OF INVISIBILITY

resignation, malignant, paradigmatic. This can be explained if the conditioning final nasals are invisible in α-final position.

(37)
    Prosodic structure required by g deletion: [consig]$_{p_\alpha}$ n
    Prosodic structure provided by C Invisibility: [consig]$_{p_\alpha}$ n

Though they must become visible at some later point, in order to be deleted by g-deletion applying at a later level, final nasals are crucially invisible to α rules. Across-the-board α-final consonant invisibility accounts for this.

Voiced Obstruent Deletion

The fourth lexical rule referring to final consonants, Voiced Obstruent Deletion systematically fails to apply to α-final consonants. The final voiced obstruent in *iamb, prolong, monophthong, diphthong* shows up in such derived α forms as *iambic, prolongation, monophthongal, diphthongic*. As will come as no surprise, the failure of obstruents to delete in these base forms follows naturally from the assumption that C Invisibility has made them invisible to the deletion rule.

(38)
    Prosodic structure required by V. O. Deletion: [diphthon]$_{p_\alpha}$ g
    Prosodic structure provided by C Invisibility: [diphthon]$_{p_\alpha}$ g

Thus, each of the four rules in English which crucially refer to final consonants uniformly ignores those consonants when applying on the α domain. Once final consonant invisibility has been assigned to α constituents, it shields those consonants from the view of all subsequent rules applying on the domain. This across-the-board effect is exactly what the domains approach to invisibility predicts.

Apparent Counterexample

An apparent counterexample to the Across-the-board prediction is found in Selkirk 1984. In an elegant analysis of English word stress couched in the diacritic framework,[17]

---

[17]Selkirk's analysis departs from that of Hayes 1981 in a number of details; for instance, she takes all extrametricality marking to be a property of underlying representation. However, because

Selkirk crucially assumes that a final closed syllable can be visible to the Heavy Syllable Basic Beat Rule (Selkirk 1984:87-98) at the same time that it is invisible to another rule (the Main Stress Rule). This pattern is exemplified by words such as *shishkabob*, shown in (39).

(39)

shishkabob

Selkirk attributes the secondary stress on *bob* to the Heavy Syllable Basic Beat Rule, which stresses all heavy syllables. However, the fact that the syllable *bob* surfaces without primary stress in *shìshkabòb* (cf. *Tènnessée*) shows that it must be invisible to the Main Stress Rule.

This simultaneous visibility and invisibility of the same constituent is made possible by Selkirk's view that invisibility is rule-specific. What makes Selkirk's proposal especially interesting is her attempt to predict whether or not a given extrametricality feature will be respected by a given rule. The generalization seems to be that extrametricality of a constituent is relevant only to rules which make crucial reference to that constituent's mother (pp. 88-89).[18] The Main Stress Rule refers to the smallest cyclic domain dominating syllables, and thus qualifies as a rule which will respect syllable extrametricality. By contrast, the Heavy Syllable Basic Beat Rule (which stresses heavy syllables) appeals only to syllables and subsyllabic structure. By Selkirk's criterion it can respect only subsyllabic (i.e. segment) extrametricality. Thus, the Heavy Syllable Basic Beat Rule ignores the extrametricality marking in (39) and assigns the last syllable of *shishkabob* a grid mark.

Though initially appealing, this intuition breaks down quickly when it comes to accounting for why final consonants in English are invisible to the three rules described earlier — all of which crucially refer to the edge of the cyclic domain. The assumption that extrametricality of an element is acknowledged only by rules referring

---

Selkirk indicates that extrametricality is marked directly on the extrametrical constituent in those underlying representations (e.g. '[... $C_{em}]_{Root}$' and '[a sto nish$_{em}$]' (p. 92)), I have classed her approach with that of Hayes for the present purpose. Both she and Hayes represent invisibility as a diacritic feature in the phonological string.

[18]Selkirk assumes that segments are dominated directly by syllables, and that syllables are dominated directly by a word-sized unit, rejecting the idea of intermediate metrical structure.

6.4. SCOPE OF INVISIBILITY

to that element's mother predicts, incorrectly, that the stem-level rules of n deletion, g deletion and Voiced Obstruent Deletion will not respect segment invisibility.

In the face of the failure to predict which rules will respect which extrametricality features, it becomes a mere stipulation that some syllable is visible to one rule but not to another. And for English, the excess power engendered by the ability to stipulate rule-specific (in)visibility appears not to be necessary. Hayes 1981 provides an alternative account of the stress of words like *shishkabob* according to which, following proposals in Selkirk 1980, a foot is marked underlyingly on the final syllable.[19] The syllable need not be visible to the Heavy Syllable Basic Beat Rule in order to receive its stress. Rather, it can remain invisible to all rules; we maintain the Across-the-board hypothesis, and end up with a more constrained theory.[20]

6.4.2 Inherited Invisibility

We turn next to the second prediction, the Inherited Invisibility hypothesis in (30) (repeated below).

(40) Inherited Invisibility: if a node n is invisible on the cycle then its daughters will be invisible as well.

This strong hypothesis would be falsified by the discovery of evidence that some rule must refer to a constituent whose mother has been made invisible by an earlier rule. Since invisibility is unrecoverable on the cycle, such a case would force us to assume a representation like that in (41), where the mother is invisible while the daughter is visible. Allowing configurations like this would weaken the theory considerably; it minimizes the consequences of making any element invisible.

---

[19] Selkirk argues against this type of analysis because the underlying foot duplicates what the Heavy Syllable Basic Beat Rule would assign if it could apply. But one could turn this complaint around and argue that if one can capture the irregularities of English stress by judicious underlying assignment of phonological features which later surface in those very positions, such an analysis would be preferred to one which, like Selkirk's, requires abstract and otherwise unmotivated diacritic features to encode idiosyncrasy.

[20] As S. Anderson has pointed out to me, another apparent case of rule-specific invisibility lies in the analysis of infixation put forth by McCarthy and Prince 1986. They treat infixes as regular affixes which show up inside the stem they attach to by virtue of following a rule specific to them which renders some peripheral part of the base invisible. Later in this chapter, however, I will argue against this analysis of infixation on other grounds.

(41) (x) or ⌉x
     | ⫽
     y   y

At least one apparent instantiation of (41) — thus a counterexample to (40) — has been described in the literature (Myers 1987). I will argue that this can be reanalyzed by ordering the rule referring to the daughter *before* the rule assigning invisibility. Thus, there is no need for representations like that in (41), and the restrictive inheritance hypothesis can be maintained.

Apparent Counterexample

Myers 1987 describes a rule of voicing assimilation in English which is conditioned by the featural content of a consonant made invisible by final C invisibility.

(42) leave + t ⟶ lef(t)

Myers suggests that only the C slot corresponding to the past tense suffix in (42) is invisible, leaving the feature matrix associated with it available to condition the loss of voicing on the preceding consonant. That is, C invisibility has scope only over the C slot, and not over the root node which is its daughter.

(43) (C)
      |
      t

However, given that both voicing assimilation and C invisibility are phonological rules, Myers's argument that invisibility is not inherited holds water only if it can be shown that voicing assimilation crucially follows C invisibility. I know of no empirical evidence for this ordering, nor of any theoretical motivation.[21] We may thus conclude that voicing assimilation in English does not falsify the strong claim in (39).

---

[21] If we assume (as most phonologists do) that the mechanism of extrinsic rule ordering is available to the theory, then it is perfectly plausible that it should affect rules assigning invisibility as well.

6.4.3 The Diacritic Feature Approach

In contrast to the domains theory, the diacritic approach seems to make no predictions with respect to the scope of invisibility. The phenomena for which [+ex] was originally proposed involved only one rule per language (the English and Spanish stress rules, in particular), so that the question of whether [+ex] means invisibility to all rules or just to one did not arise in the pioneering studies. Later interpretations have varied.

With respect to across-the-board scope, Borowsky 1986 and Myers 1987 adopt the explicit position that [+ex] pertains to all phonological rules which would manipulate the extrametrical element. However, working within the same general theory, Selkirk 1984 makes exactly the opposite assumption, as we have seen. The fact that such different interpretations are possible suggests that the theory lacks predictive power.

Whether or not invisibility is inherited is also left ambiguous by representations in which [+ex] is linked to some node in phonological structure. The analyses by Selkirk 1984 and Myers 1987, mentioned above (see also Roca 1988), show that the framework at least allows the description of cases in which invisibility is not inherited.

One could imagine imposing a general condition on phonological features that they have effect, where interpretable, over the daughters of the constituent bearing them. This would effectively constrain the diacritic theory to the point where its predictions with respect to inheritance converge with that of the domains approach. In fact, such a condition has been implicated in certain proposals in the tonal literature, where tones are linked directly to syllable nodes instead of to the syllabic elements that actually exhibit the corresponding pitch. However, the status of the syllable as tone-bearing-unit is actually somewhat controversial; Leben 1973 and Poser 1988 have argued against linking tones to any constituent higher than the segment.

A possibility which all of the theories allow is that a daughter may be rendered invisible while its mother remains in view. This possibility is manifested in certain infixation and reduplication processes cited by Kiparsky 1986 and McCarthy and Prince 1986. I will not go into these here as they do not serve to distinguish among the various treatments of invisibility.

6.5 Phonological Content of Invisible Element

The domains theory posits two sources for invisibility: rules and underlying representations. Unless further constraints are imposed, the theory predicts that any phonological material which can be referred to by phonological rules can in principle be made invisible. An additional prediction is that no phonological constraints should hold on material which is underlyingly invisible, as the location of underlying prosodic domain brackets need not be rule-governed at all.

These predictions, which I later argue to be correct, conflict sharply with certain conditions that have been proposed to hold specifically on the content of invisible material. We will examine these constraints here, concluding that they are generally stipulative, that they are too restrictive to account for the data, and that they should be abandoned. The portions of those constraints which are correct can be derived from more general conditions on phonological rules (Poser 1986b).

In most analyses of invisiblity in the literature, material made invisible by phonological rule has been some component of metrical structure, whether a C slot, a mora, a syllable, or a foot:

(44)
- a. C slot: English C Invisibility (Hayes 1981)
- b. mora: Japanese verbs (Poser 1984)
- c. rime: English noun extrametricality (Hayes 1981)
- d. syllable: English noun extrametricality (Selkirk 1984, Myers 1987)
- e. foot: English Trisyllabic Extrametricality (Hayes 1981), Japanese noun-noun compound accentuation, Japanese hypocoristics (Poser 1984, 1990), Palestinian Arabic (Hayes 1987).

Several authors have built generalizations based on portions of this data directly into their definition of invisibility. Selkirk 1984, for example, claims that only segments and syllables may be extrametrical. The more general view, taken in Hayes 1981, Myers 1987, Roca 1988, and others, is that any phonological constituent is a potential linking site for [+ex]. Poser 1986b restricts the range of linking sites to nodes in metrical structure, a stance compatible with the data considered in the literature but not explicitly taken elsewhere in that literature.

(45) Proposed candidates for invisibility:

- a. Selkirk 1984: segment, syllable
- b. Poser 1986b: nodes in metrical structure

6.5. PHONOLOGICAL CONTENT OF INVISIBLE ELEMENT

c. Hayes 1981, Myers 1987, Roca 1988: any phonological constituent

Some (e.g. Selkirk, Myers) take these constraints to hold generally on invisibility; others (e.g. Hayes, Poser) apply them only to invisibility assigned by phonological rule.[22]

A survey of some new and old data will quickly demonstrate the incorrectness of the strong claim that *all* invisibility is restricted to phonological constituents. To this end, I present below several cases of lexicalized invisibility in which what is invisible is a non-constituent.

6.5.1 Lexical Invisibility

Evidence abounds that lexically invisible morphemes do not conform to the single-phonological-constituent requirement. I will present the evidence in two stages. First, I show that morphemes which consist of floating features (i.e. 'less' than a constituent) can be lexically invisible; second, I show that the same is true of morphemes which consist of more than one constituent.

Sekani prefixes

In a discussion of the lexical phonology of Sekani, Hargus 1985 observes that certain prefixes (the 'conjugation' prefixes) have the property of assigning Low tone to a preceding vowel in the word. If no vowel precedes,[23] the tone is lost. The examples below illustrate two conjugation prefixes, /sə/ and /nə/ (p. 140). The prefixes are underlined in what follows:

(46) kǫh sə-gha-wə-<u>nə</u>-n-ʔǫ ⟶ kǫh sawənîʔǫ 'he, she gave me a house'
                                     |
                                     L

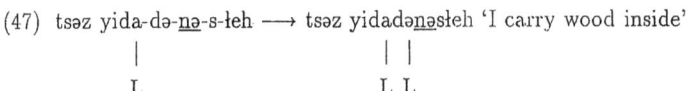

(47) tsəz yida-də-<u>nə</u>-s-łeh ⟶ tsəz yidadənəsłeh 'I carry wood inside'
     | | |
     L   L L

---

[22]Of course, Poser 1984, 1986b takes all invisibility to be of this kind.
[23]More accurately, if no level 2 or 3 prefix precedes (p. 143).

(48) nə-ts'ę u-sə-s-l-get ⟶ nəts'ę usəsget 'I crawled to you [sg]'

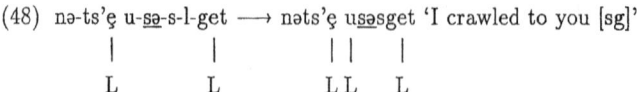

Citing work by K. Rice, Hargus analyzes conjugation prefixes as affiliated with a floating Low tone. Low docks to the preceding vowel by means of the following rule:

(49) Conjugation Tone Mapping:

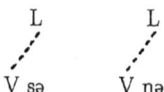

However, a more principled account of these prefixes would be to analyze their underlying tone as invisible. It becomes visible only on the next prefix cycle, at which time it docks to the leftmost available TBU.[24]

(50) Conjugation prefixes: L [sə [ ]$_p$]$_p$
                              L [nə [ ]$_p$]$_p$

Below is the relevant part of the derivation of (48). Again, conjugation prefixes are underlined:

(51)
    sə **cycle**

        Affixation:

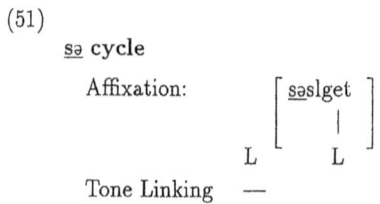

        Tone Linking —

---

[24]An similar analysis is given by Kanerva 1986 to certain prefixes in Chichewa which appear to deposit tone on the preceding syllable. Kanerva observes that on accounts (such as his and the one presented here) which attribute invisibility to the location of the edge of the rule domain, it should follow without stipulation that invisibility on one edge will disappear upon the cyclic attachment of an affix at that same edge.

6.5. PHONOLOGICAL CONTENT OF INVISIBLE ELEMENT

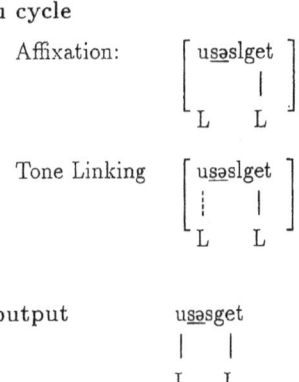

u cycle

Affixation:

Tone Linking:

output

Evidence that only the tone of the conjugation prefix is invisible, and not the segmental material as well, comes from the rule of Prefix Vowel Deletion. This rule deletes certain vowels in the environment of another vowel (p. 134).

(52) Prefix Vowel Deletion:

ə ⟶ ∅ % ___ V
i ⟶ ∅ % ___ V

Like Tone Linking, Prefix Vowel Deletion applies at levels 2 and 3 of the lexical phonology, but not at level 4. Consider the case where the conjugation prefix is the outermost prefix on level 3, as in (53).

(53) [mə- ghǫh [nə̱ - i [ya]₁]₂,₃]₄   'I got to him, her walking'

                            L

If the entire conjugation prefix was invisible, we would expect both Prefix Vowel Deletion and Tone Linking to be blocked. But this is not the case. As (54) shows, only Tone Linking is blocked. The vowel of the conjugation prefix deletes in the presence of the following i:

(54) mǫhn̰iya

To sum up, the postulation of underlyingly invisible floating tones provides a natural account of the preaccenting behavior of conjugation prefixes in Sekani, and justifies the ability of the domains approach to represent invisible nonmetrical elements.

English

While the above evidence showed that invisible elements can be 'less' than a constituent, the opposite violation of the single-constituent requirement also obtains. English provides several examples of invisible suffixes whose phonological content can be described only as sequences of constituents, but not as a single constituent of any kind.

English has at least two disyllabic adjective suffixes which are entirely invisible, yet which do not always surface as feet. These are the familiar -*ary* and -*ory* (Hayes 1981).

As is well known, stress facts indicate the necessity of analyzing these suffixes as invisible (Hayes 1981, and earlier analyses (SPE, Liberman and Prince 1977)). Yet in the words in (55), these suffixes form part of a ternary foot, and are not themselves metrical constituents:

(55) cúrsory, térnary, illúsory, infírmary

On some accounts, the suffixes have been analyzed as bearing a metrical foot which is then deleted in certain environments by a rule specific to -*ary/-ory*. However, such analyses are unacceptable in a framework which denies phonological rules access to the identity of particular morphemes. A simpler and theoretically permissable analysis is to assume the suffixes are underlyingly nonconstituents, and to assign them feet later, should they require it, by a more general rule.[25]

To sum up the past subsections, we may reject the claim that morphologically governed invisibility is subject to phonological constraints on invisibility. This is in some sense a relief, as enforcing those constraints would run into serious theoretical roadblocks. Enforcing the single-constituent constraint underlyingly would require

---

[25]In chapter 4, for example, we saw that these suffixes are assigned to a foot by the English Stress Rule when the level 1 -*ly* follows.

6.5.2 Rule-governed Invisibility

Now that we have dealt with lexicalized invisibility, let us turn to rule-governed invisibility. The first question is whether the embattled single-constituent constraint is appropriate in this arena; and, if so, how it can be derived.

I will argue here that for rule-governed invisibility the single-constituent generalization is empirically correct, with one important addition to complete the list mentioned in (44): in addition to nodes in metrical structure, floating, unlicensed melodic elements can be made invisible as well.[26] The evidence, from tone as well as segmental phenomena, will be presented below. It supports the least restrictive of the three generalizations (that of Hayes) over the other two (Selkirk's and Poser's).

Mende

We will start with a very simple case, which is more suggestive than conclusive. Leben 1973, 1978 shows that in Mende, each word is affiliated underlyingly with one of the following set of tonal melodies (Leben 1973:64):

(56) H, L, HL, LH, LHL

A simple one-to-one, left-to-right mapping algorithm links these floating tones to the syllables of the words with which they are affiliated. Leftover syllables acquire tone by left-to-right spreading; leftover tones bunch up on the leftmost syllable.

---

[26]My assumption is that features do not count as constituents in metrical structure; for example, while strict hierarchical relations obtain among the recognized constituents (mora, syllable, foot), features and feature matrices are able to belong simultaneously to more than one sister node in higher structure (resulting in ambisyllabicity and geminates). Thus, while floating features count as units (constituents) in phonological representation, they do not count as *metrical* constituents.

(57)

$$\begin{bmatrix} p\varepsilon l\varepsilon \\ H \end{bmatrix} \longrightarrow \begin{bmatrix} p\varepsilon l\varepsilon \\ \vee \\ H \end{bmatrix} \quad \text{'house'}$$

$$\begin{bmatrix} b\varepsilon l\varepsilon \\ L \end{bmatrix} \longrightarrow \begin{bmatrix} b\varepsilon l\varepsilon \\ \vee \\ L \end{bmatrix} \quad \text{'trousers'}$$

$$\begin{bmatrix} kenya \\ HL \end{bmatrix} \longrightarrow \begin{bmatrix} kenya \\ | \ | \\ H \ L \end{bmatrix} \quad \text{'uncle'}$$

$$\begin{bmatrix} nika \\ LH \end{bmatrix} \longrightarrow \begin{bmatrix} nika \\ | \ | \\ L \ H \end{bmatrix} \quad \text{'cow'}$$

$$\begin{bmatrix} nikili \\ LHL \end{bmatrix} \longrightarrow \begin{bmatrix} nikili \\ | \ | \ | \\ L \ HL \end{bmatrix} \quad \text{'groundnut'}$$

When stems are combined with a toneless suffix, the tone melody affiliated with the stem stretches to cover the suffix:

(58)

$$\begin{bmatrix} p\varepsilon l\varepsilon + hu \\ H \end{bmatrix} \longrightarrow \begin{bmatrix} p\varepsilon l\varepsilon hu \\ \vee\!\!\!\vee \\ H \end{bmatrix} \quad \text{'in a house'}$$

$$\begin{bmatrix} b\varepsilon l\varepsilon + hu \\ L \end{bmatrix} \longrightarrow \begin{bmatrix} b\varepsilon l\varepsilon hu \\ \vee\!\!\!\vee \\ L \end{bmatrix} \quad \text{'in trousers'}$$

$$\begin{bmatrix} kenya + ma \\ HL \end{bmatrix} \longrightarrow \begin{bmatrix} kenyama \\ | \ \vee\!\!\!\vee \\ H \ L \end{bmatrix} \quad \text{'on an uncle'}$$

6.5. PHONOLOGICAL CONTENT OF INVISIBLE ELEMENT 143

However, an interesting asymmetry shows up when disyllabic words with an underlying LH tone pattern are combined with a toneless suffix. In a small number of cases, the expected LHH pattern shows up, as in (59):

(59) $\begin{bmatrix} \text{navo + ma} \\ \text{LH} \end{bmatrix} \longrightarrow \begin{bmatrix} \text{navoma} \\ |\ \mathcal{V} \\ \text{L H} \end{bmatrix}$ 'on money'

But in the majority of cases, the High tone of the LH melody shows up only on the third or final syllable of the derived word:

(60) $\begin{bmatrix} \text{nika} \\ \text{LH} \end{bmatrix} \longrightarrow \begin{bmatrix} \text{nikama} \\ \mathcal{V}\ | \\ \text{L}\ \ \text{H} \end{bmatrix}$ 'on a cow'

A possible solution to this problem, suggested by W. Leben (class lecture 1986), is to posit a phonological rule which makes a melody-final floating High invisible. Exceptional stems such as *navo* will have the underlying High of the LH melody prelinked and thus will fail to undergo the invisibility rule. For all other LH words, however, on the cycle when tone is assigned, the High of a LH melody will be made unavailable. Low will spread to all available syllables.

(61)

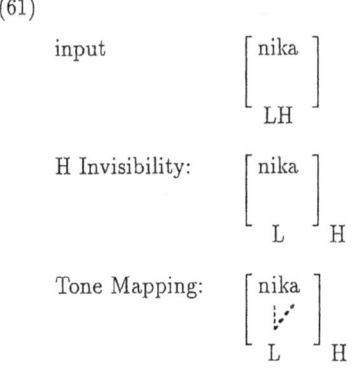

input $\begin{bmatrix} \text{nika} \\ \text{LH} \end{bmatrix}$

H Invisibility: $\begin{bmatrix} \text{nika} \\ | \\ \text{L}\ \ \text{H} \end{bmatrix}$

Tone Mapping: $\begin{bmatrix} \text{nika} \\ \mathcal{V} \\ \text{L}\ \ \text{H} \end{bmatrix}$

If a suffix is added, the floating High will become visible (see section 7) and will link to the rightmost available slot, namely that suffix vowel:

(62)

input $\begin{bmatrix} \text{nika} & + \text{ma} \\ \diagup & \\ \text{L} & \text{H} \end{bmatrix}$

Tone Mapping: $\begin{bmatrix} \text{nikama} \\ \diagup \quad \vdots \\ \text{L} \quad \text{H} \end{bmatrix}$

If no suffixes are added, High invisibility will be lost at the word level, whereupon floating High will dock to the final syllable. The resulting Low $\widehat{\text{LH}}$ contour simplifies to LH by the independently motivated rule of Tone Absorption:

(63)

input $\begin{bmatrix} \text{nika} \\ \\ \text{LH} \end{bmatrix}$

-cycle 1-

H Invisibility: $\begin{bmatrix} \text{nika} \\ \\ \cdot \text{L} \quad \text{H} \end{bmatrix}$

Tone Mapping: $\begin{bmatrix} \text{nika} \\ \vdots \diagup \\ \text{L} \quad \text{H} \end{bmatrix}$

-word cycle-

Tone Mapping: $\begin{bmatrix} \text{nika} \\ \diagup \vdots \\ \text{L H} \end{bmatrix}$

Tone Absorption: $\begin{bmatrix} \text{nika} \\ \cancel{\diagup} \\ \text{L H} \end{bmatrix}$

6.5. PHONOLOGICAL CONTENT OF INVISIBLE ELEMENT

An example strikingly similar to Mende is Kukuya (Hyman 1987), in which words are also affiliated underlyingly with one of the following tone melodies: H, L, HL, LH, LHL. As shown in Hyman 1987 (working from Paulian 1974), left-to-right, one-to-one tone association applies in all cases except for the LH words. In these cases, the High shows up only on the last vowel (unless a High-toned word follows, in which case the word is all-Low). As in Mende we could account for the association of the LH tone melody by making the floating High invisible to the initial tone assignment process.[27]

Another case where invisible elements are not incorporated into higher, metrical structure is provided by syllabification. Here, too, material which forms 'less' than a metrical constituent still qualifies for invisibility status.

Syllabification

Itô 1986 argues persuasively for a theory of prosodic licensing according to which all phonological material must be 'licensed', either by incorporation into higher (metrical) structure, or by invisibility.[28] When applied to syllabification, this principle requires all melodic elements to be syllabified or to be invisible. Material not licensed in one of these ways is deleted from the representation by stray erasure (McCarthy 1979).

Assuming that syllables are the lowest units of metrical structure[29], this view of syllabification imposes invisibility on precisely those elements which are *not* incorporated into metrical structure.[30]

To sum up, suggestive evidence from tone and more substantial evidence from syllabification converge to show that floating melodic elements can be made invisible by rule. This evidence falsifies the hypothesis that only metrical constituents can be made invisible, and is consistent with the immediately weaker hypothesis that any

---

[27]Of course, workable alternative accounts, which do not make use of invisible tone, exist both for Mende (Leben 1973, 1978, Cole and Uyechi 1988) and for Kukuya (Hyman 1987). Although these analyses are no simpler than the one motivated here, it is true that if one had independent reasons for prohibiting invisible floating features, Mende and Kukuya would probably not present crucial counterexamples.

[28]See section 6, where I argue that the domains approach to invisibility affords a simplification in the definition of prosodic licensing.

[29]The argument is exactly the same, transposed down a level in the prosodic hierarchy, if we assume the mora to be the lowest prosodic unit; this move is made implicitly in Itô 1988 and explicitly in Zec 1988b.

[30]The analysis of infixation developed by McCarthy and Prince 1986 also relies on invisibility of floating melodic elements (see e.g. p. 44). However, as far as I can tell these melodic elements become floating only after being made invisible. At the input to invisibility assignment they are all still linked to higher structure.

phonological element, or constituent, is a potential candidate for invisibility. This condition is stated below:

(64) Single-Constituent Condition: Material made invisible by phonological rules must be a phonological constituent

We may now ask whether this condition must be stipulated or whether it can be derived. The work of Poser 1986b shows that in fact (64) follows from a very general principle on phonological rules. This is the Focus Determinant Adjacency Condition of Poser 1985b, a locality constraint on the environments of phonological rules.

(65) Focus Determinant Adjacency Condition: Every focus must be adjacent on the projection to every determinant [Poser 1985b]

The scope of the FDAC extends beyond invisibility to phonological rules of all kinds. Its effect is to impose adjacency on rule environments, forcing the undergoer (focus) of each rule to be adjacent to each element in the environment (each determinant).

From this single, well-motivated constraint it follows that any context-sensitive rule can have only one focus; Poser consequently derives the result that any rule invoking invisibility can invoke it on just one element (i.e. constituent in phonological representation). This explains the generalization that invisibility tends to affect only one element at a time.

To conclude this section, we have seen that no special conditions need to be placed on the phonological content of invisible material. In the case of rule-governed invisibility, the single-constituent condition follows as a natural consequence of an independently motivated constraint on phonological rules. In the case of lexically governed invisibility, I have suggested that no phonological constraints hold at all.

It might have seemed at first glance that the domains approach is less constrained than past versions of the diacritic approach in imposing no upper bound on the phonological content of invisible material. However, precisely because the domains approach can factor apart phonologically from morphologically induced invisibility, it can impose appropriate constraints on invisibility without needing any stipulations. In this sense it is a more explanatory model.

6.6 Partial Underlying Invisibility

In this section I would like to explore further the possibilities engendered by the proposed representation of lexically invisible morphemes. The domains approach is more flexible than the diacritic approach in this regard, imposing, as I have shown, no phonological constraints on the phonological content of that material. I will argue here that the extra flexibility is needed to account for data which have not previously been the focus of attention.

On the domains account, most cases we have seen thus far of lexical invisibility have all involved lexical specifications in which the outermost prosodic domain bracket is adjacent to the innermost bracket.

(66) Invisible suffix: $[[\ ]_p\ ]_p$ suff

However, nothing we have said so far forces this to be the only option. By allowing the location of outermost prosodic domain brackets to be lexically marked, we leave open the possibility that the outermost bracket might actually interrupt the phonological material comprising the affix. That is, the theory predicts the possibility of partial invisibility.[31]

(67) Definition: an affix is partially invisible if there exist two phonological units x and y in that affix such that x and y are on opposite sides of the outermost prosodic domain bracket.

(68) Partially Invisible Suffix:

        Morphological frame   Prosodic frame
        $[[\ ]_m\ \text{xy}\ ]_m$ $[[\ ]_p\ \text{x}\ ]_p\ \text{y}$

The domains theory thus predicts a three-way suffix typology: visible, partially invisible, and totally invisible.[32]

---

[31] The representation proposed just above for the postaccenting Japanese honorific prefix *o-* displays partial invisibility.

[32] The same prediction is made for prefixes, for which I have seen considerably less data, and which I am not able to generalize about.

(69)

Totally visible:	$[[\ ]_{p_\alpha}\ xy\ ]_{p_\alpha}$
Partially visible:	$[[\ ]_{p_\alpha}\ x\ ]_{p_\alpha}\ y$
Totally invisible:	$[[\ ]_{p_\alpha}\ ]_{p_\alpha}\ xy$

I will argue in this section that precisely this ternary distinction is needed in English and in Japanese. In fact, this claim is not new: Nanni 1979 (see also Hayes 1981:199) proposes that in order to derive the stress patterns of the words in (70), the suffix *ative* must have the representation in (71). That is, it must be partially invisible.

(70)
    írritàtive
    invéstigàtive
    législàtive
    ápplicàtive
    méditàtive
    admínistràtive

(71)   -at(ive)

For details of *-ative*, the reader is referred to Nanni 1979. Here, I would like to strengthen her case by making the same argument for two other English suffixes: disyllabic *-ual* and trisyllabic *-atory*.

Both *-ual* and *atory* are weak retractors; that is, stress appears on the immediately preceding syllable.[33]

(72)

habítual	acclámatory
decídual	consólatory
rítual	decláratory
vísual	depílatory
vácual	derógatory
grádual	fecúndatory
	perspíratory
	perfúmatory

---

[33]Exception: *spiritual*

6.6. PARTIAL UNDERLYING INVISIBILITY

If *-ual* and *-atory* were visible when added to these forms, we would expect primary stress on the penultimate syllable of the suffix:

(73)
    rite   ⟶ ritual   ⟶ *ritúal (cf. discóver)

    declare ⟶ declaratory ⟶ *dèclaratóry (cf. Tàtamagóuchi)

And if *-ual* and *-atory* were completely invisible, we would expect the English Stress Rule to locate stress two syllables to the left of the suffix, in cases like these where the stem-final syllable is light. But, as the forms in (74) show, this prediction is also incorrect:[34]

(74)
    habit ⟶ habi(tual) ⟶ *hábi(tual)

    declare ⟶ decla(ratory) ⟶ *décla(ratory)

The only way to derive the stress exhibited by the words in (72) is to assume that the initial vowels of the suffixes *-ual* and *-atory* are visible — but that the remainder of each suffix is invisible.

(75)
    [ritu]$_{p_\alpha}$ al   ⟶ rítual
    [habitu]$_{p_\alpha}$ al   ⟶ habítual

    [depila]$_{p_\alpha}$ tory ⟶ depílatory
    [deroga]$_{p_\alpha}$ tory ⟶ derógatory

Supporting evidence for the claim that the initial vowels of *-ual* and *-atory* are visible comes from the α rule of Trisyllabic Shortening, which applies to the pre-suffixal syllable in words like those in (76):

---

[34]For why the stem-final consonant becomes invisible when an invisible vowel-initial suffix follows, see section 7.

(76)

gradual (< grade)	acclamatory (< acclaim)
ritual (< rite)	exclamatory (< exclaim)
residual (< reside)	explanatory (< explain)
decidual (< decide)	inflammatory (< inflame)
televisual (< televise)	provocatory (< provoke)

If *-ual* and *-atory* were completely invisible, none of the stem-final vowels in (76) would precede any visible material within an α constituent. Instead, the invisible suffix would reappear only when PCF applies to form β constituents. Since Trisyllabic Shortening applies only to closed syllables within α constituents, the rule would incorrectly fail to apply to the words in (76). Sample derivations follow:

(77)

α rules

Affixation	[exclaimatory]$_{m_\alpha}$	[gradual]$_{m_\alpha}$
	[exclaim]$_{p_\alpha}$ atory	[grad]$_{p_\alpha}$ ual
C Invisibility	[exclai]$_{p_\alpha}$ matory	[gra]$_{p_\alpha}$ dual
Trisyllabic Shortening:	—	—
β rules		
MCF	[exclaimatory]$_{m_\beta}$	[gradual]$_{m_\beta}$
	[exclaim]$_{p_\alpha}$ atory	[gra]$_{p_\alpha}$ dual
PCF	[exclaimatory]$_{m_\beta}$	[gradual]$_{m_\beta}$
	[exclaimatory]$_{p_\beta}$	[gradual]$_{p_\beta}$
(other rules)		
output:	*excl[ey]matory	*gr[ey]dual

Since Trisyllabic Shortening does not apply within β domains (e.g. *freedom, slowness, painlessness*), construing *-ual* and *-atory* as completely invisible leaves no way to derive the shortened vowel in *gradual* and *exclamatory*. However, if the first vowel of *-atory* is visible, Trisyllabic Shortening will be able to apply and generate the correct surface form.

6.6. PARTIAL UNDERLYING INVISIBILITY

(78)

    α **rules**

Affixation	[exclaimatory$]_{m_\alpha}$	[gradual $]_{m_\alpha}$
	[exclaima $]_{p_\alpha}$ tory	[gradu $]_{p_\alpha}$ al
C Invisibility	—	—
Trisyllabic Shortening:	[excl[æ]ma $]_{p_\alpha}$ tory	[gr[æ]du $]_{p_\alpha}$ al

To conclude, evidence from Trisyllabic Shortening supports the choice of a partially invisible representation for *-ual* and *-atory*:

(79)

    $[[\ ]_{p_\alpha}$ u $]_{p_\alpha}$ al
    $[[\ ]_{p_\alpha}$ a $]_{p_\alpha}$ tory

-ative, *-ual* and *-atory* combine with entirely visible suffixes like *-ic*, and entirely invisible suffixes like *-al, -ive, -ory*, to fill out the predicted three-way typology of possible suffix invisibility.

(80)

Totally visible:	$[[\ ]_{p_\alpha}$ ic $]_{p_\alpha}$
Partially visible:	$[[\ ]_{p_\alpha}$ a $]_{p_\alpha}$ tory
Totally invisible:	$[[\ ]_{p_\alpha}\ ]_{p_\alpha}$ al

Alternative

An alternative account of the English facts just discussed is to analyze *-u-* in *-ual* and *-at-* in *-atory* as bi-dependent morphemes. Empirically the consequences would be the same: *-u-* and *-at-* would not undergo phonological rules until another suffix was added, at which time the correct stress patterns would be assigned.

(81)

rite	+	$[[\ ]_{m_\alpha}$ u $[\ ]_{m_\alpha}]_{m_\alpha}$	$\longrightarrow$	$[[{\rm rit}]_{m_\alpha}$ u $[\ ]_{m_\alpha}]_{m_\alpha}$
$[[{\rm rit}]_{m_\alpha}$ u $[\ ]_{m_\alpha}]_{m_\alpha}$	+	$[[\ ]_{m_\alpha}$ al $]_{m_\alpha}$	$\longrightarrow$	$[[{\rm rit}]_{m_\alpha}$ $[{\rm u}]_{m_\alpha}$ $[{\rm al}]_{m_\alpha}]_{m_\alpha}$
		$[[\ ]_{p_\alpha}]_{p_\alpha}$ al		$[[{\rm rit}]_{p_\alpha}$ $[{\rm u}]_{p_\alpha}$ $[{\rm al}]_{p_\alpha}]_{p_\alpha}$

At present I cannot think of any way of deciding between these two analyses. Both bidirectional dependence and partial invisibility are needed independently in the theory (the Sekani and Japanese prefixes discussed elsewhere are another example of partial invisibility), so that the decision as to which to use in this case will have to be decided on grounds internal to English.

6.7 Peripherality

Perhaps the most well-known constraint on the powerful device of invisibility is that it must be peripheral. Invisible elements always occupy an edge position in the string.[35]

This constraint is motivated by three observations about the use to which invisibility has been put. Namely, it is implicated in the restricted distribution of underlying invisibility, the fact that rules assigning invisibility always assign it to an edge element, and the fact that the property of invisibility vanishes when an element bearing it ceases, via affixation, to be peripheral.

As we have seen, both rules and underlying representations can provide invisibility. A proper theory of invisibility will need to explain why neither of these invisibility sources are tapped by languages to produce nonperipheral invisibility.

An important step towards explaining the edge condition on invisibility is found in the work of Poser 1986b. Poser demonstrates that, like all other rules, those invoking invisibility are subject to a strict locality condition on rule environments. We saw above that this constraint, the Focus Determinant Adjacency Condition, predicts that only single constituents can be made invisible. Poser appeals again to the FDAC to derive an additional constraint on those rules which refer to the edge of

---

[35] One may wonder how medial invisibility would be detected in the first place. One manifestation, not attested, would be the random occurrence of ternary feet. Such feet are generally analyzed as the adjunction of a formerly extrametrical element to a binary foot, and thus would not be expected to occur medially in a monomorphemic form. Another hypothetical, unattested example of medial invisibility would be the random distribution of superheavy syllables. In many languages, e.g. Cairene Arabic, superheavy syllables (CVCC) are permitted only word finally (see e.g. McCarthy 1979:11, 53). McCarthy observes that this distribution can be explained by positing a syllable template which disallows superheavy syllables, and by rendering extrametrical the final consonants of superheavy syllables (p. 11). By virtue of extrametricality, word-final consonants escape both syllabification and stray element erasure (Itô 1986). At some later stage in the derivation, after syllabification constraints are relaxed, these consonants become visible and can be syllabified.

If consonant extrametricality were permitted word-medially, we would expect random superheavy syllables to punctuate the vocabulary of languages like Arabic. A word like *kitarkpu*, with invisible medial *rk*, would be left undisturbed by syllabification rules, and licensed. However, this is not the case; superheavy syllables occur only word-finally.

a rule domain. Since that domain edge must be present in the rule environment, and since each element in the rule environment must be adjacent to the undergoer (the element to be made invisible), it therefore follows that rules of this type can impose invisibility only on edge constituents (Poser 1985b).

(82) Domain-limit rules which invoke invisibility must invoke it on a peripheral element

This elegant result is diminished by the lack of an explanation for why only domain-end rules can assign invisibility. Poser has no (nonstipulative) means of prohibiting rules of the type Selkirk calls "domain span rules" (Selkirk 1980:111) from assigning invisibility.

(83) Rule types (Selkirk 1980)

a. Domain-limit and domain-juncture rules (refer to an edge of the rule domain)
b. Domain-span rules (do not refer to a domain edge)

A domain-span rule might, for instance, treat as invisible every light syllable, or every mora dominating a voiced obstruent, regardless of their position in the rule domain. This possibility opens a Pandora's box of peripherality violations.[36]

In the morpheme-based theory I am assuming, Poser's result also does not extend to the distribution of lexicalized invisibility, the second potential source of nonperipheral invisibility.[37][FIGURE THIS OUT] The potential for locating an inherently invisible suffix word-internally opens the door for the possibility of nonperipheral invisibility. Yet this never occurs. On the contrary, the constraint against medial invisibility appears to be an active one, as shown by the fact that invisibility, both lexical and rule-governed, systematically disappears as soon as the element bearing

---

[36]Domain-span rules have in fact been suggested in the literature as sources of invisibility. Franks 1985 (see also Halle and Vergnaud 1987, and Alsina 1988 for a similar analysis of Catalan), proposes that the assignment of invisibility to a syllable in Polish is triggered by the presence of an abstract feature +F on the preceding morpheme. In Polish, +F is found underlyingly on particular suffixes. Neither it nor the extrametrical syllable necessarily appears adjacent to the edge.

I will actually offer a reanalysis of the Polish data later on in this chapter, arguing that this method of extrametricality assignment is overly powerful and not needed for Polish. However, credit is due to Franks for pointing out that in its current unconstrained state the diacritic theory is capable of generating nonperipheral invisibility diacritics.

[37]Poser treats affixes as rules, which permits him to associate them with the invisibility parameter.

it becomes nonperipheral. In particular, elements which are invisible on one cycle systematically lose their invisiblity when affixation causes them to be nonperipheral on the next. This phenomenon has been discussed in detail by a number of authors (see e.g. Hayes 1981, Harris 1983, Pulleyblank 1983/1986, Archangeli 1984, and many others.) I will present one example here for the sake of illustration.

Consider the word *generosity*. On the *-ous* cycle, the entire final syllable is invisible, due to the lexical properties of the suffix:

(84) géne(rous)

However, that invisible syllable regains its visibility when the suffix *-ity* is attached. Evidence for this is its acquisition of stress on that cycle. (The final syllable of the suffixed form is made invisible by Noun Invisibility.)

(85) géne(rous)ity ⟶ generósi(ty)

Were *-ous* allowed to remain invisible upon the suffixation of *-ity*, we would generate the incorrect stress pattern in (86):

(86) *géne(rous)í(ty)

A similar effect emerges in constructions where an invisible suffix is added to a base which itself already ends in another invisible suffix:

(87)

	curs(ory)(ous)	⟶	*cúrsorious (cf. cursórious)
	perfunct(ory)(ous)	⟶	*perfúnctorious (cf. perfunctórious)
	pisc(atory)(ous)	⟶	*píscatorious (cf. piscatórious)
	salt(atory)(ous)	⟶	*sáltatorious (cf. saltatórious)
	accus(atory)(al)	⟶	*accúsatorial (cf. accusatórial)
	combin(atory)(al)	⟶	*cómbinatorial (cf. combinatórial)
	fund(atory)(al)	⟶	*fúndatorial (cf. fundatórial)
	observ(atory)(al)	⟶	*obsérvatorial (cf. observatórial)

If both of the two adjacent invisible suffixes remained invisible to α rules, we would expect both to be stray adjoined to the left by the same β rules which stray

6.7. PERIPHERALITY

adjoin β suffixes. (There is no evidence that any stressing rules other than Stray Syllable Adjunction and the Compound Stress Rule apply to β forms.)

(88) pérfúnct(ory)(ous) ⟶ pérfúnctorious ⟶ *pèrfùnctòrioùs

Yet, as (87) indicates, this does not happen. Stray adjunction does not incorporate both suffixes into the preceding foot; only the last suffix is stray adjoined. The first suffix surfaces with stress. Since only α rules will stress suffixes, we know that the first of the two invisible suffixes must be visible to α rules.[38]

(89) pérfúnct(ory) + (ous) ⟶ pérfúnctòry(ous)

As Poser 1986b has shown, locality constraints on the environment of rules make important inroads into explaining the peripherality constraint.[39] However, they are not sufficient. In what follows I will discuss two proposals which supplement Poser's constraints. These seek to transfer some of the burden of constraining the distribution of invisibility to the representation of invisibility itself. The first is the diacritic approach, and the second is the domains theory.

6.7.1 The Diacritic Feature Approach

From the treatment of extrametricality as a diacritic feature ([+ex]), it does not automatically follow that [+ex] can survive only on edges. To the extent that they are motivated at all, other diacritic features (e.g. accent) which have been posited in phonological theory are capable of lodging on nonperipheral material. And nondiacritic features can certainly occur in all positions in the string.

Thus, the diacritic approach to invisibility has had to incorporate a stipulative constraint: the feature [+ex] is permitted only at domain edges. The particular

---

[38]In the case of *perfunctorious*, the partial derivation in (89) feeds the Rhythm Rule and Stray Syllable Adjunction, resulting in the correct surface form *pèrfùnctórious*.

[39]Others have also suggested that the edge condition is derivable solely from properties of phonological rules; see, for example, Archangeli 1984 and Franks 1985. Both propose that the extrametricality feature can in fact exist in nonperipheral locations, but that it is simply uninterpretable by rules unless it is at the edge. However, they do not offer reasons for why this should be so. Thus this proposal simply shifts the problem from representations to rules, with no contribution toward explanation.

Peripherality Constraint proposed by Harris 1983 and adopted by Hayes 1981, Pulleyblank 1983 and others is formulated as a deletion rule. It removes [+ex] from nonperipheral locations. The following statement is taken from Pulleyblank 1986 (p. 208):[40]

(90) Peripherality Condition

$$\begin{array}{c} X \longrightarrow \\ | \\ [+\text{ex}] \quad [-\text{ex}] \end{array} \quad / \quad [\, Z \underline{} Y \,]_D$$

where $Y \neq \emptyset$ and $Z \neq \emptyset$, and D is the domain of the stress/tone rules.

This condition constrains where rules can assign the [+ex] diacritic. It has the desired effect in the analyses presented above, where invisible elements cease to be peripheral upon the addition of another affix:[41]

(92)

```
fatalist + ic  ⟶  fatalistic     ⟶  fatálistic
     |                 |
   [+ex]             [+ex]

cursory + ous  ⟶  cursoryous      ⟶  cursorious
  |      |          |     |                |
[+ex]  [+ex]      [+ex] [+ex]            [+ex]
```

---

[40]The restriction of D to stress and tone rules should not be interpreted as an inherent part of the edge constraint; I assume it merely reflects the fact that all analyses of invisibility had, at the time Pulleyblank formulated this condition, involved only stress and tone.

[41]This type of condition will also correctly eliminate from view [+ex] diacritics of the type Franks 1985 assigns to nonperipheral elements.

(91) universytet + u ⟶ universytetu ⟶ universytetu
         | | ⋮ | ≠
         F   F+ex   F+ex

Though descriptively adequate,[42] the universal Peripherality Condition lacks independent motivation in the theory, and follows from no known theoretical principles. (90) yields no insight into why edge conditions do not obtain on other features as well; thus the special status of invisibilty is merely stated, but not explained. Finally, if the Peripherality Condition is in fact a deletion rule, we have the answer to the question posed earlier as to whether or not [+ex] is to be interpreted broadly. [+ex] cannot produce across-the-board invisibility, since it and the element to which it is linked must be visible to at least one rule: that in (90).

6.7.2 The Domains Approach

We have seen that the attempt to capture the distribution of invisibility by constraining the phonological representation is handled by stipulation in the diacritic feature approach, thus not achieving the status of explanation.

In this section I will argue in support of the domain approach by showing that it is able to derive, without further stipulation, the edge condition on invisibility. That invisibility cannot be medial follows directly from the representation of invisibility itself, assuming in addition the very general, independently motivated Focus Determinant Adjacent Condition. The argument builds on that of Poser 1986b, but has as an additional crucial weapon a representation for invisibility: mismatched domain edges.

This representation is solely responsible for the disappearance of nonperipheral invisibility upon further affixation. Recall that invisibility is a property of the location of any given element with respect to the edge of the current prosodic domain. When further affixation causes, as it must, the incorporation of a string into a new prosodic domain, that new domain supplants the previous one. Bracket erasure eliminates any information that some internal element used to be outside of an embedded prosodic constituent.

This result is demonstrated below with respect to the word *generosity*. On the *-ous* cycle, the final syllable is invisible. It gets bracketed outside of the prosodic constituent containing the rest of the word:

(93) [gene]$_{p_\alpha}$ rous

---

[42]See, however, the next section, in which it is shown that the Peripherality Condition is too strong.

When -*ity* is added on the next cycle, the outermost prosodic domain of the suffix creates a new prosodic constituent around the entire form. Due to bracket erasure, the fact that -*rous* used to be outside its prosodic constituent is lost to history.[43]

(94) [gene]$_{p_\alpha}$ rous + [[ ]$_{p_\alpha}$ ity]$_{p_\alpha}$ $\longrightarrow$ [generosity]$_{p_\alpha}$

The same effect obtains, of course, in the case that two lexically invisible suffixes co-occur. That only the outermost of these will be invisible to rules applying on its affixation cycle again follows directly from the nature of prosodic subcategorization frames. Bracket erasure obliterates the information that the internal affix used to be invisible:

(95) [[perfunct]$_{p_\alpha}$]$_{p_\alpha}$ ory + [[ ]$_{p_\alpha}$]$_{p_\alpha}$ ous $\longrightarrow$ [perfunctory]$_{p_\alpha}$ ous

The predictive power of the domains approach extends also to rule-governed invisibility. Here, the representation of invisibility is not sufficient to account for its restricted distribution: we must also make appeal to Poser's universal Focus Determinant Adjacency Condition, repeated below.

(96) FDAC: Every focus must be adjacent on the projection to every determinant

To see how this principle contributes to the derivation of the edge condition, recall that on the domains theory, the invisibility of an element depends on its location with respect to the edge of a prosodic constituent. Thus in order to make some element x invisible, a rule must crucially refer to an edge (E) of the prosodic domain. As we have already seen, the FDAC requires first of all that the target x must be a single constituent. But the FDAC says one thing more: namely, that that x be adjacent to the determinant, E. This turns out to be all that is needed to predict that rules assigning invisibility can pick out only a single, peripheral element.

By forcing all rules assigning invisibility to be domain end rules, the domains representation for invisibility supplies the necessary missing link in Poser's attempt to derive the peripherality condition from the FDAC.

---

[43]Kanerva 1986 offers an explanation along the same lines for the loss of nonperipheral invisibility due to certain kinds of multiple prefixation or multiple suffixation; he shows that attaching an affix outside and adjacent to an invisible affix causes the invisibility of the inner affix to disappear. His account of the edge condition does not extend to cases where the inner invisible affix is not adjacent to the outer affix, nor to rule-governed or underlying invisibility.

6.7. PERIPHERALITY

To sum up, we have derived from the representation of invisibility the important result that no source, phonological or morphological, can produce a configuration in which an invisible element is medial in the string. This results in a further prediction: that no prosodic constituents will be discontinuous. Discontinuous constituency and medial invisibility obtain exactly the same representation in the prosodic domains theory.

(97) $x(y)z = ?[\underset{\cdot\cdot}{x}\overset{\frown}{\cdot}\underset{\cdot}{y}\overset{\cdot}{\cdot}\underset{\cdot}{z}]_p$

This result is significant for two reasons. First, it permits a simpler statement of Prosodic Licensing (Itô 1986). According to Itô, all melodic elements must be prosodically licensed either (a) by being incorporated into higher metrical structure or (b) by being extrametrical. Now that we have derived the condition that all phonological material is either contained within a prosodic constituent, or linearly ordered before or after that constituent, we can eliminate disjunct (b) from the definition of prosodic licensing.[44]

(98) Prosodic Licensing (revised): All material within the rule domain must be incorporated into higher metrical structure.

Second, as P. Kiparsky has pointed out, prohibiting discontinuous constituents correctly predicts that, for example, phonological phrases will not be able to contain interjections and parenthetical expressions. Rather, whenever such a disruptive expression occurs, it should split the string surrounding it into two separate phrases. In this respect phonological phrases differ from the domains of intonational melodies, which demonstrably persist across interruptions by parenthetical expressions. A plausible explanation for this difference is to assume that intonation 'phrases' are not part of the prosodic hierarchy, but rather units in metrical representation.

The predicted integrity of phonological phrases is borne out in English, where expressions such as *y'know* are obligatorily surrounded by phrase breaks. Evidence for this is that finite auxiliary clitics, and reduced auxiliaries, which are prohibited

---

[44]In the last chapter I will argue that from Prosodic Licensing we can derive Selkirk's Exhaustive Parsing condition as well as the Strict Layer Hypothesis. With the need for the extrametricality disjunction eliminated, we can state all three principles as a single constraint on those rules parsing strings into higher level constituents: each parse must be exhaustive.

in phrase-final position (Zec and Inkelas 1987), also cannot occur immediately before *y'know*, as shown in (99)a, b.[45]

(99)
    a. *Helen's, you know, afraid of snakes.

    b. *Helen is, you know, afraid of snakes.

    c. Helen is, you know, afraid of snakes.

To conclude, not only is the edge condition on invisibility easy to state in the domains approach; in fact, it follows directly from the architecture of prosodic and morphological structure that invisibility can be distributed in no other way. In order for the less constrained diacritic approach to enforce the same conditions, a number of otherwise unmotivated stipulations must be introduced into the theory.

6.8 Multi-source Invisibility

In this section we will examine a set of invisibility data that only the domains approach can accommodate, thus demonstrating that the domains approach is superior in descriptive as well as in explanatory power to the diacritic feature model. The data we will consider all involve cases where two different sources for invisibility are both tapped on the same cycle.

Because invisible material is not seen by any rules on the domains approach, no rule will be able to know whether any material has previously been made invisible on the cycle. It follows from this that more than one source should be able to supply invisibility to the same lexical form. As a result we expect to find cases where, on the cycle on which an invisible affix has been attached, a phonological rule applies to make an edge constituent of the stem invisible as well.

This prediction of the domains approach is supported by evidence from English. I will present two cases here.

---

[45]I am factoring out here cases where *y'know* is inserted as a hesitation, as in cases where the speaker is changing his/her mind about the utterance. This kind of hesitation can occur even morpheme internally (e.g. *Ta — y'know, Tatamagouchi*) and does not help to diagnose constituency as far as I can tell.

6.8. MULTI-SOURCE INVISIBILITY

Case 1: VC before invisible affix

The first case involves the attachment of invisible affixes to bases ending in a short vowel and single consonant, e.g. *corpor + al, mountain + ous, marvel + ous, conifer + ous*. From the representation of invisible suffixes, it follows that the prosodic domain produced by affixation will end in the final consonant of the base:

(100)

corpor	$+ [[\ ]_{p_\alpha}]_{p_\alpha}$ al	$\longrightarrow$	$[$ corpor $]_{p_\alpha}$ al
mountain	$+ [[\ ]_{p_\alpha}]_{p_\alpha}$ ous	$\longrightarrow$	$[$ mountain $]_{p_\alpha}$ ous
.narvel	$+ [[\ ]_{p_\alpha}]_{p_\alpha}$ ous	$\longrightarrow$	$[$ marvel $]_{p_\alpha}$ ous
conifer	$+ [[\ ]_{p_\alpha}]_{p_\alpha}$ ous	$\longrightarrow$	$[$ conifer $]_{p_\alpha}$ ous

In the course of the subsequent application of α rules, C invisibility will cause the final consonant in these stems to join the suffix in exile to the right of the prosodic constituent.

(101)

UR	marvel, $[[\ ]_{p_\alpha}]_{p_\alpha}$ ous
Affixation:	$[$ marvel $]_{p_\alpha}$ ous
C invisibility:	$[$ marve $]_{p_\alpha}$ lous

The resulting vowel-final prosodic constituent is the domain for the subsequent English Stress Rule, which constructs a left-headed foot over the last two syllables and correctly produces initial stress in the words in (100). Stray adjunction, applying on a later cycle, incoporates the invisible material into the preceding foot:

(102)

α rules

Affixation:	$[$ marvelous $]_{m_\alpha}$
	$[$ marvel $]_{p_\alpha}$ ous
C invisibility:	$[$ marve $]_{p_\alpha}$ lous
Stress Assignment:	$[$ márvĕ $]_{p_\alpha}$ lous

β rules

MCF: [márvelous]$_{m_\beta}$
             [márve]$_{p_\alpha}$ lous

PCF: [márvelous]$_{m_\beta}$
             [márvelous]$_{p_\beta}$

Stray Adjunction: [márvelous]$_{p_\beta}$

Thus, the cumulative effect of affix invisibility and rule-governed invisibility produces the desired output in these cases. By contrast, consider what would happen if C invisibility were not allowed to apply to a form which already had an invisible affix. Words like *marvelous* would present the stem *marvel* to the English Stress Rule; the final syllable, being closed, would receive a foot, and the word would incorrectly obtain medial stress.[46]

(103)
UR   marvel, [[ ]$_{p_\alpha}$]$_{p_\alpha}$ ous
-cycle 1-
Affixation: [marvel]$_{p_\alpha}$ ous
C invisibility: —

English Stress Rule: *[marvel]$_{p_\alpha}$ ous

Therefore, we must assume that both sources of invisibility (lexical and rule-governed) may contribute invisibility to the same representation.

Case 2: ...VCC + invisible affix

A second, similar case involves the attachment of invisible affixes to words ending

---

[46]One might suppose that medial stress assigned to *marvelous* would be deleted by Post-Stress Destressing Rule (Hayes 1981), whose environment would be met after Stray Adjunction incorporated the suffix into the foot dominating *vel*. (PSD deletes a binary sw foot whose first syllable is open and which is preceded by a unary foot.) However, as shown by analogous words with heavy medial syllables, such as *parental, incentive, magenta*, if there was a foot dominating *vel* it would be assigned prominence in the word tree. As a consequence, no destressing rule, including PSD, would be able to apply to it.

6.8. MULTI-SOURCE INVISIBILITY

in consonant clusters. For example, take the word *malignant*. Final C invisibility will prevent g deletion from applying on that first cycle:[47]

(104)
    cycle 1   [malign]$_{p_\alpha}$

    C Invisibility: [malig]$_{p_\alpha}$ n
    g deletion: —

    Stress Assignment: [malíg]$_{p_\alpha}$ n

When the invisible *-ant* is attached, its prosodic subcategorization frame provides that *malign* again forms the domain for rules.

(105)   [malig]$_{p_\alpha}$ n + [[ ]$_{p_\alpha}$]$_{p_\alpha}$ ant $\longrightarrow$ [malign]$_{p_\alpha}$ ant

Subsequent application of the cyclic rules of C Invisibility and g deletion produces exactly the right result: the g of *malignant* fails to delete.

(106)
    cycle 2   [malígn]$_{p_\alpha}$ ant

    C Invisibility: [malíg]$_{p_\alpha}$ nant

    g deletion: —

If, however, C Invisibility were blocked from applying to *malign* on the *ant* cycle, the environment for g deletion would be satisifed. A g-less **malinant* would be the unfortunate result.

Similar effects obtain with n deletion; even though the final mn sequence of *hymn* is domain-final when the invisible suffix *al* is attached, n is not deleted. Instead, it is made invisible by the cyclic rule of C invisibility, and resyllabified as an onset with *al* when that suffix becomes visible on the next cycle.

---

[47] If no α affixes are attached to *malign*, it will undergo β rules and the n will surface there, triggering g deletion and producing the correct output.

(107)
$$\begin{array}{ll} \text{C Invisibility:} & [\text{ hymn }]_{p_\alpha}\text{ al} \\ & [\text{ hym }]_{p_\alpha}\text{ nal} \\ n \text{ deletion:} & \text{—} \end{array}$$

These data show that the contributions of two independent sources of invisibility may be cumulative. Because it places no restrictions on the invisible string, constraining only the individual processes which independently contribute invisibility, the prosodic domains account extends naturally to cover multi-source, additive invisibility.[48]

6.8.1 The Diacritic Feature Approach

All cases of additive invisibility are impossible for the diacritic theory to deal with — as they are expressly prohibited by the Peripherality Condition. Consider, as an illustration, the diacritic representation of *malignant* immediately upon affixation.

(108) malign + -ant ⟶ malignant
      | ⊤   ⟋⟍
    [+ex] [+ex]   [+ex] [+ex]

The Peripherality Condition, seeing two [+ex]'s in the representation, will apply to remove the nonperipheral one:

(109) malignant ⟶ malignant (by the Peripherality Condition)
      ⟋⊤   ⊤
    [+ex] [+ex]   [+ex]

At this point, cyclic α rules start applying. Depending on the interpretation of [+ex], the first relevant rule, final C invisibility, will either assign invisibility to the stem-final *n* or it will vacuously assign it to the final consonant in the invisible suffix. Since

---

[48]The cases we have seen involve the accumulation of lexical and rule-governed invisibility; we also predict the existence of cases where two different rules can both assign invisibility to the same form. I have not found any such cases so far.

6.8. MULTI-SOURCE INVISIBILITY

the latter option obviously will not have the desired result of making the n in *malign* invisible, let us assume the former option is taken.

(110) malignant ⟶ malignant (by final C invisibility)
          T   T
       [+ex]   [+ex] [+ex]

But this puts us back exactly where we started (see (108))! The Peripherality Condition, a well-formedness condition on representations, will immediately erase the first of the two [+ex]'s. The stem-final n will be visible to g deletion, resulting in the incorrect surface form *malinant*.

(111)

                                   ma lign + ant
                                   /   T
                                [+ex] [+ex]

Peripherality Condition: malig nant
                                      ✗ T
                                  [+ex][+ex]

C Invisibility: malig nant
                                     / T
                                  [+ex][+ex]

Peripherality Condition: malig nant
                                      ✗ T
                                  [+ex][+ex]

This problem is acknowledged implicitly in Myers 1987. Recognizing the need for the onset of the syllable containing extrametrical adjective suffixes to be extrametrical as well, Myers proposes that adjective extrametricality is actually accomplished by a rule making the entire final syllable of adjectives extrametrical.[49]

(112) $\sigma \longrightarrow$ em. / ___]$_{Adj}$

Of course, (112) applies only to those adjectives ending in a subset of suffixes; this solution thus requires phonological rules to see internal morphological structure, and to know the identity of individual morphemes. Worse, it fails to accommodate invisible *disyllabic* adjective suffixes such as *-ary* and *-ory* (section 5.4) and the partially invisible *-atory* (section 5.5). I therefore assume that the invisibility of potential onset consonants which immediately precede invisible adjective suffixes is logically separate from the invisibility of the suffixes themselves.

To sum up, the Peripherality Condition, which is crucially needed elsewhere in the diacritic theory to clean up the result of overgeneration of invisibility, results in failure in cases where a vowel-initial invisible suffix attaches to a base ending in a single consonant. The Peripherality Condition fails because it cannot distinguish between those strings of invisible elements which have their source on different cycles (which we do not find), and those made invisible by different processes operating on the same cycle. The latter are attested in English. They support the domains approach, the only theory to actually predict their existence.

6.9 Bracket Erasure: Cyclic Loss of Invisibility

We have seen that both the domains approach, as well as the diacritic approach with its crucial Peripherality Condition, require that an invisible element lose its invibility when an affix is attached outside of it. On the diacritic account, this follows from loss of peripherality of the invisible element. But on the domains account it follows simply from the creation of a new prosodic domain on the new cycle.

The domains account thus makes a prediction that the diacritic account does not: namely, that *all* invisibility will disappear on the next cycle, not just in cases when the formerly invisible element ceases to be peripheral.

(113) Cyclic Erasure: invisible elements will regain visibility on each new cycle of phonological rules

---

[49]In this Myers departs from Hayes 1981, who formulates a rule making only the suffix itself extrametrical.

6.9. BRACKET ERASURE: CYCLIC LOSS OF INVISIBILITY

One example of cyclic invisibility erasure is argued for in detail in chapter 5, and the reader is referred there. Here, I will present a simpler case from English, in which α-final invisible syllables regain their visibility immediately upon construction of a β constituent.

The arguments for syllable invisibility at the right edge of nouns has already been discussed in detail; I will assume it here. What I wish to show is that these same syllables must be visible to the first cycle of β rules.

Consider the forms in (114). All are nouns; all undergo α Noun Invisibility:

(114) ci(ty), la(dy), pi(ty), etc.

As is well known, in certain dialects final i undergoes a β rule of tensing/lengthening which must crucially apply before β suffixation.

(115) cit[ii]hood, lad[ii]ship, pit[ii]less, etc.

In order to undergo lengthening on the first β cycle, final i (more specifically, the syllable containing it) must be visible on that cycle. Yet it remains peripheral in the stem. On the diacritic approach, the [+ex] diacritic is predicted to remain in place upon application of β rules. This is shown below:[50]

(116)
α PCF: [city]$_\alpha$

Noun extrametricality: [city]$_\alpha$
                            |
                           +ex

β PCF: [city]$_\beta$
                  |
                 +ex

---

[50] I am formulating the derivation within the domains model, but using the extrametricality diacritic, in order to make it more easily comparable to the following derivation. Formulating the derivation in nonprosodic terms would make no difference at all. Furthermore, I am assuming an across-the-board interpretation of [+ex]. If we do not assume this then the argument disappears.

y Lengthening: —

output: *cit[i]

On the domains approach, by contrast, a syllable which is excluded from an α constituent will be included by the Prosodic Constituent Formation algorithm into a β constituent. The relevant derivation is given below:

(117)

α PCF: [city]$_\alpha$

Noun Invisibility: [ci]$_\alpha$ ty

β PCF: [city]$_\beta$

y Lengthening: [city[ii]]$_\beta$

output: cit[ii]

No suffixation is necessary in order to reinstate these consonants into the purview of rules. Rather, building a new prosodic domain is sufficient to do the trick.

A number of apparent counterexamples to the prediction in (113) exist in the literature. These are all cases in which invisibility is argued to persist, even when nonperipheral, into a future cycle of rules. In the next three sections I will present three of the most convincing cases against cyclic erasure. For each I will argue that an alternative analysis, which maintains the edge condition, is available.

6.9.1 Persistent Invisibility I: Turkish

Poser 1984 describes a phenomenon in Turkish wherein invisibility appears to have to persist across more than one cycle of suffixation, in conflict with the Peripherality Condition and with the prediction of cyclic invisibility loss.

As Poser notes, citing Underhill 1976, the regular, final stress pattern of Turkish is perturbed by a set of invisible ('unaccented') suffixes, which induce stress on the immediately preceding syllable.

6.9. BRACKET ERASURE: CYCLIC LOSS OF INVISIBILITY

(118)
> No suffix: adám 'man'
> Visible suffix: adam-ím 'my man'
> Invisible suffix: adám-im 'I am a man'

If stress were assigned postcyclically in Turkish, we would expect the differences between visible and invisible suffixes to disappear in nonfinal position. But this does not happen. Instead, as shown in (119), stress shows up on the final syllable only if there is no invisible suffix anywhere in the word. Otherwise, stress will appear on the syllable immediately preceding the leftmost invisible suffix.

(119)
> Innermost suffix visible: adam-lar-á 'to the men'
> Innermost suffix invisible: yorgún-dur-lar 'they are tired'

Poser interprets these facts in light of a principle which extends the invisibility of a nonperipheral suffix outward to all adjacent affixes. Accordingly, the inherently invisible suffix *-dur* causes rules to treat the following, ordinarily visible suffix *-lar* as invisible as well. This is shown in the second example in (119).

However, the mechanism for propagating invisibility rightward is somewhat problematic. If, as Poser proposes, invisibility is a property of rules, then Turkish would seem to require phonological rules to be able to look down into an in principle unbounded number of morphological embeddings in order to identify the leftmost invisible suffix.

From the viewpoint of a diacritic approach, one could imagine that the requisite propagation mechanism is some sort of spreading of the invisibility feature. As far as I know, spreading has not previously been proposed as a possible operation on [+ex], but in fact such a rule would nicely account for the retention of internal invisibility upon suffixation of a visible suffix in Turkish. Suppose that on each cycle of suffixation, a rule spreads [+ex] rightwards.

(120) yorg-un + dur + lar ⟶ yorg-undurlar
```
       |                        |⋰⋯
      +ex                      +ex
```

Because spreading results in a single, multiply linked feature, the environment for the Peripherality Condition is arguably not met in (120), and the invisibility is retained.

Thus, assuming we want to endow diacritic features with the ability to spread, and give up the single-constituent constraint on rule-governed invisibility, the Turkish facts could be analyzed in a way which is compatible with the Peripherality Condition proposed in the diacritic theory.

However, they still pose a problem for the domains approach, which cannot impose the invisibility of an inner suffix onto an outer one. The very nature of the representation of such a form prevents rules from seeing that the inner suffix used to be invisible, and hence makes impossible the statement of any sort of invisibility propagation rule.

Therefore, I will propose for these Turkish facts yet another alternative analysis, this time within the domains approach. This analysis will neither violate the edge constraint nor require invisibility to persist across more than one cycle. It involves the cyclic assignment of a final, unary stress foot, along with the two destressing rules shown in (121):[51]

(121)

    a. Rightmost Wins: F F
                                        $\not=$ |
                                        σ σ

    b. Leftmost Wins: F ... F
                                         | $\not=$
                                        σ σ

As a result of the cyclic application of the Final Stress rule, a string of visible suffixes will induce cyclic creation of the environment for Rightmost Wins. Stress will thus be incrementally bumped rightward until it reaches the final syllable of the word.

(122)   adam lar a ⟶ [adamlar] a ⟶ [adamlara]
                                 | $\not=$ |
                                   F   F F

---

[51]See Barker 1989 for an independently developed argument that stress in Turkish is assigned cyclically.

6.9. BRACKET ERASURE: CYCLIC LOSS OF INVISIBILITY

By contrast, if a string of visible suffixes is preceded by an invisible suffix, a one-syllable gap will be created between the foot of the stem and the foot assigned to the first visible suffix. The foot assigned by the Final Stress Rule to the suffix is thus immediately deleted by Leftmost Wins.

(123) yorgun (dur) lar ⟶ [yorgun(dur)] lar ⟶ [yorgundurlar]
           | | ǂ
           F   F   F

A benefit of this analysis is that it extends naturally to cover polysyllabic stems with idiosyncratic initial stress. These retain their stress even when visible suffixes are added. As (124) shows, this phenomenon is exactly what the rules in (121) predict:

(124)

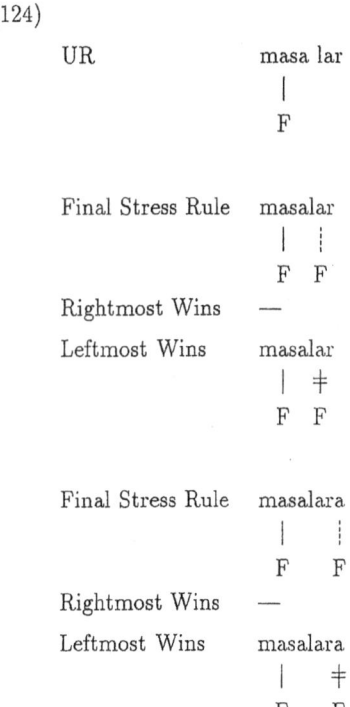

6.9.2 Persistent Invisibility II: Japanese

A second compelling case for persistent invisibility is described by Poser 1984 for Japanese. Poser discusses two 'post-accenting' prefixes, both of which normally place High tone on the following syllable. This is accomplished, on Poser's account, by making the prefix invisible, and associating its attachment with two rules. The first inserts High tone into the representation. The second links that High tone to the leftmost sonorant mora.

(125)

    ma + kura $\longrightarrow$ makkura   'total darkness'
                                    ⋮
                                    H

    o + kimono $\longrightarrow$ okimono   'clothing'
                                    ⋮
                                    H

When a postaccenting prefix attaches to a noun which already contains a High tone on a noninitial mora, that High tone is deleted by a rule removing all but the leftmost High tone in a word (p. 47).

(126) ma + shikaku $\longrightarrow$ mashikaku $\longrightarrow$ mashikaku 'perfect square'
       | ⋮ | |
       H   H H   H

The problem arises when the two postaccenting prefixes co-occur. In this case the outermost (o-) fails to exhibit postaccenting behavior. Instead, as shown below, the High tone assigned by the inner prefix (ma-) is retained.

(127) o + ma + kura $\longrightarrow$ omakura (*omakura)
                           | |
                           H   H

6.9. BRACKET ERASURE: CYCLIC LOSS OF INVISIBILITY

As Poser observes (p. 87), this fact could be explained if we assume that *ma*- remains invisible when *o*- is attached. Both prefixes will thus be skipped over by the rule(s) assigning High tone to the rightmost mora.

This example differs from Turkish in that the propagation of invisibility is lexically conditioned. Even if we were to adapt Poser's insight to the diacritic model and employ a spreading rule to get [+ex] from one prefix to another, the rule would still need to have access to morpheme identity, and is thus problematic. The Japanese example resembles Turkish in that in both cases the propagation of invisibility suggested by Poser is impossible to capture in the domains approach. Thus, to maintain the domains account of invisibility, a new analysis of these Japanese prefixes is needed.

A clue toward a possible reanalysis is Poser's observation that *o*- is not as clearly a postaccenting prefix as *ma*- is. In fact, of the forms he cites, in only one case does *o*- attach to a stem with noninitial High tone — and in that one case, the High is retained.[52]

(128)

ha'si	oha'si
hagaki	oha'gaki
ka'me	ok'ame
kimono	oki'mono
kutu'	okutu'
noroke	ono̞'roke
ta'bi	ota̞'bi
tabako	ota'bako
yasai	oya'sai

Although more data is clearly needed to resolve this problem, a plausible solution is to assume that *o*- differs from *ma*- in that *ma*- contributes a linked High to the representation, while *o*- contributes only a floating High. The active view of subcategorization proposed in chapter 5 makes this difference easy to capture representationally. Instead of assuming that *ma*- triggers a rule linking High to the rightmost mora, we may assume that *ma*- subcategorizes for a base whose initial mora is linked to High:

---

[52]There are actually two allomorphs of *o*-. One, which I am not discussing here, simply causes all tone to be deleted from the stem.

(129)

$$\text{ma } [[\ \mu\ ...\ ]_p]_p$$
$$|$$
$$H$$

$$o\ [\ \ [\ ...\ ]_p]_p$$

$$H$$

On the assumption that floating High deletes in the presence of a linked High, this analysis would explain both the behavior of *o-* before the prefix *ma-* as well as the otherwise exceptional *okųtu'*.

(130)

UR	$o\ [\ H\ [\ ...\ ]_p]_p,$	$\text{ma } [[\ \mu\ ...\ ]_p]_p,$	kura
		$\|$	
		H	

cycle 1

Affixation   ma [kura]$_p$
$|$
H

H Deletion   —

cycle 2

Affixation   o [makura]$_p$
$|$
H H

H Deletion   o [makura]$_p$
$|$
H

output   omaku'ra

6.9.3 Persistent Invisibility III: Yawelmani

Perhaps the most explicit challenge posed in the literature to the cyclic erasure of extrametricality is found in Archangeli 1984. Archangeli argues that extrametricality which is assigned in the lexicon to certain Yawelmani verbs[53] must persist all the way into the postlexical phonology. Her argument, which has to do with stress assignment, is based on the following description by Newman 1964 of phrasal stress in Yokuts:

> "A group of words composing a phrase is pronounced as a stress unit, taking the stress on the penultimate syllable. Nouns and verbs tend to keep their word stress unmodified in phrases, largely acting as the phrase nucleus in drawing to themselves any preceding unaccented words. But pronouns, demonstratives, and particles, especially those of one syllable, vary their stress according to their position in the phrase. However, the grouping of words into phrases is extremely plastic, for a given sentence may shift its words into varying phrase patterns... "(Newman 1964:28)

Newman provides the following examples to illustrate the correlation between location of stress and location of phrase boundaries (p. 29):

(131)

[ʔóhɔm]	[maʔ	ním	hiʔ]	[dab	wíyen]	[mókyi]
[ʔɔhóm	maʔ]	[ním	hiʔ]	[dab	wíyen]	[mókyi]
[ʔɔhóm	maʔ]	[nim	híʔ	dab]	[wíyen]	[mókyi]
[ʔɔhɔm	maʔ	nim	híʔ]	[dab	wíyen]	[mókyi]
not	you	my	will	then	tell-will	wife

'You, then, will not tell my wife'

In Yawelmani, stress always resides on the penultimate syllable — except in the case of durative verbs, which under certain conditions take antepenultimate stress.

---

[53]In particular, it is assigned to verbs taking the durative suffix, -xɔɔ. In the same paper, Archangeli argues for another violation of the peipherality condition, showing that even though the durative suffix is not the outermost morpheme in the word, it can still trigger final extrametricality when it is in the final syllable of the word. Her analysis involves preservation and percolation upwards of the nonperipheral extrametricality feature. Elsewhere (Inkelas 1987b) I have argued that a simpler solution would be to assign, at the word level, final mora extrametricality to words containing the morphological feature [+durative].

Archangeli attributes this property to extrametricality which, because it is triggered by the durative suffix, must be clearly assigned lexically.

Archangeli also reasons that, because the stress of the first four words in (131) depends crucially on the location of phrase boundaries, all stress must be assigned postlexically. And since the extrametricality of durative verbs must be assigned in the lexicon (because it makes reference to morphological features), Archangeli concludes that lexical extrametricality must therefore be allowed to persist into the postlexical rules as long as the extrametrical element remains peripheral.

(132) Archangeli:

> UR: [[[hɔɔyee] xɔɔ] t]
>
> Lexical rules: hɔɔye(xɔt)
> Phrasal rules: hɔ́ɔyḛ(xɔt)
> Output: hɔ́ɔyḛxɔt

However, Archangeli's logic is flawed, because she ignores a crucial distinction between verbs — which, as she shows, have lexical stress effects — and those words in (131) whose stress is conditioned by phonological phrasing. The words in (131) which undergo the stress alternations are all nonlexical (grammatical, function) words. Nonlexical words do not undergo lexical rules (Kiparsky 1982). Thus when they enter the postlexical phonology, they have no stress.

Verbs, nouns, and other content words *do* undergo lexical rules, and it is there that they receive their stress. There is no reason, on the basis of Newman's grammar, to think that the stress of these lexical words is affected by the location of phonological phrase breaks.

In sum, the only phrasal rule needed to account for the known facts is something along the lines of (133), applying in the absence of metrical structure (i.e. to nonlexical words only) to assign stress to the penultimate syllable in the phrase. Since Newman does not provide much phrasal data, I have deliberately left the rule inexplicit:

(133) Stress the penultimate syllable in the phrase

There is no need to wait until the postlexical rules to assign stress to verbs; hence, there is no need to maintain extrametricality into the postlexical rules.

6.9.4 Reappearance of Invisible Elements

The claim that invisibility disappears cyclically may appear at first glance to be contradicted by cases like that of English, where final consonants are invisible on every cycle of α phonology. However, phenomena like this are easily captured by cyclic rules reassigning invisibility to the same spot on each cycle.

The domains approach thus captures the intuition of Kiparsky 1985, Itô 1986, Rice 1990 that invisibility 'turns off' at some point in the lexical rules. Specifically, invisibility turns off precisely upon the entrance into a component within which phonological rules no longer assign invisibility. In Turkish this appears to be the postlexical component (the phonological word) (Rice 1990); in English, it is level 2.

6.10 Morphological Content of Invisibility

Possibly the most surprising prediction of the domains approach to invisibility is that only prosodically bound forms will be able to encode invisibility underlyingly.

(134) Only affixes and clitics may contain underlyingly invisible material.

This prediction follows from the typology proposed in Chapter 5. Because only prosodically bound morphemes contain information about prosodic constituency in their lexical entries, and since invisibility is represented in terms of prosodic constituency, it is a consequence of the domains treatment of invisibility that no stems or roots will contain any underlyingly invisible material.[54]

It is well known that affixes can be lexically invisible. In chapter 8 I argue that clitics, too, can enjoy this status. In this section I will defend the strong claim in (134) against several proposals made in the literature (Harris 1983, Selkirk 1984,

---

[54] As C. Condoravdi points out, prosodic dependence and the underlying representation of prosodic constituency are logically separate. For purposes of parsimony, I have coupled the two in the theory developed here, restricting the underlying mention of prosodic structure to prosodically dependent items. However, Condoravdi 1990 shows that allowing the lexical entries of a small set of (nonclitic) modifiers in Modern Greek to refer to postlexical prosodic structure offers a way around otherwise intractable distributional puzzles. In particular, allomorphy in this small let of lexical items appears to be conditioned by location in postlexical prosodic structure. If other such cases are found, then clearly my theory will have to be revised. However, the evidence at the moment does not yet warrant, in my opinion, abandoning the important predictions made by linking underlying prosodic contstituency to prosodic dependence.

178   *CHAPTER 6. THE REPRESENTATION OF INVISIBILITY*

Franks 1985, others) to the effect that invisibility can be marked in the lexical entries of certain exceptional stems. Although I cannot hope to address each of these cases here, I will offer reanalyses of two, in the hopes that other apparent counterexamples to (134) can be resolved along similar lines.

6.10.1 Spanish

Harris 1983 argues that extrametricality must be marked underlyingly on certain roots in Spanish in order to derive the exceptional stress patterns of words containing these morphemes.[55] The basic stress rule motivated by Harris builds a maximally binary, quantity-sensitive, left-dominant foot at the right edge of the word.[56] It can be stated as follows (Harris 1983:121):

(135) Stress Rule: build a s (w) foot at the right edge, where w cannot branch

Application of the Stress Rule results in the regular, penultimate stress of words like the following:

(136) páp-a   sabán-a   alemán-a

Although these words are morphologically complex, Harris argues that their bases are not cyclic domains for rules. Each word in (136) consists of a base and a 'terminal element':

(137) [[saban] a]

Terminal elements attach to what Harris calls 'derivational stems'; that is, to a root plus any derivational suffixes. According to Harris, neither the derivational stem nor any of its subconstituents form cyclic rule domains. Stress feet are thus built on the forms in (137) only after the inflectional terminal element is attached.

However, there are a number of words with the same morphological structure as those in (137) which differ from them with regard to stress. The forms in (138) all surface with antepenultimate stress, counter to what the stress rule would predict:

---

[55] For a more recent analysis by Harris, see Harris 1987.

[56] I will ignore here secondary stress, which occurs to the left of the primary stress assigned by the rule in (135). See Harris 1983 and Roca 1986 for discussion.

(138) sában-a númer-o héro-e

The difference between the roots in (138) and those in (137) is phonological in nature, and Harris proposes to capture the special status of the forms in (138) by marking the rime of the final syllable of each as extrametrical. Below I will use parentheses to indicate elements which Harris analyzes as extramtetrical.

(139) sab(a)n-a num(e)r-o her(o)-e

The stress rule ignores the extrametrical syllable when it constructs the word-final binary foot, producing the desired antepenultimate stress.

(140) $\overset{s}{\text{sab}}\text{(a)n-}\overset{w}{\text{a}}$

Observe that the extrametrical rime in (140) is allowed to remain even after a suffix — the terminal element'— has been added. This may seem odd in light of the usual assumptions about peripherality. In fact, Harris does impose a Peripherality Condition on the existence of extrametricality, but that condition says only that an extrametricality specification must be peripheral within its *morphological* domain. In (140), taken from Harris 1983 p. 105, the relevant extrametrical rime is morpheme final.

(141)

Peripherality Condition: $$\underset{\substack{| \\ [+\text{ex}]}}{a} \longrightarrow a \;/\; [_m\ X\ __\ Y\ b\ Z\ ]_m$$

where *a* and *b* are both rimes, and where the *m*'s delimit a morphological domain.

Problems

Although the above forms only a subpart of Harris's analysis, it already raises significant problems for my proposals. First, Harris's account relies on the ability to mark extrametricality underlyingly on roots, which I predict never occurs: neither bound roots nor stems possess prosodic subcategorization frames, and neither provides a location for storing information about prosodic domain edges.

Second, extrametricality must persist even when it is not at the edge of the current rule domain. We have seen that this situation is completely untenable in the domains approach.

With these difficulties in mind, I will now present a different account of the above facts which is consistent with the prosodic domain framework. The proposed account captures the elegant generalizations achieved by Harris without suffering from the problems mentioned above. In addition, it uses a simpler set of rules, thus characterizing Spanish stress in a more palatable manner.[57]

Proposed Reanalysis

My proposal treats all terminal elements as extrametrical, and includes a stress rule which stresses the final syllable in the domain.

(142)
    a. Terminal elements are invisible

    b. Final Stress Rule (FSR): Stress final syllable in domain

For regular words ending in vocalic terminal elements, my proposal converges with Harris's to predict penultimate stress:[58]

---

[57] The proposed counteranalysis converges in a number of respects with that of Roca 1988, which recently came to my attention.

[58] Harris argues on the basis of two sets of data that the basic stress pattern is penultimate. One set of data involves prepositions, which uniformly have penultimate stress. However, since prepositions are nonlexical words it would not be too surprising to find that they obey a different stress rule. The other set of data involves hypocoristics, e.g. *árquī* from *arquitécto* (p. 95), which also take penultimate stress. Recent work on such morphological formations (e.g. Poser 1984, 1990, McCarthy and Prince 1986) has posited that a template is involved; in the case of Spanish, the template would be a disyllabic foot. We can easily imagine that its stress pattern could be prespecified.

6.10. MORPHOLOGICAL CONTENT OF INVISIBILITY

(143)

[papa]$_m$ [sabana]$_m$ [alemana]$_m$
[pap]$_p$ a [saban]$_p$ a [aleman]$_p$ a

FSR: [pap]$_p$ a   [saban]$_p$ a   [aleman]$_p$ a
      ⋮   ⋮   ⋮

      pápa   sábana   alemána

However, for a different set of words, the two proposals diverge — and mine makes the correct prediction. Consider the examples in (144):

(144) papá   Perú   Panamá

The words in (144) are all monomorphemic; and, like all the monomorphemic words Harris describes, are predictably assigned final stress. But this pattern is not predicted by Harris's stress rule, and as a result he is forced to propose a separate rule just to handle monomorphemic forms.[59]

By contrast, the Final Stress Rule of my account predicts exactly the attested pattern: because the final vowel of these monomorphemic words is not a suffix, it cannot be underlyingly invisible, and is therefore subject to the Final Stress Rule.

(145) FSR: [papa]$_p$ [Peru]$_p$ [Panama]$_p$
              ⋮   ⋮   ⋮

Thus far, my proposed account has a descriptive advantage over Harris's in that it treats both simple and complex stems in a uniform manner. Instead of requiring two stress rules, one of which refers directly to morpheme boundaries, the proposed analysis requires only one rule — which, furthermore, is entirely impervious to morphological structure.

---

[59]The Strong Foot Rule (p. 118) stresses the last syllable of any word *not* ending in a terminal element, clearly referring crucially to internal morphological structure.

Exceptional stress

To handle roots which trigger exceptional stress patterns, I will rely on two tools: the marking in the lexicon of stress feet on exceptional roots (see e.g. Selkirk 1980, Hayes 1981 for English), and a cyclic, noniterative rule of stray syllable adjunction.

On this account, the roots of words like *sában-a, númer-o* and *héro-e*, which exceptionally take antepenultimate stress, enter the derivation with that stress already in place.

(146) saban   numer   hero
         | | |

When these roots combine with an (invisible) terminal element, they form a prosodic domain within which Stray Syllable Adjunction (147) can apply.

(147) Stray Syllable Adjunction: Adjoin an unstressed syllable to a preceding nonbranching foot

As shown in (148), SSA bleeds the Final Stress Rule to produce the desired antepenultimate stress.[60]

(148)
$$[\text{ sabana }]_m$$
$$|$$

$$[\text{ saban }]_p \; a$$
$$|$$

SSA: $[\text{ saban }]_p \; a$

---

[60]Although not represented here, I assume that a rule of adjunction applies at the word level to incorporate unlicensed final syllables into metrical structure.

6.10. MORPHOLOGICAL CONTENT OF INVISIBILITY

FSR: —

Stray Syllable Adjunction is independently motivated on both my account and Harris's; in both cases it is needed to incorporate formerly extrametrical elements into the representation (Harris, p. 98).

Furthermore, the marking of feet underlyingly seems also to be needed on Harris's account, as no arrangement of extrametricality features can explain the exceptional stress patterns of such monomorphemic words as *ómicron, júnior* (p.135). Rather, Harris proposes that the stress of these forms is most likely lexicalized (p. 133).

My account of roots with irregular stress thus requires a proper subset of the mechanisms needed by Harris, making crucial use of Stray Syllable Adjunction and underlying stress placement. These mechanisms are also required in English (e.g. Hayes 1981) and other languages. In contrast to Harris's account, the analysis proposed here requires neither underlying extrametricality on roots nor reference by phonological rules to morphological structure.

Complex derivational stems

Harris also makes use of underlying invisibility on stems in order to account for excpetional behavior under derivation. As Harris shows, derivational suffixation has different phonological properties from inflectional suffixation. For various reasons specific to his analysis,[61] Harris designates derivational suffixation as noncyclic, but I will not adopt this approach.

Instead, I propose that derivational and inflectional suffixes belong to two different constituent types, α (level 1) and β (level 2). (The same move is made by Alsina 1988 in an analysis of similar phenomena in Catalan.) The set of rules applying within α constituents differs from that of β constituents only in that the former does not contain Stray Syllable Adjunction.[62]

(149)
    α: Derivational affixation
         Final Stress Rule

    β: Inflectional affixation
         Stray Syllable Adjunction

---
[61] These will be discussed later.
[62] This violates the Strong Domain Hypothesis (Kiparsky 1984).

Final Stress Rule

Constituent type is not the only dimension along which Spanish suffixes vary; as Harris shows, α (derivational) suffixes further subdivide into visible and invisible. Some of these suffixes are listed below, along with the uniformly invisible β suffixes.

(150) Affixes:

	α (derivational)	β (inflectional)
Visible	-in, -an, -ism, -os	—
Invisible	-ic, -crat	-a, -o, -e (TE's)

In (151) I illustrate one example of each kind of derivational suffix, paired first with a regular root and then with one bearing underlying stress. Each example also includes a terminal element. In the leftmost column, a root with no derivational suffixes is given for comparison. Parentheses indicate Harris's proposed underlying extrametricality.

(151)

	root-(TE)	root-suff-(TE)	root-(suff)-(TE)
Unstressed root:	sabán-a	Peru-án-o	demó-crat-a
Stressed root:	héro-e	hero-ín-a	heró-ic-a

It can be seen from (152) that when derivational suffixes are attached, any underlying stress differences between roots are neutralized. Stress is predictable from the extrametricality of the rightmost derivational suffix. Harris accounts for this elegantly by enforcing, via the Peripherality Condition, the removal of extrametricality specifications to the right of the final rime in the derivational stem (pp. 104-120).

The account proposed here is equally simple, though it requires no invisibility marking on roots. Because Stray Syllable Adjunction does not apply to α constituents, the Final Stress Rule applies each time a derivational suffix is added. We

6.10. MORPHOLOGICAL CONTENT OF INVISIBILITY

know independently that Spanish has a right-dominant word tree, so that the cyclic rule of Final Stress Assignment captures nicely the generalization that the rightmost derivational suffix appears dominant in determining the stress pattern of the word.

Derivations of all the forms listed in (151) are presented in (152) and (153); the former illustrates a stressless root and the latter a root with underlying stress.

(152)

	saban-a	Peru-an-o	demo-crat-a
α rules:	—	[Peruan]$_\alpha$	[demo]$_\alpha$ crat
FSR:	—	[Peruan]$_\alpha$	[demo]$_\alpha$ crat
β rules:	[saban]$_b$ a	[Peruan]$_b$ a	[democrat]$_b$ a
SSA:	—	—	[democrat]$_b$ a
FSR:	[saban]$_b$ a	—	—
	sabána	Peruána	demócrata

(153)

	hero-e	hero-in-a	hero-ic-a

Level (a):   —   [heroin]ₐ   [hero]ₐ ic
                          | |

FSR: —   [heroín]ₐ   [hero]ₐ ic
                      | ⋮ | ⋮

Level (b): [hero]_b a   [heroín]_b a   [heroic]_b a
              | | | | |

SSA: [hero]_b e   [heroín]_b a   [heroic]_b a
              |⁄ |⁄| | ⋅|⁄
              s⁄   s⁄   s⁄
              v   v   v

FSR: —   —   —
            héroe   heroína   heróica

Although these derivations generate more stress feet than there are surface stresses, we know independently that Spanish has a rule erasing all but the rightmost foot.

(154) F ⟶ ∅ / F

Harris 1983 and Roca 1986 show that secondary stress does not derive from subordinated primary stresses left over from previous cycles; rather, all but the rightmost primary stress is simply deleted. Secondary stress is assigned by a later, word-level rule.

This fact not only tidies up the derivations in (152) and (153), but also plays an important role in constraining the proposed account. A danger in any account proposing underlying stress is that it would predict a number of irregular stress patterns which do not occur. For example, it would allow two stresses to be lexically specified on a word, or secondary stress in a position where rules would not assign it. However, these unwanted possibilities are erased by the rule in (154). Any overpopulation of stress feet in underlying representation will quickly be taken care of by Foot Erasure.

6.10. MORPHOLOGICAL CONTENT OF INVISIBILITY

Implications of the analysis

In what precedes we saw that positing underlying stress yields a description which is at least as good as, and possibly better than, one which relies on marking underlying extrametricality on roots. I will conclude with one additional argument in favor of the proposed account over Harris's.

Harris cites as an advantage of his account the prediction that no Spanish word can possibly surface with preantepenultimate stress. However, as also pointed out in Roca 1988, because Harris allows both the final vowel of roots and vowels of suffixes to be simultaneously extrametrical, it is in fact possible to derive a word with preantepenultimate stress in his model. Consider the hypothetical trisyllabic root in the following example:

(155) [[pabal(o)] (e)]

The Peripherality Condition of Harris would license both extrametricality specifications, resulting in the construction of a disyllabic foot whose strong terminal rests on the initial syllable of the root. The unbounded stray adjunction rule that Harris relies on will complete the rest of the metrical structure, resulting in the ungrammatical output in (156).

(156) pábaloe

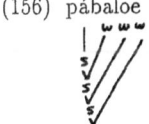

Thus, one of the most basic generalizations of Spanish stress — namely, that stress is always found among the last three syllables of any word — is an accident on Harris's analysis.

By contrast, the hypothetical word in (156) could never be derived under my proposal. Because cyclic Stray Syllable Adjunction is limited to syllables following unary feet, and because the Final Stress Rule applies on each cycle, it is impossible to generate a single foot which incorporates more than two syllables.

6.10.2 Polish

A case rather similar to that in Spanish is presented by Polish. In Polish as well as Spanish, one of the final three syllables in the word must be stressed; in both languages, certain stems cause the words containing them to exhibit exceptional stress patterns. And in both languages, underlying extrametricality has been proposed as the source of the deviant stress behavior. In what follows I will briefly summarize the arguments for stem invisibility in Polish, and then propose a counteranalysis which uses underlying feet instead of underlying invisibility to characterize exceptional forms.[63]

As mentioned in the literature (Comrie 1976, Dogil 1979, Rubach and Booij 1985, Franks 1985, Halle and Vergnaud 1987), the basic stress pattern in Polish is penultimate stress. This is most naturally captured by two rules, one which assigns a sw binary foot at the right edge of the word, and another which adjoins stray (unlicensed) syllables to an adjacent foot. We may assume here that both rules apply at the level of the phonological word.[64]

(157) Main Stress Rule: Build a binary left-dominant foot at the right edge of the word.

(158) Stray Syllable Adjunction: incorporate unlicensed syllables into an adjacent foot.

Below is an illustration of the application of these rules to the inflected forms of a regular stem, *reporter* 'reporter' (data from Rubach and Booij 1985:282):

(159)

	input:	reporter	reporter-a	reporter-owi
MSR:		repórter	repórter-a	repórter-owi
SSA:		repórter	repórter-a	repórter-owi
		(nom.sg.)	(gen.sg)	(dat.sg.)

---

[63]See Hammond 1989 for an alternative account using underlying stress, which came to my attention after this section was written.

[64]They apply to the individual members of compounds.

6.10. MORPHOLOGICAL CONTENT OF INVISIBILITY

Exceptional Stress

Polish has two classes of exceptional words, presented below. In each class, a certain set of forms surfaces with antepenultimate stress — namely the Class I stems which take monosyllabic affixes, and the Class II forms which precede no suffixes on the surface.[65]

(160) Class I:

gramátyk	'grammar (gen.pl.f.)'
gramátyk-a	'grammar (nom.sg.f.)'
gramatyk-ámi	'grammar (instr.pl.f.)'

(161) List of Class I stems:

anglistyk	'English studies'
logik	'logician'
egzamin	'examination'
fanatyk	'fantastic'
fizyk	'physics'
historyk	'historian'
katolik	'Catholic'
logik	'logic'
matematyk	'mathematics'
ogoł	'generality'
okolic	'surroundings'
pijatyk	'drinking bout'
republik	'republic'
szczegoł	'detail'
retoryk	'rhetorics'
teoretyk	'theoretician'

(162) Class II

| uniwérsitet | 'university (nom.sg.m.)' |

---

[65]In these cases, a jer-ending has been deleted.

uniwersytét-u   'university (gen.sg.m.)'
uniwersytet-ámi 'university (instr.pl.m.)'

(163) List of Class II stems:

autorytet   'authority'
dzentelmen   'gentlemen'
komitet   'committee'
leksykon   'lexicon'
prezydent   'president'
Waszyngton   'Washington'

One important generalization we can immediately draw from this data is that in all forms presented here (and in fact in all Polish words, period) stress falls on either the penultimate or on the antepenultimate syllable. This generalization forms the starting point for the literature on extrametricality in Polish.

(164) Generalization: either the penultimate or the antepenultimate syllable is stressed in Polish

All five accounts in the literature capture the generalization in (164) by assigning binary sw feet at the right edge of the word, and by making one of the final two syllables of exceptional words extrametrical. It is thus unavailable to the stress rule.

The approaches differ only in their method of assigning extrametricality [+ex]. The four different methods are summarized below.[66] Dogil, and Rubach and Booij, assign [+ex] to selected syllables by rule; Comrie and Franks view it as underlying.[67] Comrie and Rubach and Booij require a nonperipheral syllable to be extrametrical in certain suffixed words.[68] Franks has a rule that will occasionally assign [+ex] to a nonperipheral syllable, but stress rules are impervious to that diacritic when it is nonperipheral.

---

[66]Halle and Vergnaud outline essentially the same account as Franks, so I won't mention them further.

[67]Comrie has a pretheoretical view of extrametricality — he treats it as the feature [unstressable] — but the intuition is really the same.

[68]This is true despite Rubach and Booij's claim that their version of the Peripherality Condition is orthodox; perhaps they are thinking of Harris's Peripherality Condition, which allows internal [+ex] so long as [+ex] is adjacent to a morpheme boundary.

6.10. MORPHOLOGICAL CONTENT OF INVISIBILITY

(165) Summary of the four approaches

A Dogil 1979: sw feet with [+ex] assigned by rule which makes the final syllable extrametrical if both (a) and (b) hold:

  a. the word is [+foreign] (Class I) or [-derived] (Class II)

  b. the penultimate syllable contains -i- or -y-

B Rubach and Booij 1985: sw feet and two rules assigning [+ex]:

  a. Extrametricality I: mark as [+ex] the post-stem syllable in class I nouns

  b. Extrametricality II: mark as [+ex] the last stem syllable in class II nouns

C Comrie 1976: sw feet and underlying [+ex] (which he refers to as the feature [unstressable]). [+ex] vowels can't be the s member of a foot.

D Franks 1985: sw feet, underlying [+ex] (Class I), and underlying [+F] (Class II). [+F] syllables trigger a rule assigning [+ex] to the following syllable. In both Class I and Class II words, [+ex] is visible to rules only when peripheral.

These approaches all cover the facts about exceptional Polish stress.[69] However, leaving aside the more general question about whether it is correct, as these analyses assume, to treat [+ex] as a diacritic feature, each of these treatments suffers from at least one serious disadvantage. These are assembled below:

(166) Disadvantages of the [+ex] approaches:

  a. Otherwise unmotivated diacritics (Franks)
  b. Underlying marking of [+ex] on stems (Comrie, Rubach and Booij, Franks), violating the hypothesis that extrametricality will be inherent only on prosodically bound morphemes

---

[69]Dogil takes issue with Comrie's data, and Rubach and Booij present native words whose penultimate syllable is o, thus invalidating Dogil's generalization, but these details are irrelevant here; what matters is the existence of some set of exceptional forms.

c. Phonological rules referring crucially to internal morphological structure (Dogil, Rubach and Booij)

d. Nonperipheral extrametricality (Comrie, Rubach and Booij).[70]

All of these disadvantages, I believe, are symptoms of the underlying problem that stem extrametricality is not a natural, probably not even a possible, solution to Polish stress. It is certainly not a natural solution for words formed from Class II stems, for the following reasons:

(167)
    a. Idiosyncratic stress patterns in Polish are a property of stems, not of suffixes.

    b. Invisibility is known to be a property of peripheral elements only.

    c. Stress in Polish is assigned postcyclically.

Because Polish stress is assigned after all suffixes have been attached, stems will rarely be peripheral. Precisely because exceptional stress of suffixed forms is a property of *stems*, it cannot be encoded naturally via invisibility. Any attempts to do so will require incorporating globality into the derivation; stress rules will have to know, in some manner, that the string they are applying to contains a stem which wants extrametricality to be assigned to a particular syllable. The analyses in the literature represent varying methods of doing precisely this.

The considerations in (167) conspire to doom from the start any attempt to solve Polish stress using extrametricality. I therefore propose to depart from the literature and approach the problem from a different angle altogether. Suppose that instead of trying to lexically encode the idiosyncratic *absence* of stress on particular syllables, we turn things around and encode its *presence*. That is, exceptional syllables will be marked underlyingly with exactly the structure makes them exceptional on the surface: a binary stress foot. All (polysyllabic) Polish words will surface with such a foot; exceptional words are special only in that the foot occurs in a location where rules would not otherwise have put it.

In the case of Class I words, the underlying foot covers the final two syllables.

(168) repúblik

---

[70]Franks claims to have nonperipheral extrametricality, but since he arranges for his nonperipheral [+ex] features to be inaccessible to rules at the time stress is assigned, we might just as well assume that [+ex] is removed by a word-level rule when not peripheral.

6.10. MORPHOLOGICAL CONTENT OF INVISIBILITY

In the case of Class II words, the underlying foot covers the penultimate and antepenultimate syllables.

(169) uniwérsytet

The differing location of these underlying feet captures exactly the asymmetries in the behavior of the corresponding stems. Below are derivations showing the interaction of these underlying representations with the Main Stress Rule of Polish.

(170)
Class I:

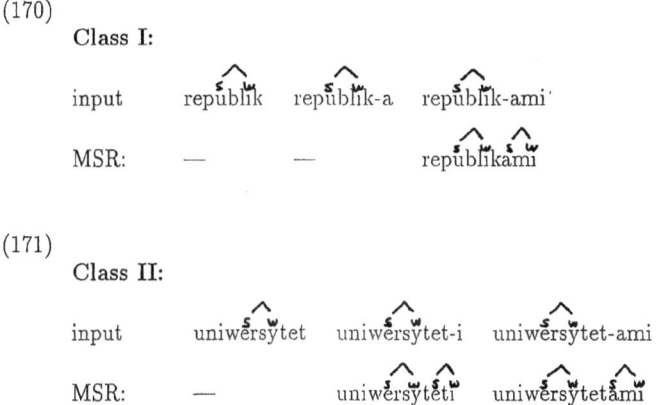

(171)
Class II:

    input   uniwérsytet   uniwérsytet-i   uniwérsytet-ami

    MSR: —   uniwérsytéti   uniwérsytetámi

As can be seen from these derivations, when two free syllables follow the underlying foot, the Main Stress Rule applies to assign an additional binary foot at the right edge of the word. Assuming a rule which deletes all but the rightmost foot (see below), the regular, penultimate stress pattern will result in these cases. Similarly, if no syllables follow the underlying foot, the stem will surface with penultimate stress. However, exactly when *one* syllable — whether part of the stem, or a suffix — follows the underlying foot, the Main Stress Rule will be unable to apply. In just these cases, the exceptional antepenultimate stress pattern results.

Thus, the generalization about which forms of the stem will bear exceptional stress and which will not is due entirely to the number of free syllables available to the Main Stress Rule at the word level. No reference needs to be made by phonological rules to morphological structure; no appeal needs to be made to extrametricality or other diacritic features.

Preventing Overgeneration of Feet

An obvious drawback of permitting feet to be marked in underlying representation is the potential for overgeneration. True, by restricting underlying feet to the two positions illustrated in (168) and (169), we capture the generalization that Polish stress is either penultimate or ultimate; but how do we arrive at the restriction in the first place?

To do this, I propose two rules, at least one of which is independently motivated in the language, and both which are needed in other languages (note that the same cannot be said for Franks's feature [+F], nor, I believe, for underlying extrametricality on stems). The first, Rightmost Wins, removes all but the rightmost stress foot in a word; the second, Unary Foot Erasure, removes all unary feet, whether spuriously existing in UR or derived by rule.

(172) Rightmost wins: Delete all but the rightmost stress foot.

As in Spanish (Roca 1986), secondary stress in Polish is completely predictable (Booij and Rubach 1985). This fact will allow us to remove all but the rightmost stress foot in a word, thus capturing the fact that underlying feet will be erased when, through suffixation, they end up to the left of the final two syllables in the word.

(173) uniwèrsytéti $\longrightarrow$ uniwersytéti

By means of this rule, a system which permits underlying feet can still capture the generalization sought by the extrametricality analyses: stress in Polish will always fall on the penult or antepenult.

Note that the Rightmost Wins rule does not make the underlying stress approach any more stipulative than the extrametricality analyses; the latter all require an analog of Rightmost Wins, namely the Peripherality Condition, to remove any overgenerated extrametricality features.

We also want to ensure that no unary stress feet will be marked underlyingly and thereby alter the normal stress pattern. Fortunately, Polish appears to require, on independent grounds, a rule of unary foot deletion which would erase such spurious feet. This is the rule referred to above as Unary Foot Erasure. It is stated below:

6.11. INFIXATION

(174) Unary Foot Erasure: Remove all degenerate feet

(174) captures the fact that Polish has no cases of finally-stressed (polysyllabic) words at all, and is also supported by facts from jer-deletion. When a word-final unary foot is produced as the result of jer-deletion (Rubach and Booij 1985), it does not surface. Instead, as shown in (175), feet produced in this manner are erased and a new, binary foot is assigned by the Main Stress Rule.[71]

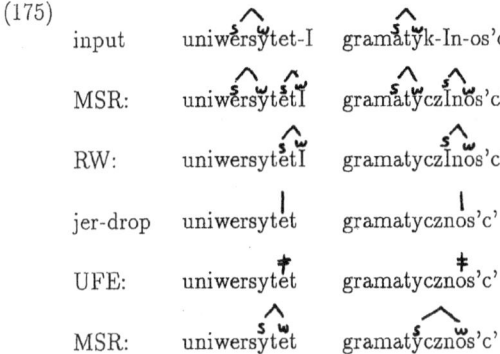

(175)
```
       input      uniwersytet-I     gramatyk-In-os'c'
       MSR:       uniwersytetI      gramatyczInos'c'
       RW:        uniwersytetI      gramatyczInos'c'
       jer-drop   uniwersytet       gramatycznos'c'
       UFE:       uniwersytet       gramatycznos'c'
       MSR:       uniwersytet       gramatycznos'c'
```

6.11 Infixation

In this section I will explore in a somewhat speculative fashion the implications of the domains account of invisibility for the analysis of infixation. An important insight to come out of recent work on this latter topic is that the conditions on what material may separate an infix from the edge of a word correspond to conditions on what may be made invisible by rule. Constraints on infixation were noted by Moravcsik 1977. To Poser 1984 (see also McCarthy and Prince 1986) is due the subsequent proposal that infixation can be insightfully treated as invisibility of some part of the base to affixation.

On such accounts, infixation results from adding an affix to a base whose peripheral element (on the edge at which affixation occurs) is invisible. The following example of a plural infixing prefix in Sundanese is taken from McCarthy and Prince 1986:48:[72]

---

[71]The palatalization of *k* in *gramatyik* is due to the following jer.
[72]McCarthy and Prince assume that the infix occupies a tier distinct from that of the base.

(176)

$$\underset{ar}{\overset{\sigma}{\wedge}} + \underset{(n)i}{\overset{\sigma}{\cancel{\wedge}}} \underset{?is}{\overset{\sigma}{\cancel{\wedge}}} \longrightarrow \underset{(n)a}{\overset{\sigma}{\wedge}} \underset{ri}{\overset{\sigma}{\wedge}} \underset{?is}{\overset{\sigma}{\wedge}}$$

How exactly to implement the insight that the material to be skipped over is invisible has not, to my knowledge, been worked out in the literature.[73] Judging from examples like that in (176), the assumption seems to be that first, invisibility is marked on the base; subsequent to this, the affix and base are concatenated.

Despite its initial appeal, this proposal falls down in certain important areas. A general problem is that it attributes infixation to some representational property of the base. But as observed in Kiparsky 1986, infixation is a property of affixes, not of bases. While there are affixes which consistently show up in infixed position, there are no stems which are idiosyncratic in that they take as infixes morphemes which would behave as normal affixes with respect to all other stems. This suggests that whatever properties are unique to infixation should be marked on the infix.

A more concrete objection with McCarthy and Prince's account is that it incorrectly predicts that *any* affix attaching to a base with peripheral invisibility will show up as an infix. This is easily refuted. Consider, for example, English, which has pervasive final consonant extrametricality, and plenty of suffixes. The interpretation given above to the schema in (176) predicts that when an α suffix is added to a stem with final consonant invisibility, that suffix will appear as an infix to the left of the invisible consonant melody. But this of course does not occur; English has no infixes at all.

(177) rhoti(c) + ize $\longrightarrow$ *rhotiize(c)

Instead, as we have seen earlier, combinations of the type in (177) result in erasure of the information that some part of the stem used to be invisible.

However, as multiple morpheme tiers are not crucial here I've simplified the representation by leaving them out.

[73] An exception is Poser 1984, who suggests that the morphological rule introducing the affix invokes invisibility on a peripheral constituent. This is consistent with Poser's program of locating the responsibility for invisibility in rule environments. While I agree with and will adopt the intuition that infix-hood is a property of the affix, proposing a separate word formation rule for each individual affix is too powerful a mechanism to adopt in a theory which also has morphological subcategorization frames.

6.11. INFIXATION

(178) [rhoti]$_p$ c + [[ ]$_p$ ize]$_p$ $\longrightarrow$ [[[rhoti]$_p$ c]$_p$ ize]$_p$ = [rhoticize]$_p$

I take these facts as evidence that the property of being an infix must be encoded in the representation of the infix itself. And prosodic subcategorization frames provide the necessary means to do this. In particular, a suffix will be an infix if its prosodic frame locates it to the left of some element of the base (vice versa for prefixes).

The Sundanese infix illustrated above will have the prosodic subcategorization frame in (179) (c represents a consonantal melodic element):

(179) ar: [c ___ [ ]$_p$]$_p$

(180) [c ar [ ]$_p$]$_p$ + [ni?is]$_p$ $\longrightarrow$ [nar [i?is]$_p$]$_p$

Thus infixation can be seen as a property of whether or not the affix has more than one sister. All affixes have at least one sister, the prosodic constituent for which they by definition subcategorize. Infixes are special in that they mention an additional sister, the material 'across' which they are attached. We may adopt Kiparsky's (1986) term 'pivot' for this material. (181) shows the representational difference between the Sundanese infix and a regular prefix, English *in-*:

(181)
           Infix   Invisible prefix

    ar: [c ___ [ ]$_p$]$_p$ in: [___ [ ]$_p$]$_p$

The proposal to represent infixes as subcategorizing for an additional sister leads to two strong predictions which I have not as yet been able to explore in full. However, I will outline their implications here with the idea that the data assembled in future studies will help to resolve the unanswered questions.

6.11.1 Invisibility × Infixation

The orthogonal, binary-valued properties in (182) together produce a five-way typology of infixes, shown in (183).

(182)
    a. a morpheme m in a prosodic subcategorization frame has one sister or more than one ([+/– infixation])
    b. an element e in a prosodic subcategorization frame is outside or inside the outer prosodic domain ([+/– invisibility])

First, affixes differ as to whether or not they have more than one sister (infixation). Second, that additional sister can be either visible or invisible. Third, the affix itself can be either visible or invisible. One slot is left unfilled: the case of an invisible affix which has a visible second sister. To represent this would require either that the affix has two sisters on the same side (this is ruled out, as we see below) or the postulation of discontinuous constituency (also prohibited).

(183)

		affix visible	affix invisible
one sister		[[ ] ─]	[[ ]] ─
more than one sister	outer sister visible	[[ ] ─ X]	∅
	outer sister invisible	[[ ] ─] X	[[ ]] ─ X

The proposed representation for infixes has the desirable consequence of correctly accounting for the cases when an infix attempts to attach to a base which its pivot, X, exhausts. Facts of this kind are discussed by Kiparsky 1986, who shows that when a prefixing infix is attached to a base which X would subsume, the infix shows up instead as a prefix. Nabak provides such an example. The reduplicating prefix is underlined in the forms below (Kiparsky 1986:161, data from Fabian, Fabian and Peck 1971):

(184)
    a. sek   se-sek-piŋ   '(don't) carry it'
       ek   e-ek-piŋ   '(don't) look'

    b. kutu   ku-tu-tu-piŋ   '(don't) fold it'

6.11. INFIXATION

c. za   zan-za-piŋ   '(don't) tie it'
ande   an-den-de-piŋ   '(don't) open it'
muŋguŋ muŋ-guŋ-guŋ-piŋ '(don't) wind it around'

The above data evince a reduplicating prefix of the form CVN,[74] which shows up as an infix after the first syllable exactly when the base consists of more than one syllable. (The suffix -piŋ is apparently attached concomitantly with reduplication and does not figure into the computation of base size.) When the base is monosyllabic, as in the case of *sek*, *ek* and *za*, the reduplicating affix shows up as a prefix.

As Kiparsky argues, this behavior is what we would expect on an analysis in which infixation is caused by invisibility on part of the base. The prohibition against exhaustive invisibility prevents an affix from rendering invisible the entire base with which it combines.

This intuitive prediction falls out naturally from the representation our theory would provide for the negative imperative infix in Nabak. The generic infix pivot X is instantiated by a syllable, as shown in (185):

(185) Nabak negative imperative infix: CVN: [σ --- [ ]$_p$]$_p$

When a bi-dependent frame of this sort encounters and attempts to unify with a monosyllabic base such as *sek*, two outcomes are logically possible. Either the base instantiates X, or it instantiates the prosodic host. Both possibilities are depicted below:

(186) Outcomes of combining the infix [σ CVN [ ]$_p$]$_p$ with the base   [sek]$_p$

      a. Base instantiates X   b. Base instantiates prosodic host

      [sek CVN [ ]$_p$]$_p$ [∅ CVN [sek]$_p$]$_p$
        | |
        σ   σ

      *sek-seN-piŋ   seN-sek-piŋ

---

[74] The nasal surfaces only before voiced obstruents (Kiparsky 1986:161).

Only one of the two outcomes is correct; happily, it is exactly the one which is licensed in our theory. The option in (186a), in which X is instantiated by the base, results in a representation containing an empty prosodic constituent. As we know, such representations are illicit; and the derivation is rejected. By contrast, option (186b) results in an empty metrical constituent, the unfilled pivot X. In contrast to empty prosodic constituents, empty metrical constituents play a role in phonological theory. They are either filled or deleted by stray erasure; we may assume the latter option is invoked in the case of Nabak. Thus, the theory allows for only one possible outcome in the case where the infixal pivot subsumes the base, and correctly predicts non-infixal attachment in just these cases.

Notice that this analysis crucially depends on the 'active' view of subcategorization, in which all of the information present in the subcategorization frame is contributed to the representation resulting from the combination of affix and host. A theory which treats subcategorization as a passive constraint would have no way of accounting for the behavior of Nabak. In order to explain the suspension of the requirement that the negative imperative affix must follow a syllable in those cases where the base is monosyllabic, such theories will have to posit two allomorphs for the affix, as shown below:

(187)

Monosyllabic base:	CVN:	$[\_\_[\,\sigma\,]_p\,]_p$
Polysyllabic base:	CVN:	$[\,\sigma\_\_[\ ]_p\,]_p$

But this solution lacks explanatory power. The relationship between the syllabic structure of the base and the presence and content of the pivot is arbitrary, and accidental. By contrast, the active approach to subcategorization is able to predict exactly when the potential for infixation will be realized.

Data which would support the passive over the active approach would be cases in which an infix fails to attach in any form when the pivot would exhaust the base. We should be on the lookout for cases of this kind.

Single-sister condition

The literature suggests that the infixal pivot, X, always corresponds to a single phonological constituent (Moravcsik 1977). Segments are the typical infixal pivot in the reduplicating infix data collected by McCarthy and Prince 1986, but cases do occur (e.g. Timogen Murut (McCarthy and Prince p. 46)) in which the melodic content of an entire syllable is rendered invisible for purposes of infixation. In addition, Hale and Lacaya Blanco 1988 have uncovered an infix in Ulwa which, as W. Poser and J. McCarthy have pointed out (p.c.), can be construed as taking as its pivot the moraic foot.[75]

A desirable result of the assumption of Poser 1984 and McCarthy and Prince 1986 that infixes trigger rules which assign invisibility to the base is that constraints on what may constitute the pivot of an infix follow directly from constraints on what rules may render invisible. That is, the single-constituent constraint following from the Focus Determinant Adjacency Condition corresponds to the observed restrictions on pivot material.

This attractive prediction appears to be lost on the proposed account, however. In the prosodic theory the invisibility required by infixation is imposed by lexical subcategorization frames, not by phonological rules.

Another prediction does arise, of course, namely that the content of the infixal pivot should obey constraints on what may constitute the subcategorized sister of an affix. But what, if anything, does constrain the content of prosodic subcategorization frames? Are there any limits on X in the above representations? A possible solution to constraining infixation would be to extend the FDAC to all constraints on phonological representation.[76] (This same approach is taken elsewhere by Itô, in a move to impose identical locality conditions on both the rules and the constraints which regulate metrical structure (Itô 1986:27).) Stated generally, the new condition will be as follows:

(188) Generalized Focus Determinant Adjacency Condition: Each phonologically constrained element must be adjacent to each constraining element

The GFDAC essentially places a one-constituent upper bound on material adjacent to the focus. Not only can the focus subcategorize for at most one sister string on each side; that sister is in addition limited by the FDAC to being a single phonological constituent.

---

[75] I have seen only that subset of the data reproduced in Bromberger and Halle 1989. They show that the construct state form of nouns is generated by infixing the syllable *ka* after the first syllable if that syllable is heavy (i.e. bimoraic), and otherwise after the second syllable.

[76] According to Poser (p.c.), the FDAC is intended to constrain everything it can; though Poser 1985 mentions only phonological rules, the extension of the FDAC to constraints is in the spirit of his proposal.

Prosodic subcategorization frames of infixes are thus an instantiation of the most fully specified frames possible: prosodically bi-dependent morphemes. The constrained element, i.e. the morpheme, has a single sister to each side: one, the prosodic constituent to which it attaches, and the other, the infixal pivot.[77]

Further Consequences

A possible further consequence of the GFDAC lies in its application to templatic phonology and morphology of the kind discussed in detail in McCarthy and Prince 1986. In a template, every element in the representation is simultaneously constrained and constraining (at the same time both focus and determinant). The prediction of the GFDAC is thus that all elements of the template should be adjacent. This would essentially put a limit of two on the number of terminal elements which such a template could mention.

This prediction accords with the list of units designated by McCarthy and Prince as possible templates (McCarthy and Prince 1986:7).[78]

(189)

	Wd	'prosodic word'
	F	'foot'
	σ	'syllable'
	σ_μ	'light (monomoraic syllable)'
	$\sigma_{\mu\mu}$	'heavy (bimoraic syllable)'
	σ_c	'core syllable'

McCarthy and Prince say that foot templates, which can dominate either syllables or moras,[79] are maximally binary-branching. They pattern with the syllables in the above list in containing at most two daughters. Though McCarthy and Prince state the binarity condition as a basic premise, we can go one step further and derive it by subjecting prosodic templates to the GFDAC.

---

[77] An obvious question to ask here is whether a prosodically bi-dependent affix could subcategorize for two prosodic sisters, as opposed to one prosodic and one metrical sister. I do not know the answer to this. The only testable instantiation I can imagine of this possibility would be a bi-dependent clitic; such cases should be looked for.

[78] σ_c, or 'core syllable', means maximal light syllable.

[79] Bimoraic feet are also postulated in Poser 1984, Poser 1990.

Chapter 7

Case Study: Carib

This chapter focuses on stress assignment in Carib, a Cariban language spoken in the coastal area of Guyana. The data support several important predictions of the theory of Prosodic Lexical Phonology. First, certain facts in Carib can be accounted for only under the assumption that there is no preaffixal stem cycle. Thus, Carib instantiates the possibility predicted in chapter 5 that a language may allow morpheme combination to precede (and preempt) Prosodic Constituent Formation. Carib also makes productive use of invisibility, the topic of Chapter 6. A good test case for the theory, Carib makes use of all three of the logically possible sources of prosodic constituency provided by the theory: underlying representation, phonological rule, and the Prosodic Constituent Formation algorithm. The data also show that suffixation triggers cyclic erasure of invisiblity, as predicted by the prosodic domain treatment of invisibility. This confirmation is especially striking when one considers that all invisibility in Carib occurs at the *left* edge of words.

7.1 Basic Stress Rule

Each lexical word in Carib contains one 'accent', which Hoff describes as a prominence in pitch (p. 96).[1] Accent shows up on the second heavy syllable in the word (or on the final syllable, if fewer than two heavy syllables precede). Heavy syllables are those ending in long vowels, diphthongs, or consonants. We may assume that in Carib, as

---

[1] All of the data I refer to are taken from the comprehensive grammar by B. J. Hoff (1968).

in Malayalam (Mohanan 1982) and English, tone is assigned to stressed syllables, and that all heavy syllables in Carib bear stress. It is the distribution of stress with which we will be concerned here.

In monomorphemic words without closed syllables or diphthongs, vowel length is systematically alternating throughout the first four syllables (subject to the restriction that no final syllables in Carib may be stressed). This suggests that vowel length is derived from stress, and that stress feet are binary and quantity sensitive. The stress rule builds up to two feet beginning at the left edge of the word.

Hoff observes that words with alternating vowel length (in our view, alternating stress) fall into two classes: those with length (stress) on the first two even-numbered syllables, as in (1), and those with length (stress) on the first two odd-numbered syllables, as in (2).[2]

(1) Even-numbered stress

# of syllables		gloss
3	akaami	'trumpeter bird'
	tonooro	'large bird'
4	araamari	'mythical snake'
	kuriiyara	'canoe'
5	asaaparaapi	'species of fish'
	wotuuropooro	'cause to ask'
6	epaanamaatoko	'listen'
	wotuuropootake	'I shall ask'
7	awiïtopootïrïkoĝ	'your (pl.) wandering

(2) Odd-numbered stress

# of syllables		gloss
1	wo	'to beat'

---

[2]In these and future examples, I have strived to exclude words with a preponderance of closed syllables and diphthongs. Due to a CVX maximal syllable template, these types of syllables never exhibit the vowel lengthening which is my only diagnostic of the presence of stress. They are also subject to a number of rules affecting coda consonants, an added complication.

7.1. BASIC STRESS RULE

2	eero	'this'	
	kuupi	'bathe'	
3	eemaka	'to comb a parting'	
	taakuwa	'polishing-stone'	
4	aarawaata	'howling monkey'	
	paayawaaru	'cassava beer'	
5	auwanoopono	'causing laughter'	
	kookapootake	'you will have me bitten'	
6	seekapootïrïkoŋ	'the fact that I keep tearing them'	
	iipokaapotïrïkoŋ	'the fact that I keep shaving them'	

Note that all disyllabic stems, because of the prohibition against final stress, surface with stress on the first syllable when they stand alone as words. However, evidence from derived forms shows that disyllabic stems split into the same two classes as polysyllabic stems. When combined with a suffix, one class of disyllabic stems yields words with even-numbered stress, while the other class of stems produces an odd-numbered stress pattern in that same context. Stems representing the two stress classes, and the corresponding derived forms, are listed in (3) and (4):[3]

(3) Even-numbered stress

aapi	'red, ripe'	apii-ro	'to cause to ripen'
aapi	'broadness'	apii-ka	'to broaden'
aaro	'take'	aroo-to	'he used to take him continually'
		aroo-ko	'you must take him'
		aroo-to?me	'[means] for taking him along'
aaru	'dryness'	aruu-ta	'become dry'
		aruu-ta-rïï-koŋ	'their getting dry'
		aruu-ka-poo-ro	'drying it'
aato	'hole'	atoo-ka	'to make a hole in'

---
[3] The *e/o* alternation observed in e.g., *oonu* 'eye' and *enuu-ta* 'understand' occurs with a small class of noun roots, and more productively with deverbal nouns (Hoff p. 214-217). In forms exhibiting the alternation, the *o*-initial variant seems to occur when the form is acting as a complement; the *e*-initial variant is found elsewhere. The morphological status of these initial vowels remains to be worked out.

		atoo-rï	'hole'
aima	'smoke'	aimaa-ko	'you must smoke it'
eemI	'louse'	emïï-rï	'lice'
eene	'see'	enee-rï	'to see'
		enee-po	'to show'
oonu	'eye'	enuu-ta	'to understand'
		enuu-ru	'eye'
		enuu-kepï	'to be dazzled'
eeta	'hear'	etaa-topo	'means of hearing'
		etaa-po	'cause to hear'
eetï	'name'	etïï-ka	'give someone a name'
		etï-mbo	'original name'
		etï-xpa	'nameless'
		otïï-waano	'names in general'
eeto	'blow'	etoo-ko	'you must blow it'
		etoo-rï	'to blow'
eewa	'hammock-line'	ewaa-rï	'hammock-line'
		owaa-koŋ	'hammock-lines'
iiro	'the one mentioned'	iroo-koŋ	'the ones mentioned'
kaarai	'blackness'	karai-ma	'blacken'
oono	'eat'	onoo-rï	'to eat it'
		onoo-to	'one who devours'
		onoo-yaŋ	'he eats it'
oxta	'cave, hole'	oxtaa-rï	'cave, hole'
paxka	'bring'	paxkaa-no	'he brings out'
uupa	'serve'	upaa-no	'she served him'
		upaa-topo	'means for serving'
uupi	'look for'	upii-kepï	'stop looking for'
		upii-keese	'stop looking for
uura	'weeping'	uraa-rï	'her weeping'
uuwa	'to dance'	uwaa-no	'being dancing'

(4) Odd-numbered stress

aarï	'foliage'	aarï-na	'to get leaves'
		aarï-ngepï	'to be stripped of leaves'

7.1. BASIC STRESS RULE

ooma	'path'	eema-rï	'path'
		ooma-mbo	'former path'
		eema-xpa	'without a path'
eepï	'little stick'	eepï-ndo	'provide somebody with a little stick'
		eepï-mbo	'former stem'
eero	'this'	eero-me	'now'
		eero-mbo	'past'
kaami	'pale red'	kaami-ro	'to cause to become pale red'
kaamu	'flame'	kaamu-ro	'cause to flare up'
		kaamu-ka	'cause to flare up'
kaawo	'high'	kaawo-mbo	'from above'
		kaawo-naaka	'up'
		kaawo-no	'a high one'
		kaawo-noo-koŋ	'high ones'
		kaawo-noo-konï-mbo	'those who are not really high'
keepu	'wet'	keepu-ro	'cause to become wet'
kuupii	'bathe'	kuupii-ma	'to bathe thoroughly'
		kuupipoo-tï	'to bathe repeatedly'
moorï	'noise'	moorï-ka	'cause to rumble'
muure	'bench'	muure-mbo	'poor benches'
naana	'pineapple'	naana-mbo	'you know, a pineapple'
		naana-koonï-mbo	'you know, pineapples'
piina	'catch/get'	piina-toopo	'means of getting.'
		piina-toʔme	'in order to get'
piipa	'flat frog pipa'	piipa-ta	'become as flat as a pipa'
taamï	'tobacco'	taamï-mbo	'poor cigar'
		taamï-rï	'tobacco'
taano	'what is in'	taano-koŋ	'which are in'
uuna	'to sieve'	uuna-toopo	'sieve (N.)'
		uuna-toʔme	'in order to sieve'
waare	'song'	waare-ta	'to sing'
		waare-ka	'to make a song on a particular event'
wo	'kill'	woo-topo	'means of killing'
		woo-toʔme	'in order to kill'

		woo-toʔma-ŋ	'something to kill with'
wooku	'cassava beer'	wooku-ta	'to prepare beer'
		wooku-xto	'make cassava beer for somebody else'
woomï	'garment'	woomï-ndo	'to dress'
wooto	'meat, fish'	wooto-rï	'meat'
		wooto-koŋ̂	'fishes'

Similar behavior is found among stems containing more than two syllables: before most suffixes, stems exhibit their isolation stress pattern. Note that in cases where stress is prohibited from appearing on the final vowel in isolation, it surfaces before a suffix.[4]

(5) Even-numbered stress

akiinu	'lazy'	akiinu-ro	'make lazy'
atïïta	'to grow up'	atïïta-xpo	'having grown up'
kareeta	'paper'	kareeta-naano	'paper in general'
kariʔna	'human being'	kariʔna-ma	'to cause to become human'
kopooseme	'on the opposite side'	kopoose-no	'one on the opposite side'
koroomo	'recent'	koroomo-no	'a recent thing'
koroona	'deep'	koroona-ka	'deep'
kowaaro	'very small'	kowaaro-no	'a very small one'
kuruuwese	'palm sheath'	kuruuwese-mbo	'old palm sheath'
pakooto	'to cut wood'	pakooto-no	'fact of wood-cutting'
pitaani	'child'	pitaani-koŋ̂	'children'
puruure	'small hand-adze'	puruure-xto	'to adze'
samaane	'overturned'	samaana-ŋ	'an overturned one'
sawoone	'lightweight'	sawoona-ŋ	'a light one'
		sawoona-paamï	'to become light'
		sawoo-no	'to make light'

---

[4]The form *atïïta-xpo* actually shows up in the text as *atïïtaapo* because of an optional rule whereby *x* and *ʔ* in the coda delete, inducing compensatory lengthening of the preceding vowel (see e.g. Hoff p. 67).

7.1. BASIC STRESS RULE

seseewu	'fringe on clothing'	seseewu-ro	'provide with a fringe'
tïyaapo	'marsh, swamp'	tïyaapo-xto	'to cause to become swampy'
tuwaaro	'thoughtful'	tuwaaro-no	'a thoughtful one'
wokïïrï	'man'	wokïïrï-yaŋ̂	'men'
wotaaro	'go hunting'	wotaaro-tooto	'one who goes hunting'
wotuuropo	'ask'	wotuuropoo-ro	'to cause to ask'
		wotuuropoo-take	'I shall ask'

(6) Odd-numbered stress

aaripaapï	'distribute'	aaripax-topo	'place for distributing'
		aaripax-to?me	'for distributing it'
aasakaarï	'fellow'	aasakaarï-koŋ̂	'his fellows'
baasiya	'deputy-chief'	baasiyaa-koŋ̂	'deputy-chiefs'
eenapoorï	'snoring'	eenapoo-wa	'to snore'
kaawono	'a high one'	kaawonoo-koŋ̂	'high ones'
kooroka	'scrub'	kookoraa-ṅo	'he scrubbed'
oomïya	'a young one'	oomïyaa-ko	'a young woman'
ooruwa	'three'	ooruwaa-no	'one who is third'
		ooruwaa-no-koŋ̂	'triple ones'
		oruuwaa-kari?na	'sixty' [compound]
weerïkï	'dirt'	weerïkïï-ko	'to cause to become dirty'

The stress pattern exemplified thus far suggests a cyclic or postcyclic rule assigning up to two binary feet at the left edge of the word. However, it is not clear whether the Carib stress foot should be iambic or trochaic, since both patterns seem to be attested in the two classes of Carib words. A piece of evidence which will help to decide this question, at least preliminarily, comes from the fact that vowel length in Carib is largely derived; vowel length is predictable from stress, we have concluded, and not the other way around. That is to say, stress appears not to be quantity-sensitive. This hypothesis is supported by evidence from monomorphemic words containing closed syllables. Since closed syllables never contain long vowels in Carib, a logical conclusion is that Carib syllables are maximally bimoraic, closed syllables patterning as heavy. Yet the stress rule is insensitive to the presence of closed syllables, as the following forms illustrate:

(7)

	Odd-numbered stress	Even-numbered stress
1st syllable closed	tuxkusi 'arrow'	wingoosi 'ant'
1st syllable open	taakuwa 'polishing-stone'	tonooro 'large bird'
1st syllable closed	kaŋkasaapa 'lizard'	ma?maatakaara 'sp. of fish'
1st syllable open	paayawaaru 'cassava beer'	kuriiyara 'canoe'

Hayes 1987 has argued that iambic feet are always quantity-sensitive. Since this property appears not to characterize Carib feet, we are left only with the option of trochaic feet. I will thus propose for the present that Carib stress feet are syllabic trochees, and furthermore, that initial moras are invisible to the stress rule.[5]

(8) Initial mora invisibility: $[\, \mu \, \ldots \, \longrightarrow \, \mu \, [\, \ldots$

(9) Basic Stress Rule: build up to two syllabic trochees at the left edge of the word

These principles together account for the class of words with even-numbered stress.

(10)
    [asaparapi] ⟶ a [saparapi] ⟶ a [sáapàraápi]

    [kuriyara] ⟶ ku [riyara] ⟶ ku [ríiyara]

But what of the words with odd-numbered stress? I propose that this set of words are exceptional underlyingly in that they all contain a long first vowel. Because only initial moras are made invisible by the rule in (8), the initial, bimoraic syllable of

---

[5] We will later argue that what appears to be initial mora invisibility is actually the convergence of two independent processes: across-the-board initial vowel invisibility, and context-sensitive initial consonant invisibility.

7.2. CYCLICITY

words like those in (11) will still be available to the stress rule. As a consequence such words will obtain initial (odd-numbered) stress.[6]

(11)   [aarawata]   ⟶ a [arawata]   ⟶ a [áarawáata]

[paayawaru]   ⟶ pa [ayawaru]   ⟶ pa [áayawáaru]

Some support for the decision to lexically mark the forms inducing odd-numbered stress, as opposed to those inducing even-numbered stress, comes from Hoff's observation that "[w]here two types of vocalic structure are possible, those with a long first vowel are the least frequent" (p. 73). Thus, the extra structure in the lexical entry of forms that later obtain odd-numbered stress correlates with their comparatively marked status in Carib.[7]

7.2 Cyclicity

Given the data we have seen so far, stress could be assigned either cyclically or postcyclically. We know that the rule assigning initial stress to those disyllabic words with short initial vowels is bled by suffixation. (This ordering was deemed necessary in order to account for the difference in stress between e.g., *aapi* 'ripe' and *apii-ro* 'cause to ripen'.)

But this observation does not serve to distinguish the cyclic from the noncyclic approach. Our rule of initial invisibility prevents even a cyclic stress rule from assigning stress to the first, short syllable of unaffixed disyllabic stems.[8]

---

[6] Some mechanism will needed to guarantee that length is contrastive only in first position; one possibility is a general shortening rule that applies after initial invisibility has been assigned. An additional assumption needed here is that when the initial mora becomes visible and has to form a syllable with a vowel lengthened as a result of stress, the resulting syllable will lose one of its three moras and surface as a regular long (bimoraic) syllable. Carib syllables are never trimoraic.

[7] In support of vowel length as the means of marking these forms, as opposed to some diacritic which might, for example, block the initial mora invisibility rule from applying, note that the vowels marked underlyingly as long always surface as long. Thus, though it is arguably used diacritically, initial vowel length is the most economical diacritic possible, as it can safely persist throughout the derivation and need not be erased. By contrast, a rule-blocking feature would serve no other purpose and would added unneeded complexity to the grammar.

[8] Only at some later level, e.g., the phrase, will initial invisibility be turned off. At that point words which still lack stress will receive a trochee.

However, facts from the interaction of prefixation and suffixation crucially argue that stress must be assigned cyclically. Consider the following forms:[9]

(12)

akiima	'tease'	kïn-aakiimaa-no	'he teases her'
awoomï	'to get up'	ay-aawoomï-i	'you must not get up'
epaanopï	'help'	ay-eepaanopï	'your being helped'
emeepa	'to teach'	kïn-eemeepaa-no	'he teaches them'
etamboka	'untie'	kïn-eetambokaa-no	'she unties it'
eyaato	'call'	kïn-eeyaato-yaa-toŷ	'they call him'
kuraama	'cure'	si-kuuraama-e	'I cure him'
kuraama	'look after'	kï-kuuraama-ko	'you must look after me'
		kï-kuuraama-i	'you must not look after me'
		i-kuuraama-ko	'you must look after him'
		kï-kuuraama-ko	'you must look after me'
poroopï	'stop'	ni-pooroopï-i	'actually he has stopped'
		ni-pooroopïi-se	'so that he may stop'
		a-pooroopï-i	'you must not stop'

Both the derived and the underived words listed in the first and third columns of (12) exhibit stress on the second syllable, as predicted by the stress and invisibility rules presented earlier. However, note that the derived stems also exhibit stress on their own second syllable — that is, the third syllable of the derived word, where no postcyclic rule would place it. Of course, the stem-medial syllable is exactly where stress would be assigned were the prefix not present. We may thus conclude that these stems undergo stress assignment both before and after the prefix is added. Stress assignment in Carib is cyclic, and structure-building in nature. Carib thus patterns with Diyari and Warlpiri, as analyzed in Poser 1989, and with Greek, as analyzed in Steriade 1988.

(13)
PCF	[kurama]
μ Invisibility	ku [rama]

---

[9]Note that the suffixes -no, -toŷ, -se, and -ma always impose length on the preceding vowel; the penultimate long vowels of words ending in these suffixes is thus a local effect and can be overlooked for present purposes.

7.2. CYCLICITY

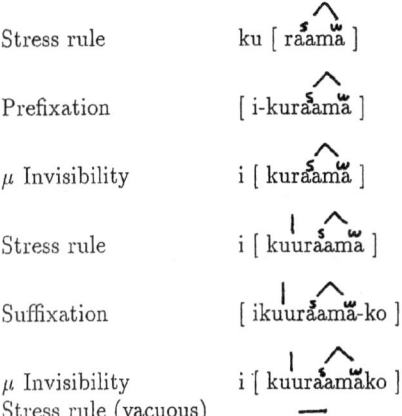

Of course, nothing we have seen so far requires that suffixation take place after prefixation, as was presented in (13). On the assumption that a stem cycle takes place before affixation, the correct form would still be generated if the order of affixation were reversed, as it is in (14):

(14)

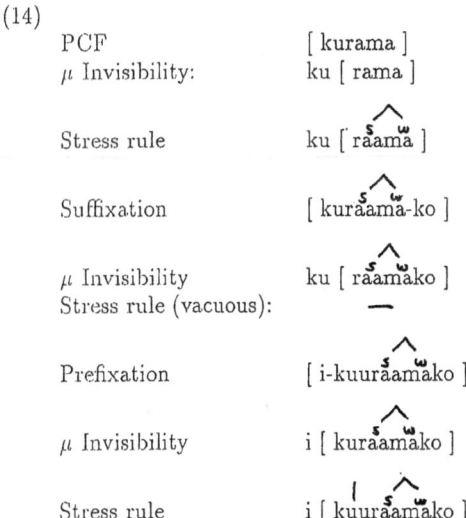

On the basis of data from "strong" suffixes, to be introduced in a subsequent section, we will actually find reason to challenge the assumption of a preaffixal stem cycle. I will argue not only that no such cycle takes place, but also that suffixation is crucially ordered before prefixation; thus the ordering ambiguity will be resolved. Before proceeding to that argument, however, I would like first to solidify the premise that the surface stress of forms like *i-kuuraama-ko* results from the cyclic application of the same two rules (invisibility and stress assignment). Accordingly, I will argue in the following subsection against the most obvious alternative hypothesis, namely that prefixes are somehow lexically marked to place stress on the following syllable.[10]

7.2.1 Prefixation

Prefixation in Carib is both inflectional and derivational; most of the work of person-marking is performed by prefixes, and they thus show up frequently on verbs and possessed nouns.

As we observed above, prefixes tend to incur the assignment of stress on the following syllable. This is true even if the following syllable is itself a prefix:[11]

(15)

kuupi	'to bathe'	a-wee-kuupi	'your taking a bath'
uxku	'draw'	tu-woot-uuku	'having drawn'
paxka	'to bring'	kĩn-(w)ee-paxka-nopo-yaŋ̃	'he caused himself to
		3pers-refl-bring_out-caus-TNS	be brought out'

A first difficulty for a hypothetical rule stressing the syllable following a prefix is

---

[10]Motivation for considering this hypothesis, aside from the fact that it is a logical possibility, comes from the fact that, as noted in an earlier footnote, certain suffixes obligatorily lengthen the preceding vowel (by some means not entirely clear to me). One might expect prefixes to perform the mirror image operation. However, as we will see, none do.

[11]The appearance of x in the unaffixed form of 'draw' is due to a phenomenon which I do not fully understand, whereby long vowels sometimes alternate with Vx and $V?$ sequences. According to Hoff (p. 67), certain forms exhibit these sequences in free variation (e.g., *sexpa/seepa* 'refusing', *yuxpa/yuupa/yu?pa* 'good', *axta/aata* 'if', *i?me/iime* 'child') while in other forms (e.g., *moxko*, **mooko* 'he', *pooko*, **poxko* 'with') only one alternant is possible. Given Hoff's observation (p. 67) that exactly those Vx sequences which do alternate with long vowels can surface with an h-like consonant instead of the velar fricative, a possibility is that the alternating forms are underlyingly Vh; not being a surface phoneme in Carib, the underlying, abstract h must be realized either as a velar fricative, a glottal stop or as a vowel. Non-alternating Vx or VV sequences would thus not contain an h underlyingly.

7.2. CYCLICITY

that many prefixes are consonantal, forming the onset of the initial syllable where possible.[12]

(16)

aaro	'to take'	k-aroo-ko	'you must take me'
aaru (aru)	'dryness'	t-aruu-re	'dry'
aato (ato)	'hole'	t-aroo-re	'full of holes'
eene	'see'	s-enee-ya	'I see him'
		s-enee-yakoŋ̂	'I saw him then'
		s-enee-yaine	'I see him continually'
		s-enee-to	'I used to see him then continually'
		s-enee-se	'so that I may see him'
		n-enee-se	'so that he may see it'
		s-enee-rï	'I would/could see him (but I didn't)'
		n-enee-rï	'he would see it (but he didn't)'
		s-enee-take	'I'll see him'
		n-enee-se-ŋ̂	'did he really see them then?'
eeta	'to hear'	s-etaa-e	'I hear him'
		m-etaa-e	'you hear him'
		s-etaa-no	'do I hear him?'
		m-etaa-no	'do you hear him?'
		k-otaa-e	'I hear you/you hear me'
eetï	'sound'	t-otïï-po-re	'sounding beautiful'
utaapï	'to lose one's way'	k-utaa-sa	'the two of us lose our way'
		k-utaa-sa-ŋ̂	'do the two of us lose our way?'
		k-utax-take	'both of us will lose our way'
		n-utaa-sa-ŋ̂	'does he lose his way?'
awoomï	'to get up'	n-awoomï-rï	'he would get up

---

[12] Otherwise they trigger a rule of epenthesis (inserting, I believe, *i*).

			(but he didn't)'
eneepï	'bring'	n-eneepï-xpo	'brought by __'
epoorï	'to find'	s-epoorï	'I would find it
			(but didn't)'
eneepï	'to bring'	s-eneepïï-se	'so that I may bring it'
onaapi	'lie'	t-onaapi-me	'given to lying'
t-akoono	'friend'	t-akoono-mbo	'her so-called friend'

In these cases, the first syllable of the stem does *not* receive stress. This suggests that an analysis whereby the prefix deposits stress on the "following" syllable is not correct. Instead, the true generalization over all the prefixed words we have seen thus far is that the syllable containing the second mora of the derived word is stressed.

This is confirmed by the behavior of disyllabic prefixes. Instead of placing stress on the following, stem-initial syllable, disyllabic prefixes themselves surface with stress. As one might predict it lands on the second syllable of the prefix.[13] Some examples are given in (17):

(17)

kïïri	'to make'	kïnii-kïrïï-taŋ	'he'll make it'
		kïnii-kïrïï-yaŋ	'he makes it'
		kïnii-kïrïï-yaa-toŋ	'they make it'
korootï	'??'	kïnii-korootï-ʔmaa-no	'it becomes fully
			burned off'
			3pers-burn_off-
			compl-pres
kuraama	'look after'	kïsii-kuraama-ko	'you must look after
			him'
		kïsii-kuraamaa-toŋ	'you must not look after
			them, you (pl) must not
			look after him, them'
		kïsii-kuraama-i	'you must not look after
			him'
		kïsii-kuraamaa-toŋ	'you (pl) must not look

---

[13]Since I have allowed the initial vowel of certain stems to be marked as long underlyingly, one might expect the same phenomenon to occur with prefixes. However, I have not found any prefixes which attract stress to their first syllable, and conclude that no prefixes have underlying long vowels.

7.3. STRONG SUFFIXES

			after him'
kuupi	'bathe'	kïsii-kupii-ya	'the two of us bathe him'
		kïnii-kupii-yaŋ̂	'he bathes him'
		kïnii-kupi-ŋ̂	'he really bathed him then'
		kïnii-kupii-po-yaŋ̂	'he has him bathed'
		kïsii-kuupi-potï-i	'you must not bathe him repeatedly'
		kïsii-kupii-take	'the two of us will bathe him'
		kïsii-kupii-taŋ̂	'shall the two of us bathe him?'
		kïsii-kupii-ya	'both of us bathe him'
		kïsii-kupii-ya-ŋ̂	'do both of us bathe him?'
mooroma	'overcome'	kïnii-mooromaa-no	'it overpowers him'
pakooto		kïnii-pakooto-yaa-toŋ̂	'they slash her'
paasama	'to pass'	kïnii-paasama-ʔmaa-toŋ̂	'he passed all of them'
piika	'to peel'	kïnii-pikaa-no	'she peels it'
pooka	'to shoot'	kïnii-pokaa-toŋ̂	'they shoot him'
poroopï	'to stop'	kïnii-poroo-saŋ̂	'he stops'
		kïnii-poroo-saa-toŋ̂	'they stop'

From these facts, we may safely conclude that stress is assigned by a single phonological rule. Moreover, the seemingly unexpected pattern of adjacent stressed syllables found in certain complex words can be generated only if the Carib stress rule applies cyclically, from which it follows as a natural consequence.

7.3 Strong Suffixes

With the case for cyclicity fairly well established, we now turn to a complexity in the data which elucidates the more subtle properties of the phonology-morphology interaction in Carib. This added complexity enters with what I will term the "strong" suffixes. Their most prominent representative is the nominal suffix -*rï*.

As noted by Hoff (pp. 74, 79, 216), -*rï* has a peculiar effect on the nouns it attaches to: consonant-initial stems with even-numbered stress systematically shift to an odd-numbered stress pattern upon suffixation with -rï. The phenomenon is illustrated in (18), where eight stems are shown in isolation and in combination with -rï. The suffix encodes the fact that the noun is possessed, or modified by an adjective:[14]

(18)

kuriita	'day'	kuuritaa-no-rï	'day'
kuriiyara	'canoe'	kuuriyaara-rï	'canoe'
paraapi	'bowl'	paarapii-rï	'bowl'
tampooko	'old man'	tampokoo-rï	'my old man = tremendous!'
waramba	'mat'	waarambaa-rï	'(my) mat'
wïrïïpo	'sweepings'	wïïrïpoo-rï	'sweepings'
yakuuwa	'spirit'	yaakuwaa-rï-koŋ	'spirits'
yamaatu	'basket'	yaamatuu-ru	'basket'
yopooto	'chief'	yoopotoo-rï	'chief'

The stress patterns of stems with initial short vowels in isolation and those with initial long vowels in isolation are neutralized when the stems are directly affixed with a strong suffix, as (19) illustrates:

(19)

	isolation	before strong suffix	gloss
a.	suurabaŋ	suurabaa-nï	'beam of roof'
	yamaatu	yaamatuu-ru	'basket'
b.	kaarawaasi	kaarawaasi-rï	'rattle'
	kuriiyara	kuuriyaa-rï	'canoe'

In this the strong suffix differ from the "weak" suffixes, i.e. those we have seen in preceding sections. In contrast to -rï, "weak" suffixes do not perturb the stress of the base they attach to.

---

[14] -rï shows up as -nï following nasals (e.g. suurabaŋ, şuurabaa-nï) and as -ru after u (e.g. yamaatu, yaamatuu-ru). This suffix encodes the same information about complement status that the e/o alternation discussed earlier revolves around; forms undergoing that alternation exhibit an o vowel when suffixed with -rï. However, the e/o alternation also takes place in contexts where the suffix is absent. Thus the two phenomena must be regarded as independent.

7.3. STRONG SUFFIXES

(20)

	isolation	gloss	before weak suffix	gloss
a.	kooroka	'scrub'	kookokaa-no	'he scrubbed'
	koroomo	'recent'	koroomo-no	'a recent thing'
b.	baasiya	'deputy-chief'	baasiyaa-koŋ̂	'deputy-chiefs'
	pakooto	'to cut wood'	pakooto-no	'fact of wood-cutting'
c.	kuruuwese	'palm shell'	kuruuwese-mbo	'old palm sheath'

(21) illustrates the one perfect minimal pair that I found in which the influence of strong and weak suffixes contrasts for the same stem.[15]

(21)

Isolation	Weak suffix	Strong suffix
kuriiyara	kuriiyaraa-koŋ̂	kuuriyaa-rï
'canoe'	'canoes'	'canoe'

A further unique property of the strong suffixes is that their stress-perturbing behavior is localized to consonant-initial stems. As (22) shows, vowel-initial stems do not display the same alternation that consonant-initial ones do. Instead they exhibit their isolation stress pattern when -rï is attached. In these forms, the strong suffix behaves in just the same manner as the weak suffixes we observed earlier.

(22)

akiinu	'laziness'	akiinu-ru	'his laziness'
areepa	'cassava bread'	ereepa-rï	'his cassava bread'
ineeku	'liana'	ineeku-ru	'liana'
ïraapa	'bow'	ïraapa-rï	'my bow'
okoomo	'wasp'	okoomo-rï	'wasp'
ooruwa	'three'	yooruwaano-rï	'third member'
oreeki	'wound'	ereeki-rï	'wound'

---

[15]There is no reason to think that such pairs are rare in the language (on the contrary, they ought to be abundant), but because of the nature of his exposition, Hoff does not actually happen to explicitly present any. This example was culled from the glossary.

oreemi	'medicine man's song'	ereemi-rï	'medicine man's song'
otïï-po	'beautiful sound of musical instrument'	etïï-po-rï	'beautiful sound of musical instrument'

In order to account for the behavior of this strong suffix[16] (opposed to the sixty or so 'weak' suffixes, which do not perturb the stress pattern normally associated with the stem), we must solve two problems: first, how strong suffixes avert the usual initial mora invisibility displayed by all the other (derived and underived) forms we have seen, and second, how strong suffixes are able to override the stress on the base. A cyclic analysis in standard Lexical Phonology would have assumed that stress is assigned to the stem on the very first cycle. If we follow suit, then we are obliged to explain why forms like *kuuriyaa-rï* bear no stress on the second syllable. Rules applying only to the stem would, as we have seen, assign stress there (cf. *kuriiyara*).

I will address the latter puzzle first, by making use of a property peculiar to the theory of Prosodic Lexical Phonology developed in the preceding chapters. In particular, I propose that, like English and Dakota, Carib has no preaffixal stem cycle. This twist has the consequence that a word directly suffixed with a strong suffix will possess no stress at the time that suffix is attached. We thus directly account for the lack of residue of stress from a previous stem cycle in just these cases.[17] In effect, it is as if stress rules applying to forms which acquire strong suffixes are subject to the Strict Cycle Condition, although that particular condition is impossible to implement here for two reasons. It would need look-ahead power (rules fail to apply only to those stems which later acquire strong suffixes) and also would require stress rules to be considered structure-changing — which they are patently not. At least in recent conceptions (Kiparsky 1982), only structure-changing rules are ever subject to strict cyclicity.

Recall that in the examples seen earlier where evidence from prefixation showed that stress must be assigned before the prefix is attached, the forms in question also bore suffixes. Although we had no reason at the time to question whether or not the stem underwent stress assignment before or after suffixation (empirically there would be no difference), we may now assume that in fact, the prefix cycle is only the *second* cycle — not the third — to take place in such words. The first cycle of rules takes

---

[16] Since the number of relevant forms is so small I cannot be sure, but the homophonous subordinating verbal suffix *rï*, and two allomorphs of the causative marker (*-po* and *-nopo*), appear to be members of the strong class as well.

[17] The strong suffix(es) can attach to complex stems, and in this case stress is preserved, as we will shortly see.

7.3. STRONG SUFFIXES

place upon suffixation.

(23)

    Morphological structure   Prosodic structure

    [i [[kurama] ko]]   [i [kurama ko]]

This mismatch in morphological and prosodic structure may be generated quite simply given the usual assumption that underived stems acquire prosodic constituency by the rule of Prosodic Constituent Formation. In Carib, we need only say that Prosodic Constituent Formation is ordered after affixation in order to derive the result that wherever affixation is possible, no cycle will take place beforehand on underived stems. Just as we suggested with respect to the English and Dakota facts in chapter , Prosodic Constituent Formation in Carib is a default, elsewhere process. It applies only to those stems which fail to achieve prosodic constituency by any other means.

(24) Carib: Affixation < PCF

Now that we have accounted for why the strong suffixes are oblivious to the isolation stress pattern of the stems they attach to, we may address the issue of why consonant-initial words ending in these suffixes fail to undergo the systematic initial mora invisibility which characterizes all other forms in the language.

I propose to solve this problem by decomposing initial mora invisibility into two subcomponents: initial consonant invisibility, and initial vowel invisibility.[18]

(25) Initial Vowel Invisibility: [v ...] ⟶ v [...]

Although all forms undergo the cyclic rule in (25) assigning invisibility to initial vowels, initial consonant invisibility comes not from a rule but from the subcategorization frames of affixes. If we suppose that weak suffixes, and all prefixes, impose invisibility on the word-initial consonant, then all we need to say about strong suffixes is that they make no special demands in this area. They are unique in *not* assigning initial consonant invisibility to the prosodic constituents that they form.

---

[18]To be precise, I mean initial vocalic mora.

(26)
                          Prosodic subcategorization frame

```
     prefix    kïni-    k [ ïni [   ] ]
weak suffix    -topo    c [[   ] topo ]
strong suffix  -rï      [[   ] rï ]
```

When both initial consonant and initial vowel invisibility take effect, as is the case in most consonant-initial forms, initial mora invisibility is achieved. As we have seen, this is generally the desired result.

(27)
```
UR                    kowaro,  c [[   ] no ]
Affixation            k [ owarono ]
Initial V Invisibility ko [ warono ]

Stress rule           ko [ wåaróno ]
                           s  w

                      'a very small one'
```

However, when a suffix in the strong class is attached to a consonant-initial stem, that initial consonant does not become invisible. As a consequence, the following vowel will be ineligible for Initial Vowel Invisibility (not being initial), and that entire first mora will be visible to the stress rule.

(28)
```
UR                    parapi,  [[   ] rï ]
Affixation            [ parapirï ]
Initial V Invisibility  —

Stress rule           [ påarápiirï ]
                        s  w  s  w

                      'bowl'
```

In case any suffix, either strong or weak, is attached to a stem begining with

7.3. STRONG SUFFIXES

a vowel, that vowel will become invisible by virtue of Initial Vowel Invisibility, and stress will land on the following syllable.

(29)

UR	akinu, c [[ ] ro]	arepa, [[ ] rï]
Affixation	[akinuro]	[areparï]
Initial V Invisibility	a [kinuro]	a [reparï]
Stress rule	a [kíinuro]	a [réeparï]
	'make lazy, languid'	'cassava bread'

Thus by decomposing initial invisibility into its two component parts, and assigning different prosodic subcategorization frames to the two different sets of suffixes, we are able to explain the asymmetry between consonant- and vowel-initial forms ending in the strong suffixes, as well as the asymmetry between strong and weak suffixes in Carib.

One may question whether this analysis, which must state consonant invisibility in the underlying prosodic subcategorization frame for each affix, truly captures the generalization that invisibility is the normal case. However, recall from the Appendix to chapter 5 that subcategorization frames are themselves entities to which rules can apply. A sample rule posited there provides that "a prosodically bound morpheme will form a prosodic constituent with the base. (i.e. construct the outermost bracketing in the prosodic subcategorization frame such that it includes the bound morpheme and the host.)" For Carib, we may amend this rule slightly so that the inserted frame omits the initial consonant of the base.

(30) Default rule for Carib lexical entries: "a prosodically bound morpheme will form a prosodic constituent with the base such that the initial consonant of the string forming the resulting morphological constituent is omitted from the corresponding prosodic constituent."

The standard assumption in this thesis has been that rules which assign prosodic structure apply only in the absence of structure of the type they would insert. Taking this to be true of (30) as well, we may leave the prosodic subcategorization frames for weak affixes underlyingly unspecified, while supplying the strong suffix with a fully specified prosodic frame which overrides the default rule in (30). Only the lexical entries for weak affixes will undergo the rule.

(31)

	Prefix	Weak suffix	Strong suffix
Lexical entry	kïni [ ]$_p$	[ ]$_p$ ko	[[ ]$_p$ rï]$_p$
Default rules	k [ini [ ]$_p$]$_p$	c [[ ]$_p$ ko]$_p$	—

The fact that additional lexical information must be stated for the strong suffix captures its more marked status with respect to the larger set of weak affixes.

7.4 Unaffixed Forms

As it stands, the analysis we have proposed has as its only source of initial consonant invisibility the subcategorization frames of prefixes and weak suffixes. However, this mechanism is not sufficient to account for the consonant invisibility evidenced in words consisting of unaffixed stems. (Sufficiently long) stems with a short first vowel consistently receive stress on the second syllable when they stand alone (see (1)), indicating that initial consonant invisibility (which feeds Initial Vowel Invisibility) must apply in these cases as well.

Because all unaffixed stems acquire their prosodic constituency by the default mechanism of Prosodic Constituent Formation, this rule is an obvious location for stating a generalization about the prosodic constituency of unaffixed stems. I therefore propose that in Carib, PCF forms prosodic rule domains which omit the initial consonant (if any) of the input morpheme.[19]

---

[19]Maintaining the active, unification approach to phonological processes, we must assume that the template in the PCF rule is imposed on the input regardless of whether that input has an initial consonant. If it does not, then the effect of the rule is simply to insert an empty skeletal position, subsequently erased by Stray Erasure.

7.4. UNAFFIXED FORMS

(32) Prosodic Constituent Formation (Carib):

Morphological constituency	Prosodic constituency		Morphological constituency	Prosodic constituency
[cv ...]		$\longrightarrow$	[cv ...]	c [v ...]

PCF sets up the environment for Initial Vowel Invisibility, and ensures the correct stress pattern for monomorphemic words.

(33)
```
UR                      yamatu
Affixation              —
PCF                     y [ amatu ]
Initial V Invisibility  ya [ matu ]

Stress rule             ya [ máatu ]
Output                  yamaatu
                        'basket [–poss]'
```

The Carib-specific version of PCF in (32) captures the fact that in the unmarked case, initial consonants will be invisible. Because PCF is bled by affixation in Carib, however, it will not have a chance to apply to any stem which acquires an affix. Thus, initial consonant invisibility can potentially be overridden by the information present in prosodic subcategorization frames. This is precisely what occurs in the case of strong suffixes, as shown below:

(34)
```
UR                      yamatu, [[  ] ru ]
Affixation              [ yamaturu ]
PCF                     —
Initial V Invisibility  —

Stress rule             [ yáamatúuru ]

Output                  yaamatuuru
                        'basket [+poss]'
```

In English, both PCF and the default parameters governing underspecified subcategorization frames build prosodic constituency around the entire morphological constituent; in Carib, both omit the initial consonant. If other languages turn out to exhibit similarities of this kind between the PCF and default parameters, the theory really ought to to relate the two by deriving both from a common source. One obvious possibility would be to allow underspecification of the PCF rule as well, and subject both it and prosodic subcategorization frames to the same default parameters. I leave it to future work to determine if this move is called for.

7.5 Prefixes and Strong Suffixes

Earlier, we saw that prefixes must attach after the weak suffixes, since stress assignment triggered by those suffixes crucially precedes the stress assignment triggered by prefixes. Crucial examples were of the type shown in (35), where the two adjacent long vowels in the second case represent the effects of cyclic stress assignment:

(35)
[k [aro - ko]] $\longrightarrow$ karooko   (*kaaroko)
[si [kurama - ko]] $\longrightarrow$ sikuuraamako   (*sikuuramaako)

The situation appears different with the strong suffix -rï. Consider the following forms:

(36)

aaro	'take'	n-aaro-rï	'be taken (sub.)'
		n-aaro-xto-rï	'what ___ cannot take'
		tï-n-aaro-rï	'what is taken by himself'
			3refl-PASS-take-rï
eene	'see'	n-eene-rï	'be seen(sub.)'
		n-eene-xto-rï	'what ___ cannot see'
		w-oone-po	'cause oneself to be visible'
eeta	'hear'	n-eeta-rï	'its being heard by ___'

Note that in each of the above examples, the consonant contributed by the prefix is made visible to -rï, inducing stress on the syllable whose onset it forms. Because

7.5. PREFIXES AND STRONG SUFFIXES

all prefix consonants are underlyingly invisible, the visibility of these consonants can only be accounted for on the assumption that -rï is added *after* the prefix. Cyclic invisibility erasure reincorporates the prefix into the prosodic domain, and the lexical specifications of -rï ensure that it remains visible.

(37)

UR	n [[ ]], ene, c [[ ] xto], [[ ] rï]
Affixation	[enexto]
Initial V Invisibility	e [nexto]
Stress rule	e [néxtŏ]
Affixation	n [enéxtŏ]
Initial V Invisibility	ne [néxtŏ]
Stress rule	—
Affixation	[nenéxtŏrï]
Initial V Invisibility	—
Stress rule	[neenéxtŏrï]

Thus, invisibility of the prefix consonant disappears upon subsequent attachment of the suffix.

To further illustrate the phenomenon, consider the following minimal pair. Though homophonous, the first contains contains an irrealis suffix of the large weak class, and the second contains the verbal -rï suffix of the small strong class.

(38)

n-enee-rï   'he would see it, but didn't'
n-eene-rï   'be seen (sub.)'

The difference in stress between these two words is accounted for by a difference in bracketing: the weak irrealis suffix -rï is added before prefixation, while the strong, subordinating verbal -rï is added after. Derivations of the two forms are shown below.

(39)

	UR	n [[ ]], ene, [[ ] -rï]
	Affixation	[enerï]
	Initial V Invisibility	e [nerï]
	Stress rule	e [née͡rï]
	Affixation	n [enée͡rï]
	Initial V Invisibility Stress rule	ne [née͡rï] —
	Output	neneerï 'he would see it, but didn't'

(40)

	UR	n [[ ]], ene, [[ ] -rï]
	Affixation	n [ene]
	Initial V Invisibility Stress rule	ne [ne] —
	Affixation Initial V Invisibility	[nenerï] —
	Stress rule	[née͡nerï]
	Output	neenerï 'be seen (sub.)'

There are two exceptions to the generalization that strong suffixes are attached last: the distancer suffix *-mbo* and the plural marker *-koŋ*, both of which occur word-finally in the forms I found.

7.6. MULTIPLE SUFFIXATION

(41)

aaro	'take'	an-aaro-rïï-koŋ	'being taken by you pl.'
		an-aaro-rï-mbo	'not really being taken by you'
aaru	'dryness'	aruu-ta-rïï-koŋ	'their getting dry'
kaapï	'to make'	kaapï-rï-mbo	'his former making'
wooma	'to fall'	wooma-rï-mbo	'nearly falling down'
ukuutï	'to know'	tï-n-uukutïï-rï-koŋ	'what is known by them'

The ordering claim could still be maintained if we could show that these two suffixes are, like the strong suffix rï, also attached after prefixation. The only examples which would test this hypothesis would be of the form prefix-CVCVCV-suffix; if the suffix is attached after the monosyllabic prefix, then the first and third syllables of the stem would be stressed. If the suffix is attached before the prefix, then the first and second syllables of the stems would be stressed. Unfortunately, however, I could find only one example of this kind, involving -koŋ. Although this one form supports the hypothesis that -koŋ is attached after prefixation, the paucity of data leaves the prediction essentially untested.[20]

(42) weemï 'basket' tu-weemï-koŋ 'his baskets'

7.6 Multiple Suffixation

The foregoing analysis makes certain predictions regarding the interaction of the strong and weak suffixes. In particular, it predicts that strong suffixes should not cause any disruption in the pre-existing stress pattern when they attach to a complex form.

Because the only direct effect of a strong suffix on a word is to make the entirety of consonant-initial words visible to the stress and invisibility rules, strong suffixes will trigger the incorporation of the first syllable of such words into a foot. In the case that the second syllable already belongs to a foot, the initial syllable ought to then

---

[20] Also, this form is taken from a narrative text collected by Hoff, unlike the rest of the data cited here, for which Hoff gives citation forms. By looking at some words which appear in both contexts, it seems that in connected speech subtle differences among words may sometimes be neutralized. This further weakens the significance of the one form in (41).

receive a unary foot. This is, in fact, what occurs, as demonstrated by the following examples.

In (43), the addition of *-rï* to a derived form *(n-aro-xto)*, which already bears stress on the second syllable, produces a form with stress on both the first and the second syllables.

(43)

UR	surface	gloss
aro-xto	aróxto	'who does not want to take'
n-aro-xpo	naróxpo	'having been taken by ___'
n-aro-xto-rï	naaróxtorï	'what ___ cannot take'

Under the assumption (motivated earlier) that strong suffixes are attached outside of prefixes, stress rules will already have built a single binary foot over the second and third syllables of the form *naaroxtori* by the time *-rï* is added. On that cycle, an additional unary foot is built on the initial syllable.

(44)
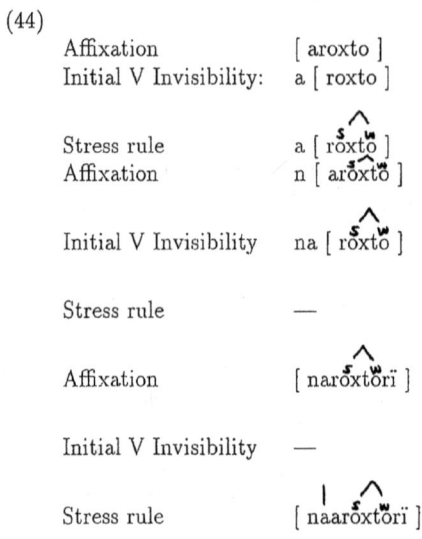

By contrast, if the strong suffix were stress-deleting, we would expect *naaroxtorï* to display the stress of a monomorphemic word suffixed with *-rï*. However, as we have seen, such forms exhibit alternating stress (e.g. *kuuriyaa-rï* 'canoe').

(45) *[nǎaróxtǒorï]

A similar example may be constructed using the verb *eene* 'see'. This verb has a short first vowel, as we can see from its behavior before the suffix *-xpo* in (46), and receives stress on the second syllable when the suffix is attached. However, when *-rï* is subsequently added, together with the accompanying prefix *ni-*, the first vowel becomes visible and receives a unary foot. We know that the prefix is not directly responsible for the stress pattern, as that same prefix does not contribute stress in the absence of *-rï* (in *n-enee-se*).

(46)

UR	surface	gloss
ene-xpo	enexpo	'having been seen'
n-ene-se	neneese	'so that he may see it'
n-ene-xto-rï	neenextorï	'what ___ cannot see'

Again, if *-rï* were stress deleting, it would cause two binary feet to be constructed on *n-ene-xto-ri*, resulting in the incorrect surface form **neenextoorï*.

7.7 Summary

To conclude this chapter, we have developed an analysis of Carib stress which makes crucial use of several unique aspects of Prosodic Lexical Phonology. First, an explanation of why suffixes appear to override the stress of underived but not of derived bases is attributed to the lack of a preaffixal stem cycle in Carib. While the failure of structure-building stress rules to apply in nonderived environments could only be stipulated in standard frameworks, it can be made to follow naturally in the prosodic theory, as a consequence of reversing the order of the only two extrinsically ordered rules in the set of lexical constituent formation processes.

Second, Carib provides important support for the domains account of invisibility, in at least two ways. First, the predicted cyclic loss of invisibility is borne out in Carib by the fact that invisible initial material will regain visibility upon attachment of a (strong) suffix. Not predicted by the Peripherality Condition of nonprosodic theories, this effect follows straightforwardly from the mechanisms for prosodic constituent creation provided in the prosodic approach to invisibility. Second, the ability of subcategorization frames to impose invisibility on the base, predicted in chapter 5, is attested in Carib, where certain suffixes render invisible the leftmost consonant of the base to which they attach.

Chapter 8

Clitics

In this chapter we will turn from lexical processes to clitics and see that postlexically, too, prosodic subcategorization frames help to solve a number of formerly intractable problems. To begin with, prosodic frames provide a formal means of distinguishing clitics from other words, instantiating in a principled way the descriptive feature [+clitic]. From this representation we can derive many of the categorial restrictions on what can be a clitic. Furthermore, the representation plays a non-diacritic role in the derivation of higher order structure. Not only do subcategorization frames affect the syntactic distribution of clitics by constraining the type of word that a clitic may lean on; they also actively contribute to the prosodic structure that differentiates clitics from nonclitic words. On this account, the surface representation of clitics follows directly from their lexical entries and independently motivated principles of the theory. No further machinery or stipulation is required.

The chapter is structured in the following way: First, clitics are identified as a set of words whose prosodic dependence must be indicated in the lexicon. Second, I show that certain of the defining phonological and syntactic characteristics of clitics follow naturally from the proposed lexical representation: prosodic subcategorization frames.

8.1 Clitics vs. Nonclitics

Given the wide range of phenomena for which the term 'clitic' has been used in the literature, it is important at the outset to be as explicit as possible about what exactly a clitic is. I take as a starting point that clitics are syntactic terminal elements — i.e. morphological 'words' — with the special property of being prosodically dependent on some other element (Zwicky 1977, 1985). A further generalization is that clitics are always function words, i.e. determiner, conjunction, pronoun, complementizer, preposition, etc.[1]

In the literature a one-to-one correspondence has often been assumed between function word status and clitichood (see e.g. Selkirk 1984, Hayes 1984/1989a, Berendsen 1986,[2] Selkirk and Shen 1990). For example, in a discussion of English Selkirk 1984 treats as clitic 'a word that is stressless and immediately adjacent, juncturally or rhythmically speaking, to what follows or what precedes' (Selkirk 1984:340). Along similar lines, Hayes 1984 characterizes the clitic group as 'a single content word together with all contiguous grammatical words in the same syntactic constituent' (Hayes 1984:12).

I will argue here, on the basis of English, that the implication between function word and clitic status does not hold universally.[3] That is, within the class of function words, important distinctions exist which the definitions of Selkirk and Hayes do not capture.

As pointed out by Kaisse 1985, there is a systematic difference among unstressed function words in English. For example, the voicing assimilation rule which we observed applying to the *'s* form of the auxiliary in chapter 5 does not apply to the unstressed function words *to, as, so* and *at* in similar environments:

(1)
    a. I don't know what I could've said to John. (*said /d/ə*)
    b. That dog's as tall as a horse. (*a/s/ tall*)
    c. She had never told so many lies in her life. (*told /z/o*)
    d. We sail at dawn.
    e. (*a/d́/ dawn*)

---

[1] See e.g. Carstairs 1981, who suggests that clitics are members of closed classes, Klavans 1982, who notes the absence of examples of lexical noun and lexical verb clitics across languages, and Zwicky 1985.

[2] Berendsen draws a distinction between word and phrase level adjunction which might be equivalent in some cases to the distinction between clitic and reduced function words.

[3] Parts of this analysis also appear in Zec and Inkelas 1987.

8.1. CLITICS VS. NONCLITICS

Second, unstressed function words differ with respect to the transparency of their phonological relationship to the corresponding full form. English has a rule of vowel reduction which takes short, unstressed vowels into ə, and as a result a function word, when unstressed, can surface sounding reduced. In some cases, the relationship between an unstressed function word and its full-form counterpart is quite regular, as provided by this reduction rule.

(2)

		Stressed form	Derived reduced form
Auxiliaries:	is	[ɨ]s
	can	c[ə]n
	will	w[ə]l
	has	h[ə]s
	have	h[ə]v
Prepositions:	in	[ɨ]n
	on	[ə]n
Pronouns:	them	th[ə]m
	us	[ə]s

However, this predictable correspondence does not obtain between all nonstressed function words and their full form (stressed) counterpart. In some cases, the reduced form is not derivable by any known phonological rules from the corresponding full form. In other cases, the unstressed function word has no full form counterpart at all (e.g. the English possessive 's). Function words whose unstressed form is not (synchronically) derivationally related to the stressed form are given below.

(3)

		Stressed form	Nonderived reduced form
Auxiliaries:	is	's
	would	'd
	has	's
	have	've
Prepositions:	of	o'

Pronouns: them   'əm
            him   'əm

I will assume, with Kaisse 1985, that the predictable and unpredictable subclasses of function words correspond to clitics and nonclitics, respectively. The latter category will henceforth be referred to as 'reduced'. Clitics are idiosyncratic, lexically listed bound forms, while reduced forms are simply the derived surface form of function words in unstressed phrasal position. The fact that clitics are lexically listed explains why their phonological relationship with a corresponding full form (if any) is not necessarily transparent.

It also explains why some some full form function words in English have two unstressed counterparts, while others have only one. All function words whose vowels are subject to reduction to begin with will surface as reduced in unstressed position; the alternation between reduced and unreduced forms is entirely predictable from the environment. In addition to this potential alternation, however, certain function words also possess a lexically listed clitic allomorph. In some cases, these independent dimensions conspire to produce three alternate realizations for what appears to be the same function word.

(4)

		stressed form (derived)	reduced form (nonderived)	clitic form
Auxiliaries:		has	h[ə]s	's
		have	h[ə]v	'v
		is	[ɨ]s	's
		will	w[ə]l	'l
Pronouns:		them	th[ə]m	[ə]m

In addition to phonological asymmetries, syntactic differences support the subclassification into clitics and reduced function words. Neither reduced function words (as in (5)) nor clitics (in (6)) can appear at the end of a phonological phrase:[4]

---

[4]Pronouns and nonfinite auxiliaries are a systematic exception to this generalization, e.g. *Yes, she could've* or *Yes, she left'əm*. Zec and Inkelas 1987 derive the asymmetry between finite auxiliary

(5)
   a. *That's the chair Sarah sat ən.
   b. *I don't know where the party əs.
   c. *I don't know who Max gave the potato tə.
   d. *What did Max stand on his head fər?
   e. *Is that the paper you think so well əf?

(6)
   a. *I don't know where the party's.
   b. *What weight of paper would you like a ream o'?
   c. *I doubt that she'll.

But the two categories are separated out in phrase-initial position, where reduced function words can occur but (en)clitics can not. (7) illustrates phrase-initial reduced forms of the preposition *of* and the auxiliaries *is* and *will*:

(7)
   a. əf the many good-hitting first basemen in the National League, I think I like Will Clark the best.
   b. əf all the books in the library, she had to check out just the one we needed.
   c. əz Anne eating peanut butter for a reason?
   d. əll Eric renew his driver's license before driving to Boston?

(8) shows that the corresponding clitic forms are not licensed in the same phrase-initial context:

---

clitics on the one hand, and nonfinite auxiliary and pronoun clitics on the other, by proposing that members of the the first subclass of clitics subcategorize, in the style proposed by Klavans, for a syntactic phrasal sister. This condition, which pronouns are exempt from, is not met when a finite auxiliary is stranded. Another apparent exception is forms like *wanna, gotta, hafta,* which can occur phrase-finally for some speakers in sentences like *I know I gotta but I just don't wanna.* However, even for these speakers the phenomenon appears to be localized to a small set of verbs. It is not at all productive. I therefore assume that forms like *wanna* are fossilized, nonderived and therefore not relevant to our discussion of clitics.

(8)
    a. *ə the many good-hitting first basemen in the National League, I think I like Will Clark the best.

    b. *ə all the books in the library, she had to check out just the one we needed.

    c. *Z Anne eating peanut butter for a reason?

    d. *L Eric ever renew his ACLU membership?

On the basis of distributional and phonological facts like the above we can safely conclude, as does Kaisse 1985, that there is a systematic difference between clitics and those function words that are reduced by phonological rules applying to unstressed syllables. We cannot automatically assume that just because a word is unstressed, or reduced, or a member of a minor category, that it is necessarily a clitic.

To sum up this discusion, the conditions we have claimed necessary for clitichood are given below:

(9)
    a. Clitics are separate syntactic terminals.

    b. Clitics cannot be pronounced in isolation.

    c. Clitics are always function words.

8.2 Clitics and Prosodic Subcategorization

In the previous section I argued that 'function word' does not entail 'clitic'. However, as I will argue in this section, the opposite is true: 'clitic' does entail 'function word.' Furthermore, I show that this implication can be derived without stipulation in the proposed framework. It follows from the representation proposed for clitics in chapter 4, namely that clitics possess a prosodic but not a morphological subcategorization frame.

(10) Clitic: -z :   [[ ]$_p$ ---]$_p$

The generalizations in (9a) and (9b) are encapsulated in this representation. Because they lack a morphological frame, clitics do not require a morphological sister, and can form syntactic terminals. Because they possess a prosodic frame, they must

8.2. CLITICS AND PROSODIC SUBCATEGORIZATION

be a proper subpart of some prosodic constituent. Prosodic restrictions prevent clitics from standing on their own.

From the simple representation in (10) we can also derive generalization (9c), above. Instead of being an accident, the restriction of clitics to function word classes follows naturally from the proposed framework.

To prove that the implication expressed in (9c) is correct, let us first consider the alternative hypothesis. Suppose some content word, x, possessed the underlying representation attributed to clitics:

(11) Hypothetical content word enclitic:

> Morphological structure   Prosodic structure.
>
> $[[\ ]_p \text{ x }]_p$

Like all other content words, $[[\ ]_p \ x \ ]_p$ will be subject to lexical rules. Thus it undergoes the rule of Morphological Constituent Formation:

(12) Hypothetical content word enclitic (after undergoing MCF):

> * Morphological structure   Prosodic structure
>
> $[\text{ x }]_m$ $\qquad\qquad\qquad [[\ ]_p \text{ x }]_p$

But this representation is ill-formed: its prosodic subcategorization frame is not satisfied. If the form in (12) does not combine with any other morpheme, it will, as a non-constituent, not be allowed to leave the lexicon, and the derivation cannot continue.[5]

Suppose, then, that the content word clitic does combine with another morpheme in the lexicon. In (13) we see the result of combining x with some stem, y. The requirements of x's prosodic subcategorization frame are now satisfied. (We can abstract away from the details of constituent type — they are unimportant here.)

---

[5]The constraint against empty constituents is, of course, needed independently in order to prevent bound roots and affixes from being inserted as syntactic terminal elements (chapter 5); it also serves the important function of prohibiting exhaustive invisibility (chapter 6).

(13)

	Morphological structure	Prosodic structure
Combination:	$[[\ y\ ]_m\ x\ ]_m$	$[[\ y\ ]_p\ x\ ]_p$
Bracket Erasure:	$[\ yx\ ]_m$	$[\ yx\ ]_p$

The output of this process, yx, corresponds to well-formed constituents in both the morphological and the prosodic hierarchies. All is well — except that the hypothetical content word clitic, x, no longer has any prosodic requirements left. It is part of a well-formed independent word that fills a single syntactic terminal position. In the postlexical phonology, there is no reason to expect any special prosodic behavior from either x or yx. x is not, in other words, a clitic.

We have now shown that there is no way to generate a content word clitic in this framework. At the output of the lexicon, the clitic will either be ill-formed, and hence rejected; or it will have already satisfied its subcategorization requirements, failing to meet the definition of clitichood. Thus even if prosodic subcategorization frames were overgenerated on content words in underlying representation, the resultant forms would not be allowed by the theory to surface as clitics. The learner will have no reason ever to postulate the existence of such entities.

Now compare the bad results of hypothesizing a content word clitic to the situation of a *function* word clitic, e.g. the English auxiliary *'s*. Unaffected by lexical rules, *'s* enters the prosodic hierarchy only postlexically, where it will successfully combine with the preceding word according to the demands of its prosodic subcategorization frame.

(14) $[\text{John}]_\omega + [\ [\ ]_\omega\ \text{'s}]_\omega \longrightarrow [\text{John's}]_\omega$

In conclusion, given the rules of prosodic and morphological constituent formation, we have shown that the only way for a morpheme with lexically encoded postlexical dependence to survive a derivation is if that morpheme is a function word. We thus explain the distributional generalization about the syntactic category of clitics.

(15) All clitics are function words, although not all function words are clitics.

This result provides an account of another previously unexplained cross-linguistic generalization about clitics: they are morphologically simplex.[6] If clitics underwent lexical rules, we would have no account for this phenomenon. But it is explained by our conclusion that clitics never undergo lexical rules — and thus never encounter affixation processes.

A third implication of this result is that it helps to explain certain phonological asymmetries obtaining between clitics and nonclitics. Past definitions of clitics have distinguished clitics from nonclitics on certain phonological grounds. For example, Neijt 1984 claims that clitics are universally monosyllabic, and weakly or not at all stressed.

While it is true that clitics tend to be phonologically 'weaker' than nonclitic words, it is not quite true to claim universal stresslessness or monosyllabicity. Greek clitics can surface with (postlexically assigned) stress; disyllabic clitics occur in Serbo-Croatian.

I suspect that, in languages where clitics do systematically lack some phonological feature that full words possess, we can actually derive this asymmetry from the more general fact that clitics, as function words, do not undergo lexical rules. In Serbo-Croatian, for example, clitics never receive the stress and High tone that characterize all content words. In English, clitics, unlike content words, never receive word stress. The crucial generalization is that in both these languages, the phonological properties which clitics lack are assigned only by *lexical* rules.

8.3 Prosodic Category of Clitic

The banishment of clitics from lexical rules sharply limits the number of possible prosodic candidates for the their prosodic subcategorization frames. In particular, only the constituents available postlexically are predicted to be able to host a clitic:

(16) phonological word, phonological phrase, intonation phrase, utterance

I will have nothing to say about the largest two constituents, which have received relatively less attention in the literature.[7] However, I will propose that both of the

---

[6]One possible exception is discussed in Klavans 1983, who characterizes Ngiyambaa as having inflected clitics.

[7]See, however, Rice 1987, Selkirk and Tateishi 1988, Selkirk and Shen 1990 for detailed studies of intonational phrasing.

smaller postlexical constituents are possible candidates for the target of prosodic subcategorization. In Serbo-Croatian and English, the clitic host is the phonological word. In Hausa and Kivunjo Chaga it is the phonological phrase.[8]

8.3.1 Phonological Word: Serbo-Croatian

Serbo-Croatian, like other Slavic languages, has a number of second position clitics. As they are typically described, these clitics can follow either the first word or the first syntactic constituent of a sentence. Thus, any sentence containing clitics which begins with a complex initial constituent has two possible variants: one where the clitics follow that constituent and one in which the clitics follow the first word.

But as Browne 1974 observes, Serbo-Croatian clitics may not follow just any initial word. Inkelas and Zec 1988 and Zec and Inkelas 1990 show that in fact the clitics are restricted to following a *phonological* word. As mentioned back in chapter 2, the distribution of these clitics is prosodically as well as syntactically constrained.

According to Inkelas and Zec, phonological words may be identified by three phonological criteria: they always surface with High tone and stress, whereas non-phonological words do not; they are the only words which can be emphasized;[9] and they constitute exactly the class of words which may host clitics. Phonological words are formed in the lexicon, so that the set of phonological words subsumes the set of content words. Thus, second position clitics may follow a noun, verb or adjective. But they may *not* follow a preposition.

That the conditions on second word clitics are crucially prosodic as opposed to syntactic is demonstrated by the behavior of conjunctions. According to Browne 1974, in clauses introduced by a conjunction, enclitics may follow the conjunction if and only if it is 'accented' (i.e. if it bears High tone and stress.) Certain conjunctions are always High-toned, and others are never High. But two conjunctions, *ali* 'but' and *pa* 'and, and so', have the option of surfacing as either High or Low. And second position clitics can follow only when the High-toned variant is selected. Inkelas and

---

[8]As Condoravdi 1990 has shown, Greek requires a constituent intermediate in size between the word and phonological phrase; and Kanerva 1989 introduces a new Focal phrase, above the level of the phonological phrase, to handle a number of postlexical rules in Chicheŵa. It is likely that more evidence will soon accrue from other languages that the prosodic hierarchy is more language particular than has previously been assumed. I thus do not mean to claim here that the word and 'phonological phrase' universally exhaust the types of host a clitic might select for. However, in regard to clitics I have so far examined only languages with evidence for just two smallish postlexical prosodic constituents.

[9]Not all phonological words may be emphasized. The implication holds only in one direction.

8.3. PROSODIC CATEGORY OF CLITIC

Zec 1988 interpret all of these facts to mean that the two conjunctions have two lexically listed allomorphs, one of which constitutes a phonological word. In their phonological word guise they receive High tone and stress — and may host clitics.

While a purely syntactic treatment would have no account for these clitic facts, our prosodic framework handles them straightforwardly. We build into the lexical entry of each Serbo-Croatian second position enclitic the following prosodic subcategorization frame:

(17) $[\ [\quad]_{p_\omega}\ \text{---}\ ]_{p_\omega}$

I consider it an open question at this point whether or not all clitics in a given language will subcategorize for the same type of prosodic constituent. We know that affixes can choose among constituents of different types; it is logically possible that in some language different clitics might also opt for different postlexical constituents. However, at least in Serbo-Croatian all enclitics seem to subcategorize for the phonological word. I propose to capture this generalization by means of a rule. Like the redundancy rules posited at the end of chapter 5 to eliminate the need for redundant underlying information, this rule applies to subcategorization frames. It adds to underspecified clitic frames the specification that the subcategorized constituent is of type ω.[10]

(18) $[\ [\quad]_p\ \text{---}\ ]_p\quad \longrightarrow\quad [\ [\quad]_{p_\omega}\ \text{---}\ ]_{p_\omega}$

An additional fact about Serbo-Croatian second position clitics is that quite commonly, more than one clitic follows the first word (or constituent). For example, the sentence in (19) contains four clitics:[11]

(19) Zašto=li=mu=ga=je   poklonila?
     Why=Q=to-him=him=AUX   presented
     'Why did she present it to him?'

---

[10] Note that, as stated, the rule appears to apply to all prosodic frames. Of course that is not what we want, as the rule should not apply to the frames of affixes. Recall from chapter 5 that these receive their constituent type specification by a rule copying information from the morphological frame onto the prosodic frame. However, suppose we take the usual road and construe (18) as a feature-filling rule. Then by ordering it after the rule copying morphological constituent type onto prosodic frames, we derive the correct result that (18) will apply only to those frames which are still unspecified for constituent type— i.e., to the frames of clitics.

[11] Thanks to Draga Zec for providing this example.

Each one of these clitics has a lexical representation containing a prosodic subcategorization frame like that given in (17). After concatenation, the sentence in (19) acquires the prosodic representation in (20):

(20)   [[[[[Zašto]ω li]ω mu]ω ga]ω je]ω [poklonila]ω

This representation is entirely consistent with the generalization that clitics must attach to a phonological word. The innermost clitic forms a phonological word with the first lexical phonological word in the sentence, *Zašto*; this complex phonological word, *Zašto=li*, in turn acts as host for the second clitic, and so on.[12]

Prosodic constraints on clitic positioning like those holding in Serbo-Croatian have been noted for other languages in the literature (e.g., Pashto, Ancient Greek, and Ngiyambaa (Kaisse 1985:79-80)). The proposal advanced here offers a unified formal means for encoding these constraints in the grammar.

8.3.2 Phonological Word: English

In Serbo-Croatian, as we saw, only content words end phonological words, and as a consequence only content words can host clitics.[13]

But this situation is not the only logical possibility. Suppose that some language had the same constraint as Serbo-Croatian on what clitics can attach to, but a different mapping between syntactic terminals and phonological words. We would thus expect the distribution of clitics to vary accordingly.

I would like to suggest English as such a language. Zec and Inkelas 1987 motivate treating every nonclitic word in English as a phonological word. Among nonclitic words are included a number of function words. Thus, English differs from Serbo-Croatian, in which virtually no function words are phonological words.

The argument, which we saw above, has to do with stress. While only those words which undergo lexical rules acquire word stress, disyllabic (nonclitic) function words do receive secondary stress. Moreover, the location of that stress is predictable. Zec and Inkelas conclude from this that nonclitic function words form domains for the application of postlexical phonological stress rules. In order for this to be true they must constitute phonological words.

---

[12] An unresolved question is how to derive the relative order of the clitics, which is predictable; I do not attempt an analysis here.

[13] Excepting, of course, the two conjunctions.

8.3. PROSODIC CATEGORY OF CLITIC

It ought to follow from this claim, then, that if clitics in English subcategorize for the phonological word,[14] they should in principle be able to attach to a word of any syntactic category.[15] English should not have the prosodic constraints against clitic attachment to function words exhibited by Serbo-Croatian. And this turns out to be true. (21) shows a verb, a noun, an adjective, a preposition, a pronoun, and a complementizer acting as host of an English auxiliary clitic:

(21)
   a. Everyone I meet's asking for free copies.
   b. President Duck's giving a news conference in April.
   c. The woman we all considered laconic's really a famous stand-up comedian.
   d. The reporter Hart snapped at's writing an article for the National Enquirer.
   e. The guy who saw it's gonna testify in court tomorrow.
   f. We'll talk no longer than's necessary to get the point across.

We thus tentatively confirm a prediction of our framework: that if we hold clitic subcategorization constant, and vary the distribution of phonological words, then the distribution of clitics ought to vary accordingly. A framework without prosodic subcategorization would have no explanation for this correlation.

8.3.3 Phonological Phrase: Hausa

As argued in Inkelas 1988,[16] the distribution of the conversational particle *fa* in Hausa provides evidence for the existence in Hausa of the phonological phrase. In particular, *fa* is licensed only at the right edge of such a phrase. Because *fa* is not separable by pause from what precedes, I take it to be a clitic; the fact of its distribution suggests that it is enclitic onto the phonological phrase.

---

[14] There is no way to analyze English enclitics as attaching to the phonological phrase, for the simple reason that there is a constraint against clitics in phrase-final position (for more discussion, see Zec and Inkelas 1987).

[15] Of course, this is an overstatement. Like other words, clitics are subject to word order constraints imposed by the syntax. What I am really claiming is that *if* an enclitic is blocked from attaching to a word on its left, the reason will not be that the word on the left has the wrong prosodic status.

[16] This section was presented at WCCFL 7, and a more detailed writeup is to be found in the proceedings of that conference. The original investigations were undertaken together with Lawan Yalwa, to whom I am greatly indebted. Aaron Halpern provided comments of a crucial nature at a crucial juncture. Parts of the analysis also appear in Inkelas and Zec 1988.

highlights the word or constituent that it follows. Never allowed at the beginning of an utterance, *fa* can always occur utterance-finally, and is inseparable by pause from the preceding word. *fa* is also found utterance-medially, but it cannot show up just anywhere.

Fa can occur between two words iff at least one of the following conditions holds:

(22)
    a. The second word is the first element of a branching maximal projection

    b. The second word is intonationally emphasized

    c. The first word belongs to the first constituent in the sentence

The examples in (23)-(25) show sentences in which one of the conditions in (22) is met, and where *fa* is licensed.

(23)
    a.   Ya sayi **fa** babbar riga.
           he bought big shirt
           'He bought a gown'

    b.   Ya sayi **fa** riga babba.
           he bought shirt big
           'He bought a gown'

    c.   Ya sayi **fa** rigar Audu.
           he bought shirt-of Audu
           'He bought Audu's shirt'

    d.   Ya sayi **fa** riga da wando.
           he bought shirt and pants
           'He bought a shirt and pants'

    e.   Ta dubi **fa** tebur guda shida.
           She looked-at table unit six
           'She looked at six tables'

    f.   Mun sauka a **fa** birnin Kano.
           we arrived at town-of Kano
           'We arrived at the town of Kano'

8.3. PROSODIC CATEGORY OF CLITIC

g. Sun zo da **fa** can yamma.
they came in far afternoon
'They came that afternoon'

h. Sun zo da **fa** ƙarfe takwas.
they came at o'clock eight
'They came at eight o'clock'

(24)

a. Ya sayi **fa** *teburin*.
he bought table-def.
'He bought the *table*'

b. Ya sayi **fa** *rigar*.
he bought shirt-def.
'He bought the *shirt*'

c. An haife shi a **fa** *Kano*
one gave-birth-to him in *Kano*
'He was born in Kano'

d. Ya zo da **fa** *ƙafa*
he came by *foot*
'He came by foot'

(25)

a. Yaron **fa** alaramma ya nemi nama.
Boy-of alaramma he looked-for meat
'The boy of the alaramma looked for meat'

b. Sabon **fa** littafi ya yi tsada.
new book it does expensiveness
'The new book is expensive'

c. Tebur **fa** babba yana waje.
table big it-masc.-cont. outside
'The big table is outside'

d. Babbar **fa** riga na saya.

>   big shirt I bought
>   'A gown, I bought'
>
> e. Guda fa shida muka rubuta.
>   unit six we wrote
>   'Six of them, we wrote'
>
> f. A fa Kano aka haife shi.
>   in Kano one gave-birth-to him
>   'In Kano, he was born'

The examples in (26) show that if none of the conditions in (22) is met, sentences with medial *fa* will be ungrammatical.

(26)
> a. *Ya sayi fa abinci
>   'He bought food'
>
> b. *Ya sayi fa abinci jiya
>   'He bought food yesterday'
>
> c. *Mun sauka a fa Kano.
>   'We arrived at Kano'
>
> d. *Sun zo da fa yamma.
>   they came in afternoon
>   'They came in the afternoon'
>
> e. *An haife shi a fa Kano.
>   one gave-birth-to him in Kano
>   'He was born in Kano'
>
> f. *Mun rubuta wasiƙa guda fa shida.
>   we wrote letter unit six
>   'We wrote six letters'
>
> g. *Ta siffanta wa Audu fa riga.
>   she described to Audu shirt
>   'She described a shirt to Audu'

Analysis

Attempting to state the conditions on the occurrence of *fa* in syntactic terms results in the following list of constraints:

(27)
    a. No utterance may begin with *fa*.

    b. If *fa* immediately precedes any material, then that material must be (i) a branching constituent or (ii) emphasized.

    c. Condition (b) is suspended within the initial constituent of an utterance.

We can reduce the arbitrariness of this list somewhat by isolating a common thread connecting two of the four post-*fa* environments where branching is irrelevant, i.e. within the initial constituent (c) and immediately preceding any emphasized material (b). These two environments pattern together in Hausa as methods of prominence.

(28) Prominent constituents:

    a. Initial
    b. Emphasized

Locating a constituent at the beginning of the utterance alternates with special uses of intonation as a means of emphasis in Hausa. The intuition that the syntactic and intonational mechanisms are just different manifestations of the same entity, which I call here 'prominence', is supported by the fact that when speakers highlight a word or phrase by fronting it, they do not have to employ any intonational tactics to get the emphatic effect across. Special intonation is by contrast obligatory for non-initial prominent material.[17]

Even if we find a way of representing prominence syntactically, however, the 'account' in (27) would still amount to little more than a description of the facts; it lists environments without capturing their relationship. Among the unexplained generalizations are the following:

---

[17]Although Hausa does exhibit quite complex intonational phenomena, it fits the general pattern of lexical tone languages in providing syntactic outlets for some of the effects that are expressed intonationally in stress languages like English.

(29)   a. Why *fa* should care about emphasis on the right — when its function is to highlight the material on the left
       b. Why branching constituents, prominence, and utterance-final position pattern together as the possible right-hand environments for *fa*
       c. Why the utterance-initial element does not share whatever property connects the positions enumerated in (b)
       d. Why *fa*, an element whose semantic effect is felt on the left, and which is prosodically bound to the material on the left, should be conditioned by any material on the right at all

The severity of these problems for a purely syntactic account of the distribution of *fa* suggests that perhaps syntax is not the proper arena in which to seek a solution. When the problem is viewed from the point of prosodic structure things fall into place much more nicely.

In Inkelas 1988 the following phrasing algorithm is proposed for Hausa.

(30) Hausa Phrasing Algorithm:

   a. From the bottom up, branching nodes are mapped into phonological phrases.
   b. Phonological words unphrased by (a) will be grouped into maximally large phonological phrases, subject to the condition that no two phonological words on opposite sides of an XP boundary may be phrased together to the exclusion of any other material in either XP.

Each clause of this general algorithm is paralleled by clauses of phrasing algorithms in other languages.[18] In fact, it is virtually identical to that proposed for English by Zec and Inkelas 1987. Both clauses of the algorithm are overridden by a third provision, namely the phrasing of prominent elements. That is, where the clauses would produce different phrasings, the Elsewhere Condition provides that the requirements of the more specific clause prevail.[19]

---

[18]Branching plays a role in the phrasing algorithms developed for Mende by Cowper and Rice 1987, and for Kinyambo by Bickmore 1990. The proviso against straddling XP breaks occurs generally in the algorithms of Nespor and Vogel 1986, and in the parameters of Selkirk 1986, among others.

[19]Prominence, or focus of some sort, is another well-known cross-linguistic factor in phonological phrasing; see e.g. Cho 1990; Vogel and Kenesei 1990; Zec and Inkelas 1987, 1990;, Condoravdi 1990;

8.3. PROSODIC CATEGORY OF CLITIC

(31) Prominent elements (emphasized words, daughters of initial constituents) will begin a new phonological phrase

With these conditions in place, all that needs to be said for *fa* is the following:

(32) *fa* must follow a phonological phrase.

To see how the algorithm works, let us consider a few of the examples seen earlier.

Part (a) accounts for all of the simple branching conditions to the right of *fa* which we observed earlier. For example, it explains why *fa* can precede the branching NP in (33):

(33) [Ta]$_\phi$ [[sayi]$_\phi$ fa]$_\phi$ [babban tebur]$_\phi$
     she   bought   big   table
     'She bought a big table'

Part (b) deals with those words left unphrased by the more specific clause (a). By grouping together adjacent unphrased elements it explains why, for example, a non-branching NP direct object like that in (34) will phrase with the preceding verb:

(34) [[Ya]$_\phi$ fa]$_\phi$ [sayi tebur]$_\phi$
     he   bought table
     'He bought a table'

It correctly predicts that non-branching objects in double object constructions will phrase together:

(35) [[Mun]$_\phi$ fa]$_\phi$ [biya Audu kuɗi]$_\phi$
     we   paid Audu money
     'We paid Audu money'

and that they will phrase with a following adverb, if any:

Kanerva 1989, 1990; and Selkirk and Shen 1990 for related examples analyzed in a similar way in the prosodic hierarchy framework.

(36) [[Mun]$_\phi$ fa]$_\phi$ [biya Audu kuɗi jiya]$_\phi$
we   paid Audu money yesterday
'We paid Audu money yesterday'

The proviso in (30b) against allowing a phonological phrase to straddle only one of the edges of a maximal projection is designed to handle the phrasing of words dominated by maximal projections that themselves already contain a phonological phrase. Take, for example, the NP *tebur guda shida* 'table unit six = six tables'. *guda shida* is a maximal projection and will be mapped into a phonological phrase by part (a) of the phrasing algorithm. The question now is, will the head noun *tebur* phrase with the preceding verb, as in (34), or will it constitute its own phonological phrase? The answer is the latter. As the algorithm predicts, *fa* is possible before any branching NP, regardless of the details of that NP's internal constituent structure.

(37)

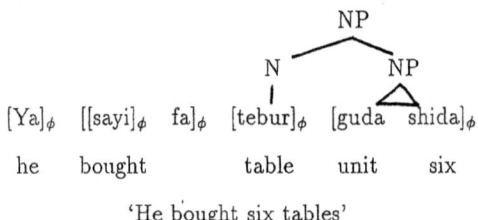

[Ya]$_\phi$ [[sayi]$_\phi$ fa]$_\phi$ [tebur]$_\phi$ [guda shida]$_\phi$
he   bought   table   unit   six
'He bought six tables'

The same is true of prepositional phrases which contain branching NP's: *fa* is always allowed to precede, indicating that the head preposition itself forms a phonological phrase, as in (38). As clause (30b) predicts, the phonological phrase containing the preposition is bounded by the left edge of the PP, and does not group the preposition together with the preceding element.[20]

---

[20]It may seem counterintuitive to attribute phonological phrase status to a preposition, but the theory forces this analysis. The possibility of treating the preposition as a proclitic is simply unavailable, due to the observed possibility of separating it from what follows by pause or by *fa*. True clitics in Hausa, such as direct object pronouns and, for that matter, *fa* itself, are not separable in this manner from their host.

8.3. PROSODIC CATEGORY OF CLITIC

(38)

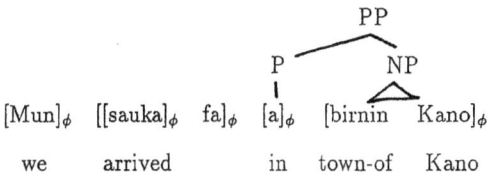

[Mun]$_\phi$ [[sauka]$_\phi$ fa]$_\phi$ [a]$_\phi$ [birnin Kano]$_\phi$
we   arrived   in   town-of Kano

'We arrived in the town of Kano'

In formal terms, I treat *fa* as a clitic, and assign to it a prosodic subcategorization frame which mentions the phonological phrase. The frame given in (39) ensures that *fa* will be incorporated into the phonological phrase which it follows, satisfying the requirements of the Exhaustive Parsing constraint — and explaining why it is impossible to pause before *fa*.

(39) [[   ]$_\phi$ fa]$_\phi$

By attributing the constraints on the syntactic distribution of *fa* to the presence of a phonological phrase break at each potential *fa* site, we capture several important generalizations:

(40)
   a. The constraint in (32(=39)) refers only to the the left-hand context of *fa*, consistent with *fa*'s leftward syntactic and prosodic attachments.
   b. We explain why intonational emphasis, branching constituents, and zero pattern together as the possible right-hand contexts for *fa*; these are exactly the environments which can follow the end of a phrase.
   c. We correctly predict that *fa* is blocked utterance-initially — as no phonological phrase precedes.
   d. We explain why speakers cannot pause between *fa* and what precedes: *fa* is an enclitic

Thus on both descriptive and explanatory grounds, the prosodic account for the distribution of *fa* is supported over a nonprosodic account.

Active Subcategorization Revisited

In the preceding analyses of English and Hausa, I have been implicitly referring to subcategorization as though it were of the passive kind, implying the phrasal clitics in Hausa can only attach to something that is already marked as a phrase. This may seem incompatible with the proclamation of chapter 5 that all subcategorization is 'active'. Recall that in that chapter, I argued for the active interpretation of subcategorization by observing that affixes can combine with bound roots, though these have no pre-existing prosodic structure. The claim is that affixes contribute to the representation the information that what they are attaching to is a prosodic constituent of type i. Unless this information conflicts with information already present, the combination is allowed. In the case of bound roots, no information about prosodic constituency exists on the base, and so combination with affixes is always permitted.

One may wonder why phrasal clitics do not behave in the same way as affixes which attach to bound roots. Before the phrasing algorithm applies, no information about phonological phrase structure exists in the string. Why, then, is the phrasal clitic *fa* not allowed to be inserted freely, imposing phrasal constituency on whatever it follows, thereby overriding the default phrasing algorithm?

(41) ... sayi fa tebur $\longrightarrow$ [[sayi]$_\phi$ fa]$_\phi$ tebur

The answer is that although phrasal constituency is not present upon entrance to the postlexical phonology, information about phonological word status is. If a phrasal clitic attempted to combine directly with a phonological word, before the phrasing algorithm had applied, a feature clash would result with respect to the category of the host constituent.

(42) *[[sayi]$_{\phi,\omega}$ fa]$_\phi$ [tebur]$_\omega$

This is exactly the same behavior exhibited by β suffixes in English. As we saw in chapter 5, these suffixes cannot combine directly with an α constituent. Instead they must wait for the β Prosodic Constituent Formation algorithm to apply. Only after the base has been mapped into a β constituent is it able to combine with the β suffix. Thus cliticization patterns with β affixation in that both take place after the requisite prosodic structure is already in place. The subcategorization frame of

8.3. PROSODIC CATEGORY OF CLITIC

fa is unable to be satisfied until the phrasing algorithm has parsed the sentence into phonological phrases.

We have answered the question of why *fa* doesn't override the phrasing algorithm; we may now ask the opposite, also legitimate question, namely why the phrasing algorithm doesn't override the prosodic requirements of *fa*, grouping *fa* into phrases just like any other words? The answer is that the phrasing algorithm is, like all of the other rules proposed here, strictly structure-building, i.e. subject to the Elsewhere Condition. Though it builds prosodic constituency largely on the basis of syntactic structure, the algorithm is sensitive to the prosodic structure of its input. It operates as an elsewhere case, assigning phrasal constituency only to material already lacking it. Because the phrasal clitic *fa* already has prosodic specifications, it will not be touched by the algorithm. Instead, *fa* will be incorporated into phrasal structure only after phrases are built. We must assume that the prosodic requirements of *fa* are held in abeyance until that point.

8.3.4 Phonological Phrase: Kivunjo Chaga

Kivunjo Chaga is a member of the Chaga family of Bantu languages, spoken in Tanzania. I argue here that, like Hausa, Kivunjo possesses 'phrasal clitics' — clitics which subcategorize for the phonological phrase. Kivunjo is perhaps a more convincing case than Hausa from a phonologist's point of view, as it exhibits an abundance of phrasal phonological rules (McHugh 1985, 1990) to diagnose the existence of phonological phrases.

Kivunjo clitics also exhibit an additional complication, one which is predicted to be possible by the proposed framework. Recall that a property of prosodically bound forms is that they possess the ability to be lexically invisible. This parameter is selected by the Kivunjo determiners: I will argue that they are invisible, phrasal clitics.

(43) Kivunjo clitics: $[[\ ]_{P_\phi}]_{P_\phi}$ clitic

Data

Determiners in Kivunjo take the form of enclitics following the noun, which is always initial in its NP (Kivunjo is a head-initial SVO language). Examples (44) and (45) show a class 1 determiner attaching to a class 1 noun, regardless of any adjectives which may occur in the NP; example (46) is ungrammatical because an adjective is interposed between the noun and the determiner.

(44) Mana=cu naleenenga msudi kite.
child=this gave nobleman dog
'This child gave the nobleman a dog'

(45) Mana=cu mtutu naleenenga msudi kite
child=this small gave nobleman dog
'This small child gave the nobleman a dog'

(46) *Mana mtutu=cu naleenenga msudi kite.

Unlike full word post-nominal modifiers, determiner clitics cannot be separated from the preceding word by pause, nor can they be cited in isolation. They contrast with the related deictic, pronominal full-word determiners which can stand alone; the two kinds of determiners are historically related and segmentally similar, though their syntax is synchronically quite different.

Strong evidence for clitichood, as opposed to affixhood, of the determiner comes from Kivunjo's phonological phrases. As we shall see, phrasal rules indicate that there is a phonological phrase boundary between the clitic and its host. This suggests it is not an affix.[21] Yet it does not behave like full word modifiers with respect to phonological phrasing.

Phrasing

Like many of its Bantu relatives (e.g. Luganda, Digo) Kivunjo divides its utterances up into phonological phrases. McHugh 1985 proposes the following general algorithm for generating phrasal structure:

(47) Phonological phrases: Two adjacent words X and Y form a phonological phrase if X is the head of a maximal projection which dominates Y.

---

[21]See, however, Poser 1984, 1990b, who argues that a prefix in Japanese actually induces a phonological phrase break between itself and its host.

8.3. PROSODIC CATEGORY OF CLITIC

This algorithm correctly predicts that a verb and following object will phrase together, as will a noun and following adjective. Unexpectedly, however, if a determiner follows the noun, we find a phrase boundary occurring between the two. This is true even though they are inseparable by pause.

As demonstrated in detail by McHugh, phrase boundaries are signalled phonologically by the application of a number of tone rules which apply at the right edge of the phrase. One of these rules, High Raising, takes a penultimate High tone (H) to Superhigh (S) before a final Low tone (L). As shown below, High Raising feeds a later rule of Superhigh Spread which spreads S one syllable to the right (McHugh 1984).[22] (Brackets indicate phrase boundaries.)

(48)

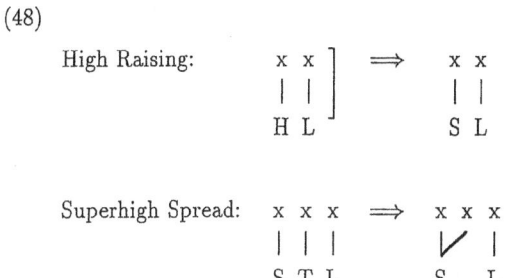

High Raising: x x]   ⟹   x x
                 | | | |
                 H L   S L

Superhigh Spread: x x x ⟹   x x x
                   | | | ⩘ |
                   S T L   S   L

The data in (49) demonstrate the application of High Raising to nouns in a variety of syntactic contexts. High Raising applies to the noun if it is phrase-final, as in (a), but not if it is followed by an adjective, as in (b). Crucially, however, if the noun precedes a determiner clitic as in (c), High Raising *will* apply. The hypothesis that (c) contains a phrase boundary before the determiner is supported by (d), a single noun with the same tonal pattern (HLL) of (c). We find no application of High Raising in (d), since the conditioning Low is not phrase-final. (Instead, another phrasal rule applies — for details see McHugh 1985.)

(49)

a. nyama]   ⟹   nyama
   | | | |
   H L   S L

---

[22]In the rule for Superhigh Spread, 'T' represents any tone (i.e. H or L).

```
b. nyama ngitutu  ]      ⟹    nyama ngitutu
   |    \|/                      |    \|/
   H    L  H                     H    L  H

c. nyama  ] =yi   ⟹    nyama=yi
   | |      |              \/    |
   H L      L              S     L

d. wasudi ]       ⟹    wasudi
   | \/                    | | |
   H  L                    H!H L
```

The presence of a phonological phrase boundary between the determiner and its host noun in (c) poses a problem for the phonological phrase algorithm, which will not generate a phrase-boundary in this environment. Instead, the algorithm should place a phrase boundary after the determiner, as the closest sister to the head noun.

One possibility is to allow the algorithm to admit exceptions, and supply special phrasing just in the case of these determiners. This is the option suggested in McHugh 1985, who discusses the problem posed by determiners. However, resorting to exceptionality would require abandoning two restrictive, well-supported and desirable hypotheses in the literature. One, arising from work in Lexical Phonology, is that postlexical rules do not admit lexical exceptions (Kiparsky 1982, 1983).[23] The other is the general claim of the prosodic hierarchy theory that postlexical prosodic constituency is built without regard to the category of the syntactic nodes to which prosodic algorithms refer (Selkirk 1986, Inkelas 1988, Zec and Inkelas 1990).[24] Kivunjo determiner enclitics are not only a subset of the set of function words in the language — they are also a proper subset even of the class of determiners. (Also in this class are the nonclitic, full word determiners.) Allowing the Kivunjo phrasing algorithm to pick out the determiner clitics would violate both of the important constraints mentioned above.

---

[23]However, Kaisse 1986, 1990 argues that the postlexical English Rhythm Rule admits lexical exceptions.

[24]This subsumes an earlier, less general hypothesis, Selkirk's 'Principle of the Categorial Invisibility of Function Words' (Selkirk 1984:315). (According to the PCIFW the syntactic category of function words is not available to postlexical rules.) Rotenberg 1978, working in a nonprosodic framework, also noted the general irrelevance of syntactic category to the statement of syntactically conditioned rules.

However, the prosodic framework proposed here allows us to create a lexical representation for determiner clitics which will make the derivation of their phrasing properties quite straightforward, and which does not require postlexical rules to admit exceptions. First, we assign to determiner clitics a prosodic subcategorization frame along the lines of that in (50), annotated for the phonological phrase.

(50) $[[\ ]_{p_\phi} \text{---}]_{p_\phi}$

This is exactly the frame we assigned to the Hausa particle *fa*. Of course, if the Kivunjo determiner were exactly like *fa*, we would expect it to end the phonological phrase that it forms with its host. But as the above data has shown, this is not quite accurate. Instead of undergoing phrase-final rule themselves, Kivunjo determiners appear to immediately follow the phrase-final element. We may capture this by marking them lexically as invisible. Just like English adjective suffixes are lexically specified to occur outside of the constituent which they form upon combining with a host, Kivunjo determiners land outside of the phrase for which they subcategorize.

(51) Kivunjo determiner (**cu**): $[[\ ]_{p_\phi}\ ]_{p_\phi}$ cu

Just as in the case of Hausa *fa*, the phrasal clitic *cu* remains untouched by the phrasing algorithm, which operates as an elsewhere condition. It groups into phrases only that material which is not already specified for phonological phrase structure. Thus, we must assume that Kivunjo clitics will be incorporated into prosodic structure only at a higher level.

8.4 The Clitic Group

Prosodic subcategorization frames provide a straightforward means of capturing the fact that certain words are prosodically dependent, as well as the direction of their dependence, and the nature of the item that they are dependent upon.

However, another proposal exists within prosodic hierarchy theory for accomplishing some of these same ends. In its original form, the theory did not have much to say about the status of clitics in the prosodic hierarchy. A major step towards illuminating the nature of cliticization was taken by Hayes 1984/1989a (and subsequently Nespor and Vogel 1986). This is the notion that the relation between clitic and host can be captured by encapsulating both in a new, special constituent in the prosodic hierarchy, called the 'clitic group.'

Clitic groups consist of one phonological word together with and adjacent clitics. In the work of Hayes and Nespor and Vogel, the clitic group occupies a position in the prosodic hierarchy above the phonological word and below the phonological phrase.

(52) phonological phrase
             |
          clitic group
             |
       phonological word

While this proposal nicely captures the intuition that prosodic constituent structure is what binds clitics to their hosts, it suffers from a number of empirical and theoretical difficulties.

Deriving the domains is the first such problem. Due to the irregular distribution of clitics across syntactic categories, the formation of the clitic group cannot be governed by a simple syntax-to-phonology mapping algorithm in the way that phrasing is. Further complicating matters is the fact, convincingly demonstrated by Klavans 1985, that clitics vary in often unpredictable ways along the parameter of the direction of phonological attachment. Thus, any analysis which builds clitic groups will have to refer to a certain amount of lexical information associated with clitics in order to know which words to apply to — and which other words to combine them with.

To this end, Nespor and Vogel propose an indeterminate lexical feature [+Clitic], which may be further specified as to the direction of attachment.[25] The clitic group algorithm simply follows the instructions of this feature. This type of account thus requires both lexical marking of clitics and rules deriving their cliticization; by contrast,

---

[25] Nespor and Vogel 1986, following Hayes 1984, treat all function words as clitics, not distinguishing between what I have called true clitics and reduced function words. As a result, they group into clitic groups certain elements whose higher prosodic structure is predictable from the syntactic structure surrounding them — namely, reduced function words. (On the account of Zec and Inkelas 1987 these are phonological words on their own, and get grouped into phrases by the phrasing algorithm.) The directionality parameter which Nespor and Vogel posit for clitics seems to be relevant only for true clitics. Thus, though Nespor and Vogel are not explicit on this issue, it may be that the distinction they draw between directional and nondirectional clitics corresponds to the distinction I have drawn between reduced function words and true clitics. In Hayes 1984/1989a, however, and Selkirk and Shen 1990, the direction of cliticization is assumed to be predictable from syntactic factors alone.

8.4. THE CLITIC GROUP

my proposal requires only lexical marking of clitics. The feature [+Clitic] of Nespor and Vogel plays no role in the grammar other than triggering the clitic group rule. It is purely diacritic in function, in contrast to prosodic subcategorization frames, which not only identify clitics but also contribute actual, functioning structure to the representation.

A second problem for the proposed clitic group is the current lack of evidence that any language crucially needs the phonological word, the clitic group, *and* the phonological phrase in its postlexical phonology.

It is true that languages with phonological word clitics may distinguish between the lexical phonological word and the postlexical unit that contains clitics, but this does not itself argue for the existence of the clitic group. According to the discussion in Nespor and Vogel 1986, Greek appears to be an example of this kind. Five phonological rules (Stress Readjustment, Nasal Deletion, Stop Voicing, Nasal Assimilation, and Mirror Image Deletion) apply postlexically within the clitic group. Two of these rules (Nasal Assimilation and Stop Voicing) also apply within phonological words. Evidence for identifying two possible domains for these rules is that when the rules apply within the phonological word, they are obligatory. Only in their application across word boundaries within the clitic group are they optional.[26] As is well-known, the distinction between obligatory and optional rule application often characterizes the division between lexical and postlexical rules. Thus a natural way of accounting for these Greek facts is to assume that only one prosodic constituent is implicated: the phonological word. Lexically, the phonological word is the last lexical cycle and corresponds to syntactic terminals. Rules (except for Nasal Deletion) apply obligatorily in this domain. Postlexically, the phonological word is enlarged to include clitics; Nasal Assimilation and Stop Voicing apply optionally within this domain.

While Nespor and Vogel 1986 take the Greek facts to argue for a contrast between the levels of phonological word and clitic group in the prosodic hierarchy, an equally plausible and more parsimonious analysis can be obtained without needing to invoke the clitic group as a unique constituent. Greek can thus be seen as a neat illustration of the contrast betwen lexical and postlexical rule application in the same prosodic constituent.

What would be needed to motivate the clitic group, and what is thus far missing from the literature, is an example of a language in which *postlexical* rules crucially distinguish between the phonological word and the clitic group. This gap is of course

---

[26]A third rule, the juncture rule of Nasal Deletion, is obligatory within clitic groups. However, it is optional within phonological words, where it applies (on the rare occasions that its environment is met in the first place) not as a juncture rule but as a domain span rule.

predicted by the more restrictive subcategorization account, in which clitics belong either to a phonological word or to a phrase. Unless it can be shown that some language rules distinguish the lexical phonological word, the postlexical phonological word, the clitic group, *and* the phonological phrase, the addition of the clitic group to the prosodic hierarchy adds unnecessary power to the theory.

A third, insuperable problem with adding the clitic group to the prosodic hierarchy is that doing so fails to accommodate the distinction between word and phrasal clitics. According to prosodic hierarchy theory, within which the clitic group proposal is inextricably couched, the hierarchical relationship among prosodic constituents is fixed. The idea is that to the extent that constituents are comparable across languages, their hierarchical relationship will be identical. Thus the discovery that dominance relations between two constituents are reversed in different languages, to the extent that it can be tested at all, would falsify this theory. Yet that is precisely the position we are forced into by the data presented in this chapter. In Hausa and Kivunjo Chaga the 'clitic group' dominates the phrase, while in Serbo-Croatian and English the relative dominance is reversed.

(53) *clitic group
    |
  phonological phrase
    |
  clitic group

This unresolvable paradox for theories taking the clitic group to be a special constituent in the prosodic hierarchy theory disappears on the proposal advocated in this chapter, in which the 'clitic group' is recognized as either the phonological word or the phonological phrase. The subcategorization account is at the same time more constrained and more flexible than the clitic group proposal. It is more constrained because it requires fewer constituents in the prosodic hierarchy, and makes use of no diacritic features. It is more flexible by virtue of its ability to describe the different levels of clitic attachment which languages seem to require.

8.5 Lexical 'Clitics'

As Zwicky 1985 points out, it is sometimes, though erroneously, assumed that a word can be classed as a clitic on the basis of its syntactic distribution alone. Zwicky argues that this assumption is invalidated by Wackernagel's (1892) and Zwicky's own (1985) observation that there are are words whose phonology clearly labels them free words, and not clitics, although they too exhibit the kind of distributional regularities — e.g. restriction to second position — that some have viewed as peculiar to clitics. I will not discuss such cases here. They pose a general problem for syntax, but not specifically for the theoretical claims I am developing here.

However, I would like to support Zwicky's position by addressing another kind of counterexample to the generalization that phrasal distribution implies clitic status. These are cases where, instead of being a full word, the phrasally distributed morpheme in question is actually an affix: it undergoes lexical phonological rules. Such morphemes have sometimes been analyzed in the literature as clitics which are attached in the lexicon. However, such analyses require the assumption that a form which leaves the lexical rules as a unit can somehow contain two syntactic terminal elements.

Since this is not a possible outcome under the assumptions I am operating under, I will examine a few of the relevant cases here. My general aim will be to argue, with Poser 1985a, that apparent cases of lexically attached clitics are merely affixes which restrict the phrasal distribution of the word they are morphologically part of.

Klavans 1983 argues that in Ngiyambaa, particle enclitics (such as the topic marker) are attached by lexical rules. They contrast with the postlexically attached pronominal clitics. The argument is based on a lexical rule (Nasal Linking: Klavans 1983:103), which applies to suffixes and to particle clitics, but not across word boundaries or to pronominal clitics. Further, particle clitics are ordered outside of all affixes and inside of all pronominal clitics (ordering is with respect to the prosodic host word). However, the facts Klavans presents are consistent with an alternative analysis, that the putative lexical clitic is in fact a suffix which happens to be able to attach to a wide range of words.

This is the type of approach taken by Poser 1985a in his analysis of the definitive accent marker in Tongan. This accent has a phrasal distibution, always falling on the rightmost word on the NP, yet undergoes demonstrably lexical rules. Poser's solution for Tongan is to assign the accent lexically, yet allow it to be "visible" to the syntax by virtue of adding a definiteness feature to the word it is part of. See Poser 1985a for an account, formulated in GPSG, of why the word bearing the definiteness marker must be final in NP.

A similar phenomenon occurs in Serbo-Croatian (Zec 1986), and here again the facts argue that the relevant particle is actually a suffix which affects word order. The future auxiliary in Serbo-Croatian is a second position enclitic:

(54) On   =će   čita-ti
      3sg FUT3sg   read-INF
      'He will read'

However, Zec shows that if the verb is in initial position, the future auxiliary behaves differently. It is attached to the verb stem, blocking the affixation of the infinitival marker *ti*:

(55)
    Čita-će
    read-FUT3sg
    'He will read'

When attached to verb stems, the auxiliary triggers a lexical rule of palatalization, which does not apply between clitics and their hosts:

(56)
    Pas-će $\Rightarrow$ Paš-će
    graze-FUT3sg
    'He will graze'

    Pas=će ... $\Rightarrow$ *Paš=će ...
    dog=(CL)FUT3sg ...
    'Dog will ...'

Finally, Zec demonstrates that the future auxiliary is also subject to two strictly lexical tone rules (see Inkelas and Zec 1988).

Because the future auxiliary attaches to the verb stem, which no other clitics do, and because it undergoes at least three lexical rules, Zec concludes that it must be treated as a suffix. But this suffix may only occur on initial verbs, just as the lexical Tongan accent analyzed by Poser may only occur on the final word in the phrase, and

8.5. LEXICAL 'CLITICS'

just as Ngiyambaa particle 'enclitics' — which we have hypothesized to be suffixes — are only found on the first word, or on the final word of the first or last phrase, in S.

Chapter 9

Implications

In this final chapter we turn to the implications of the proposals developed in preceding chapters for several important principles that have governed phonological analyses in recent years. These are the Strict Layer Hypothesis (Selkirk 1984, Nespor and Vogel 1986), the Exhaustive Parsing Constraint (Selkirk 1986), and the Strict Cycle Condition (Mascaro 1976, Kiparsky 1982). We also return to a topic deferred back in chapter 2, namely those rules which have been described as applying within metrical constituents.

All four of these proposals (the Strict Layer Hypothesis, the Exhaustive Parsing Constraint, the Strict Cycle Condition, and the claim that syllables and feet are rule domains) conflict with pivotal constraints in Prosodic Lexical Phonology, and cannot be maintained. Fortunately, however, discarding these statements does not lead to loss of generalization. On the contrary, the proposed, more constrained theory is able to provide its own principled accounts of the phenomena which prompted the original introduction of these proposals.

9.1 Strict Layering and Exhaustive Parsing

Motivated by the desire to enforce strict hierarchical relations among prosodic constituents, Selkirk's Strict Layer Hypothesis (Selkirk 1984) imposes the following constraints on prosodic trees (the statement in (1) comes from from Nespor and Vogel 1986:7):

9.1. STRICT LAYERING AND EXHAUSTIVE PARSING

(1) Strict Layer Hypothesis:

a. A given nonterminal unit of the prosodic hierarchy, X^p, is composed of one or more units of the immediately lower category, X^{p-1}.
b. A unit of a given level of the hierarchy is exhaustively contained in the superordinate unit of which it is a part.

The Strict Layer Hypothesis is usually interpreted in tandem with a constraint on exhaustive parsing, made explicit in Selkirk 1986:384.

(2) Exhaustive Parsing Constraint: For any prosodic category, the sentence is exhaustively parsed into a sequence of such categories

These constraints cooperate to produce a tightly restricted range of possible prosodic trees. They are also riddled with violations in the proposals that I have made.

First, the prosodic representations for affixes and clitics make it impossible to maintain the condition that each node in the prosodic hierarchy must branch exhaustively into other nodes in the prosodic hierarchy (as required by clause (a) of the Strict Layer Hypothesis). Neither affixes nor clitics are prosodic constituents. Thus, the nodes immediately dominating them in the hierarchy necessarily dominate two unlike elements: one, the host, a node in the prosodic hierarchy, and the other, the 'raw' phonological material corresponding to the affix or clitic.

(3)
    Affixation   Cliticization

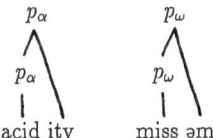

To accommodate lexical cyclicity, our theory is forced into a second class of crucial violations of the Strict Layer Hypothesis. On the assumption that postlexical rules apply noncyclically, the literature on the postlexical prosodic hierarchy has largely been able to maintain the no-nesting constraint implicit in clause (a) of the Strict

Layer Hypothesis.[1] However, any attempt to incorporate cyclic lexical phonological rule application into the theory of prosodic domains forces representations such as those in (4), where a node p_i must dominate another node of the same type.

(4)

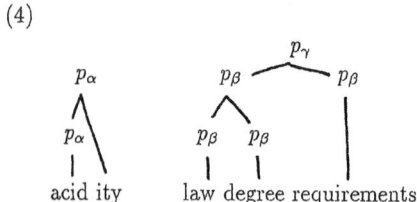

acid ity   law degree requirements

Another requirement of clause (a) of the Strict Layer Hypothesis is that every terminal element must be dominated by each of the node types in the prosodic hierarchy. We can point to two by now familiar constructions which falsify this claim as well, namely prosodic attachment to constituents other than α;[2] and, invisibility in all its forms.

Any morpheme which subcategorizes for attachment to a constituent ranked higher than α in the prosodic hierarchy automatically presents a case where some terminal element(s) will be dominated by only a subset of the possible node types in the hierarchy. A simple example is shown in (5):

(5)

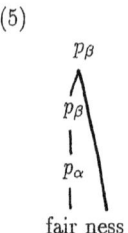

fair ness

---

[1] See, however, McHugh's arguments for cyclic phonological phrasing in Chaga.

[2] Hayes 1984/1989a and Nespor and Vogel 1986 avoid this problem for clitics by treating clitics as phonological words, specially marked so that they cannot constitute a clitic group on their own. However, no evidence supports the claim that clitics are phonological words; clitics do not undergo the same word level rules that apply to nonclitic phonological words in the languages discussed in the references cited. And as for affixes, these are not discussed by Hayes or by Nespor and Vogel.

9.1. STRICT LAYERING AND EXHAUSTIVE PARSING

Representations like that in (5) present a serious challenge to the Exhaustive Parsing Constraint and clause (a) of the Strict Layer Hypothesis, both of which it violates. The structure in question is implicated not only in β affixation but also in the representation of invisibility, where it plays a central role. For example, consider (6), a noun in English. Its final syllable is, as we know, invisible to α rules — hence excluded from the α constituent of which it was originally a part. Since this stem is unsuffixed, the reincorporation of its final syllable into prosodic structure occurs only at the level of β constituency. Thus, as shown in (6), a noun-final syllable will be dominated by only a proper subset of the nodes dominating the phonological material to its left.

(6)

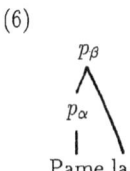

My contention at this juncture is that the four violations of the Strict Layer Hypothesis presented above all point to the same conclusion: the Strict Layer Hypothesis, and the Exhaustive Parsing Condition, have been stated as conditions on the wrong part of the grammar. They have always been viewed as a constraint on representations. I would like to propose here that we take the intuition behind the Strict Layer Hypothesis and Exhaustive Parsing Constraint and apply it instead to the algorithms which parse strings into prosodic constituents. The effect will be to require each algorithm to supply the entire string which it scans with appropriate prosodic structure. We may term the new constraint the Strict Parsing Condition:

(7) Strict Parsing Condition: Group a string of prosodic units of type X^p into units of the immediately higher category, X^{p-1}.

The Strict Parsing Condition constrains only the construction of constituents which immediately dominate prosodically licensed material. It is mute with respect to the manner by which non-constituents — i.e. affixes, clitics, and invisible material — are included into higher structure. All of the violations of the Strict Layer Hypothesis observed in (3)-(6) crucially involve non-constituents. They are derived by means other than the Prosodic Constituent Formation Algorithm. Therefore, the proposed Strict Parsing Condition is not even implicated; it is certainly not violated by them. The problems posed for the earlier Strict Layer Hypothesis and Exhaustive Parsing Constraint are thus circumvented on the proposed account.

The Strict Parsing Condition does retain the important generalization of the supplanted Strict Layer Hypothesis that each type of node in prosodic structure will dominate some part of every underived stem. Like the stronger Strict Layer Hypothesis, it correctly rules out unattested contrasts such as that in (8):

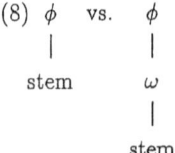

The Strict Parsing Condition also ensures that the distance, stated in terms of positions on the prosodic scale, between a mother and daughter node will never exceed one. Thus the new constraint shares with the old constraints the property of correctly prohibiting algorithms which would assign, for example, phonological word status only to the second half of a compound, or phrasal status only to the first and last phonological word in the string, or phonological word status to just those lower constituents which end in a voiced obstruent.

A consequence of restricting the scope of the well-formedness condition is that it becomes redundant. In the theory proposed in this thesis, the only algorithm to which the new Strict Parsing Constraint could apply is the Prosodic Constituent Formation Algorithm — essentially an exact restatement of the Strict Parsing Condition itself. The question is now which of these we want to keep: a universal constraint on algorithms, or a universal algorithm which obeys that constraint. In what follows I will opt for keeping the constraint, since while the PCF algorithm is specific to Prosodic Lexical Phonology, the constraint which would derive it has more general application in phonological theory.

Generalizing the Condition

As formulated in (7), the Strict Parsing Condition resembles closely a principle developed previously in the literature to cover a different set of phenomena. It is

9.1. STRICT LAYERING AND EXHAUSTIVE PARSING

Itô's principle of Prosodic Licensing (1986). As we saw in chapter 6, this principle guarantees membership in higher phonological structure to each visible element in the string. The version below is changed slightly from Itô's formulation. It incorporates the simplification afforded as a result of chapter 6.

(9) Prosodic Licensing: All phonological units in the string must be prosodically licensed, i.e., belong to higher prosodic structure

Note that while this constraint is stated generally, with reference to the standard prosodic hierarchy, in practice its main results have derived from its applications to what I am calling 'metrical' structure — moras (Itô 1988, Zec 1988b) and syllables (Itô 1986). Fortunately the terminological confusion is fleeting in nature, for what I want to argue here is that Prosodic Licensing and the Strict Parsing Condition are virtually identical constraints anyway. One holds on the rules building the 'metrical' hierarchy and the other on the rules building the 'prosodic' hierarchy. The natural move is to collapse the two into one more general condition on parsing algorithms. In short, the constraint is simply that any algorithm building prosodic or metrical structure must exhaustively parse the string into units of the next highest level.[3]

(10) Generalized Strict Parsing Condition: Parsing algorithms must group all phonological constituents of type $i\text{-}1$ into constituents of type i.

One important empirical difference obtains between the metrical and the prosodic trees generated by a theory incorporating the Generalized Strict Parsing Condition. While a licit prosodic tree will allow non-terminal prosodic nodes (e.g. β, ω) to immediately dominate otherwise unlicensed segmental material in certain well-defined cases, the same is not true of the metrical tree. As Itô shows, *all* melodic elements must eventually be incorporated into syllables (or moras, depending on which unit is taken to bottom out the hierarchy).

---

[3] This has some implications for the status of stray syllable adjunction rules. Languages in which stress is non-alternating (e.g. Polish, Ossetic, Winnebago, and many others), have been analyzed as having a rule which builds a single binary foot, followed by a process of stray syllable adjunction which incorporates unfooted syllables into that single foot (Prince 1985). A consequence of the Generalized Strict Parsing Condition is that the stray adjunction process must be viewed as part of the foot-building algorithm in these languages, yielding the strong prediction that no rules can intervene between foot-construction and stray adjunction. Though I know of no counterexamples offhand, this requires further investigation.

This difference between the hierarchies does not, however, threaten the move to subject the algorithms constructing metrical and prosodic trees to the same well-formedness constraints. Rather, the difference in permissible structures traces back to differences in the sources for metrical and prosodic constituency. Because of bracket erasure, each algorithm building prosodic structure can apply at most once per derivation. The remainder, and proportionally the largest bulk, of prosodic constituency is supplied by subcategorization frames (or compounding rules). But no version of bracket erasure applies to metrical structure. As a consequence the algorithms constructing syllables and feet are able to apply more than once in the derivation; in fact, Itô 1986 argues on independent grounds that the construction of metrical structure is a continuous process. The syllabification process reapplies every time unsyllabified/unfooted material becomes available (Itô 1986). It is the difference in bracket erasure, hence in the applicability of parsing algorithms, that derives the structural differences between the prosodic and metrical hierarchies.

A further simplification?

The Generalized Strict Parsing Condition breaks down into two parts: (a) exhaustive parsing and (b) the condition that the constituent type of the affected mothers and daughters differ by exactly one level. I will attempt here to simplify this constraint even further, by deriving one part from the other.

(11)
    a. Algorithms parse exhaustively

    b. Algorithms parse constituents into constituents of the next higher type

Let us take as our premise (a), the condition that each constituent-forming algorithm exhaustively parses the string. My contention is that it follows necessarily that these algorithms will group constituents of type p_{i-1} into constituents of type p_i. Algorithms of any other kind would be impossible to learn. Hence (b) is predictable and need not be stipulated.

To prove this, consider what kind of evidence would falsify the claim that mother and daughter nodes in the prosodic hierarchy are no more than one level apart. We would need to find a case where the two structures in (12) contrast in some language.

9.1. STRICT LAYERING AND EXHAUSTIVE PARSING

(12) p_i p_{i+1}
        | |
    p_{i-1} p_{i-1}

As we have seen, Prosodic Lexical Phonology provides only one mechanism for building higher-order prosodic structure around lower level prosodic constituents: context-free parsing algorithms.[4] The same is true of Itô's templatic approach to building metrical structure. Mapping elements to templates can be seen as context-free parsing. As Itô points out, a desirable property of the templatic approach to syllabification is that it enforces locality on syllabification, correctly capturing the generalization that "the wellformedness of a syllable or a metrical foot is determined solely within the syllable or foot and is crucially *not* dependent on information outside of that structure" (Itô 1986:7). Thus even if metrical structure, e.g. a foot, were marked underlyingly on a phonological string, the syllabification algorithm would still apply to any unsyllabified material in that string.

In order to derive both representations in (12), we would need two algorithms/templates for the same language, one which groups constituents of type p_{i-1} into constituents of type i, and another which groups them into constituents of type p_{i+1}.

But if all algorithms parse strings exhaustively, and if algorithms are context-free, then it will never be the case that more than one of the two hypothetical algorithms in (12) will ever have a chance to apply to constituents of type p_{i-1}. Therefore, only one of the structures in (12) can ever arise. And in the absence of the critical contrast in (12), the learner will have no evidence that a mother is separated by more than one level in the hierarchy from its daughter. We can thus omit the condition in (11b) from the grammar. The result is the simple statement below, which replaces the intricate set of conditions imposed on the prosodic and metrical hierarchies in past work.

(13) Parsing Condition: algorithms which build constituent structure must exhaustively parse the string.

To sum up, the fact that proposals within Prosodic Lexical Phonology violate the traditional Strict Layer Hypothesis and Exhaustive Parsing Constraint is not a defect.

---

[4]It is not clear what guarantees the context-free property. Actually, requiring constituent formation algorithms to be context-free would have the same effect as imposing an exhaustive parsing condition on them. This might be easier, and more intuitive; future investigation is required to discover whether in fact it would be too restrictive.

In fact, it has motivated a rethinking of these conditions, leading to the positive result of being able to collapse them with another independently needed constraint (Prosodic Licensing), and to subsume all three under an even simpler, more general principle.

An issue which this discussion raises is why, in a model which attempts to attribute as much responsibility as possible to representations, critical well-formedness conditions on prosodic trees must be accomplished by constraints on rules. At present the only avenue which I see towards restating the Parsing Condition as a condition on representations will require different conditions for the metrical and for the prosodic hierarchies. Worse, the condition required for the latter will be quite complex: Every nonmaximal prosodic constituent must be immediately dominated by a node which is either identical or immediately adjacent to it in the ordered list of prosodic constituent types. I leave to future work the questions of whether the Parsing Condition can be restated in terms of constraints on representations and if not, why not.

9.2 Bracket Erasure and the Strict Cycle

A second guiding principle of phonology which the framework developed here calls into question is the Strict Cycle Condition. Various attempts falling under this name have been made in order to formalize the generalization that certain phonological rules appear to apply only in derived environments (Kean 1974, Mascaro 1976, Halle 1978, Kiparsky 1982, Rubach 1984, others). What is meant by 'derived' can be phonological, but is typically stated in morphological terms. For example, Halle 1978 proposed that strict cycle rules must have a morphological boundary symbol in their environment to ensure that they apply only at morphological junctures.[5]

(14) The Strict Cyclicity Principle

A cyclic rule R applies properly on cycle j only if either (a) or (b) is satisfied:
    a. R makes specific use of information, part of which is available on a prior pass through the cyclic rules, and part of which becomes first available on cycle j. There are three separate cases subsumed under (a). R refers specifically to some A or B in:

---

[5] This statement of the Strict Cycle Condition is taken from Rubach 1984, who provides a comprehensive summary of the literature on strict cyclicity.

9.2. BRACKET ERASURE AND THE STRICT CYCLE

    i. [XAY ... [... B ... $]_{j-1}$ Z $]_j$;
    ii. [Z [... B $]_{j-i}$ XAY $]_j$;
    iii. [X [... A $]_{j-1}$ Y [... B ... $]_{j-1}$ Z $]_j$;

  b. R makes specific use of information assigned on cycle j by a rule applying before R.

Access by phonological rules to morphological derivational history is crucial to the statement of the conditions in (a). Past theories have provided a formal means by which to encode this global knowledge: morphological brackets. However, in Prosodic Lexical Phonology, morphological bracketing is inaccessible to phonological rules. The problem is not solved by translating the morphological brackets into prosodic brackets either; according to the strict bracket erasure principle which we are crucially assuming, only the requisite internal brackets in (14aiii) will be available. As a reminder of why bracket erasure is critical, consider (15). If we relaxed bracket erasure enough to permit the representation in (15a), needed in order to satisfy the environment for standard strict cycle rules, we would also have to admit the one in (15b), which incorrectly predicts a cycle of phonological rules on bound roots.[6]

(15)
    a. [[stem $]_m$ affix $]_m$ b.   [[root $]_m$ [affix $]_m$ $]_m$
       [[stem $]_p$ affix $]_p$ [[root $]_p$ affix $]_p$

A possible way out of this problem is to adopt the analysis of Kiparsky 1982, who proposes to derive the Strict Cycle Condition without needing to mention internal morphological (or, in our terms, prosodic) bracketing in rule environments. Kiparsky construes all lexically listed forms as lexical identity rules. He then allows structure-changing rules to apply wherever their phonological environment is met — while invoking the Elsewhere Condition (e.g. Kiparsky 1982:136) to prevent rules from applying in a structure-changing fashion to a form which is listed in the lexicon. The idea is that the lexical identity rules corresponding to listed forms are more specific than any phonological rules. By the Elsewhere Condition, listed forms thus block the application of any rule whose output would be distinct from its input.

---

[6]Again, this argument relies on the fundamental assumption that phonological rules apply immediately upon construction of the prosodic constituent which forms their environment.

(16) Elsewhere Condition: Rules A, B in the same component apply disjunctively to a form ϕ if and only if

i. the structural description of A (the specific rule) properly includes the structural description of B (the general rule)
ii. the result of applying A to ϕ is distinct from the result of applying B to ϕ.

In that case A is applied first, and if it takes effect, then B is not applied.

Underived stems are listed in the lexicon. So is the output of every cycle of rules.[7] Thus, the only forms to which structure-changing rules will be able to apply are unlisted forms, i.e. derived forms on the cycle at which they are derived, before they get listed.

This contrast in behavior is illustrated by the following example, in which *vanilla* and *original* are both input to the English Stress Rule. Left to its own devices, the ESR would assign antepenultimate stress to unstressed words with the same syllable structure as these two forms. But both *vanilla* and *original* come in with preassigned stress; *vanilla* because it has exceptional stress marked underlyingly, and *original* because it has already undergone stress rules on the *origin* cycle. Note that the ESR applies in a structure-changing fashion only to *original*, the only derived form. Because *vanilla* is underived, the ESR is blocked from reassigning a different stress pattern to it.

(17)   vanilla   origin + al

ESR: —[SCC]—   original

Non-structure-changing rules will apply to underived forms, however. Consider (18), which illustrates the lexical identity rule corresponding to the underived word *nightingale*, and the resulting of applying the (cyclic) syllabification rule to that same form. In this case, syllabification is not bocked, even though it is applying to an underived form. The reason is that its output wholly subsumes its input. The identity rule and the output of syllabification are technically nondistinct (Stanley 1967); the Elsewhere Condition is not activated.

---

[7]See Rubach 1984:239 for why the output of every cycle should be listed lexically. Kiparsky 1982 takes this to be true only of the output of each level.

(18)
 Lexical Identity Rule: /naytɪngeyl/ ⟶ /naytɪngeyl/

 Syllabification: /naytɪngeyl/ ⟶ $\overset{\sigma\;\;\;\sigma\;\;\;\sigma}{\overset{\frown\;\frown\;\frown}{\text{naytɪngeyl}}}$

Though seemingly effective in these examples, the Elsewhere Condition falls down in a large number of other cases as a means of blocking the application of structure-changing rules to underived forms. We will look at one representative example here, the well-known case of Trisyllabic Shortening in English (*divine, divinity* etc.). This rule is not supposed to apply to underived forms, even though its phonological environment might be met, as in the familiar example of *nightingale*. Kiparsky (1982) attributes this blocking to the Elsewhere Condition, noting that Trisyllabic Shortening would produce an output which is distinct from the underlying form — that is, from the lexical identity rule for *nightingale*.

(19)
 Lexical Identity Rule: /naytɪngeyl/ ⟶ /naytɪngeyl/
 Trisyllabic Shortening: /naytɪngeyl/ ⟶ /nɪtɪngeyl/

Though the insight behind this account is appealing and ought to be maintained, its implementation is problematic. A general criticism[8] is that identifying affixes as rules which can be ordered (even disjunctively) with respect to phonological rules opens the door to the possibility that extrinsic ordering might also play a role. That is, the insertion of some affixes might be ordered before certain rules on the cycle, and others after.

A more specific problem with this approach is that it does not work for more recent formulations of Trisyllabic Shortening. As recent work has shown (Myers 1987), Trisyllabic Shortening is properly characterized as a set of two rules each of which makes crucial reference to syllable structure: Resyllabification (or ambisyllabification) and Closed Syllable Shortening. On the assumption that syllabification is predictable, syllable structure will not be present underlyingly on nonderived words. Therefore, the lexical identity rule corresponding to *nightingale* will not properly contain the structural description of the rules effecting Trisyllabic Shortening. Thus the criteria imposed by the Elsewhere Condition for disjunctive ordering are not met; thus, the lexical identity rule should not block Trisyllabic Shortening.

---
[8]See Mohanan and Mohanan 1984 for general remarks on this topic.

(20) Lexical Identity Rule: /naytɪngeyl/ ⟶ /naytɪngeyl/

    Resyllabification: σ σ [-str] ⟶ σ σ [-str]

                              ... V C...   ... V C...

    Closed Syllable Shortening: σ   ⟶   σ

                                  CVVC   CVVC
                                                 |
                                                 ∅

Though one could imagine ways around this particular difficulty,[9] it shows up a more general problem with accounts of this type. In particular, in every situation where a structure-changing rule is crucially fed by a structure-building rule (e.g. syllabification), the Elsewhere Condition will be powerless to block the structure-changing rule from applying. This is at odds with the original intent of the Elsewhere Condition and the Strict Cycle Condition, which was to make the set of environments in which cyclic structure-changing rules were blocked coextensive with the set of underived environments. Of course, at the time the Elsewhere account of strict cyclicity was formulated, most rules making reference to syllable structure were stress rules, which accorded with the fact that stress rules did seem to apply cyclically in nonderived environments. But in recent years, more and more 'segmental' rules have been reanalyzed as dependent upon syllable structure, so that the dichotomy between stress rules and others is disappearing. The number of cyclic structure-changing rules which the Elsewhere Condition is able to order disjunctively with lexical identity rules has dwindled sufficiently far that the account in Kiparsky 1982, and the Strict Cycle Condition itself (given clause (b)), no longer cover all cases of strict cycle effects.

For these reasons I have decided not to rely on the reduction of the Strict Cycle Condition to the Elsewhere Condition as a solution for the bracketing problem which

---

[9] As Kiparsky has noted, we could simply mark the syllable structure of exceptional words like *nightingale* underlyingly. They would thus become part of the lexical identity rule, which would be able to block subsequent distinct syllabification processes.

9.2. BRACKET ERASURE AND THE STRICT CYCLE

the Strict Cycle Condition poses for Prosodic Lexical Phonology.. We must therefore search for another explanation for the phenomenon of strict cyclicity. Though I cannot offer a definitive answer here to all of the strict cycle puzzles presented in the literature, I would like to suggest several possible alternative methods of accounting for apparent strict cyclicity, none of which appeal directly to internal morphological structure. In some cases, apparently structure-changing operations can be reanalyzed as structure-preserving; in others, ways can be found to encode morphological boundaries in phonological structure, obviating the need for phonological rules to refer to morphological structure directly.

One means at our disposal is the option provided in Prosodic Lexical Phonology of avoiding a stem cycle on derived words. As I suggested earlier, this may allow us to reanalyze the English Stress Rule as structure-preserving. If so, we could dispense with the argument that the Strict Cycle Condition is needed to constrain the structure-changing application of the English Stress Rule.

(21)   vanilla   origin

Affixation: —   [origin]$_p$ al

Invisibility: —   [origi]$_p$ nal
ESR: —   [orígi]$_p$ nal

PCF: [vanilla]$_p$ —

Invisibility: [vani]$_p$ lla
ESR: —   —

This method also allows us to explain why the Carib stress rule (chapter 7) appears subject to strict cyclicity even though it is crucially *not* structure-changing.

Another tactic is to encode morphological information phonologically. Due to cyclic rule application, stems will possess phonological structure which is absent on just-attached affixes. With this in mind, we may be able to reanalyze some rules which appear to apply only in morphologically derived environments as, in fact, merely sensitive to the difference between fully specified and underspecified representations. This type of solution has already been implemented in the literature in at least two ways: cyclic application of redundancy rules, and cyclic syllabification.

In Kiparsky 1988 (see also Archangeli and Pulleyblank 1986, Rice 1988) it is suggested that rules supplying redundant values to an underspecified representation can apply cyclically. Upon affixation, then, stems will be more specified than will newly attached affixes, since the stems will already have undergone the fill-in rules on a previous cycle. It follows from this asymmetry that cyclic feature-filling rules will apply only to the affix: hence the apparent effect of strict cyclicity. This was seen in Kiparsky's analysis of Warlpiri, presented in chapter 3.

A second possible means of exploiting the more specified nature of the stem to explain apparent strict cycle effects is provided by cyclic syllabification.[10] The contrast between syllabified vs. unsyllabified material may permit a phonological characterization of morphological juncture. This solution incorporates the insight of Kiparsky 1982 and others that rules assigning metrical structure play a role in the analysis of strict cyclicity.

As one example of how this approach might account for alternations previously attributed to the Strict Cycle Condition, consider the following familiar facts from Polish (Rubach 1984:13). Polish has the two ordered rules in (22):

(22)
    a. c ⟶ č / ___ i   (Palatalization)
    b. k ⟶ c / ___ i

Strict cycle effects are claimed to hold on these rules, as shown below. In (23a) (from Rubach 1984:13,118), the output of Rule (b) ($k \longrightarrow c$) produces the phonological environment for the first, Palatalization. But the first rule only encounters that environment on a subsequent cycle, at which point the environment is no longer morphologically 'derived'. Palatalization is thus correctly blocked from applying. Note that in (23b), a derived /ci/ sequence *does* trigger Palatalization – because the rule encounters it on the came cycle at which it is derived.

(23)

                            (a)   (b)

                       [[[kozak] i] #]   [[[chłopiec] in] a]

      Cycle 1:   — [SCC] —   — [SCC] —

---

[10]For a similar account of postlexical 'derived environment' effects, see Rice 1990.

9.2. BRACKET ERASURE AND THE STRICT CYCLE

Cycle 2:		kozak+i	chłopiec+in
	Palatalization:	—	chłopieč+in
	Rule (b):	kozac+i	—
Cycle 3:		kozaci#	chłopiečin+a
	Palatalization:	— [SCC] —	—
	Rule (b):	—	—

Of course, determining which cycle a configuration was derived on requires reference to morphological structure, which is fine on Rubach's account but problematic in Prosodic Lexical Phonology. An alternative way of stating that the kind of /ci/ sequence which will undergo Palatalization must straddle a morpheme boundary is to refer to syllable structure. Assuming cyclic syllabification in Polish,[11] a heteromorphemic /ci/ sequence will, at the beginning of the cycle on which it is created by affixation, consist of a /c/ which is already syllabified leftward as a coda, and an /i/ which is not yet syllabified at all. Only later, after syllabification has applied, will the two segments belong to the same syllable. Suppose we apply Palatalization before syllabification on the cycle. If we simply make the rule dependent on the syllabic asymmetry between c and i, then we capture just those environments where it ought to apply.

(24) Palatalization: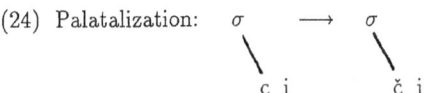

Adopting this analysis allows us to formulate the derivation seen above without making reference to morphological (or, for that matter, prosodic) boundaries. In *kozaci*, the /ci/ sequence never satisfies the environment for Palatalization. On the i cycle, the k has not yet become a c; on the next cycle, though the requisite c is now in place, the syllable structure is all wrong: the /ci/ sequence is by now tautosyllabic. Palatalization is thus blocked again, not by the absence of a morpheme boundary, but by the absence of its phonological environment. By contrast, in *chłopiečin* the /ci/ sequence exhibits the requisite syllable structure on the first affixal cycle; Palatalization is able to take effect.

---

[11]For arguments in favor of cyclic syllabification even of stem-final codas, see Rubach and Booij ms.

(25)

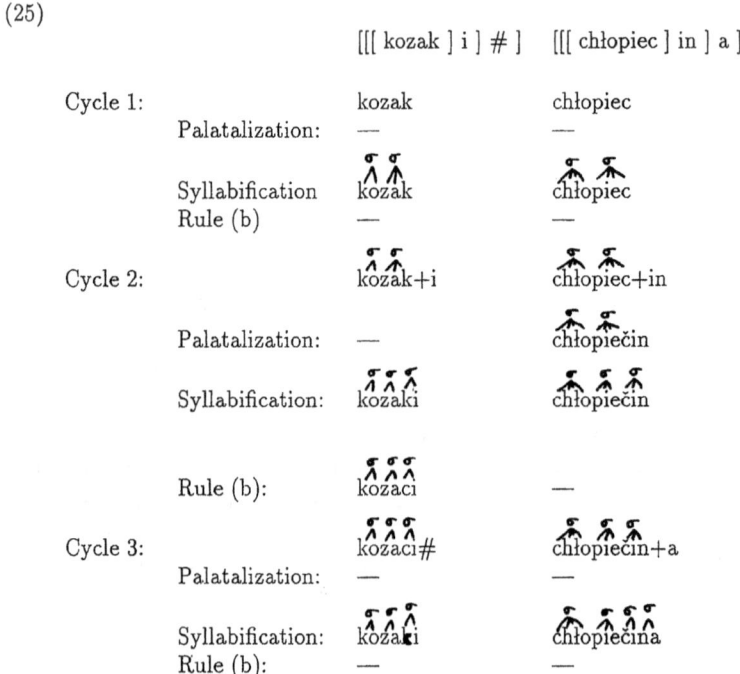

Although this represents only a very preliminary inroad into the forest of analyses relying on the Strict Cycle Condition, it is hoped that future work will be able to reduce strict cycle effects to the structure-preserving properties of cyclic phonological rules.

9.3 Metrical 'Domains'

In this section I turn to a rather different consequence of the proposed theory of Prosodic Lexical Phonology. In this case it is not a principle which the theory prevents from being stated, but a class of analyses. In particular, claims that a given phonological rule has as its domain the syllable, or the foot, cannot be supported in a theory which identifies all phonological rule domains as constituents in the prosodic hierarchy.

9.3. METRICAL 'DOMAINS'

One well-known example of such a rule is pharyngealization in (among others) Cairene Arabic (see e.g. van der Hulst and Smith 1982) and Azerbaijani Jewish Aramaic (Hoberman 1988). This rule spreads pharyngealization (emphasis) from one segment to all other tautosyllabic segments, prompting descriptions which restrict the domain of the rule to the syllable (see e.g. Nespor and Vogel 1986).

However, in the proposed theory, metrical structure is available at all stages of the derivation. Thus no matter which prosodic constituent a rule applies within, it should always be able to refer to a metrical constituent in its environment, emulating the effect of selecting that constituents as the rule's domain. For instance, the Arabic pharyngealization rule can be stated as follows:

(26) σ (mirror image, iterative
 $\wedge$
 o o
 $\searrow\!\!\downarrow$
 +F

It is precisely because metrical constituents (as opposed to prosodic ones) are not subject to bracket erasure that this reanalysis is possible. Thus, the theory predicts exactly which kind of phonological constituents can appear in the environment of phonological rules: metrical ones.[12]

In any case, the existence of rules which apply only within a metrical constituent poses no problems for a theory which limits rule domains to the set of prosodic constituents.

Summary

To conclude this chapter, we have seen that a number of distinctions in the behavior of prosodic and metrical constituents follow from the fact that bracket erasure applies to the former hierarchy but not to the latter. Perhaps the most important benefit is that the many well-formedness conditions which have been proposed in the past to hold on prosodic and metrical structure can be collapsed into one simple condition on the algorithms parsing phonological material into higher-order structure: the parsing must be exhaustive. No further stipulations appear necessary.

---
[12]Actually, prosodic constituents may also appear in rule environments if we accept the weaker version of bracketing erasure needed to allow for the statement of juncture rules. (See chapter 3.)

References

Abaev, V. 1964. "A Grammatical Sketch of Ossetic." *International Journal of American Lingustics* 30.4.

Allen, M. 1978. *Morphological Investigations*. Doctoral dissertation, University of Connecticut.

Alsina, A. 1988. "Catalan Stress and the Autonomy of the CV Tier." Unpublished manuscript, Stanford University.

Archangeli, D. and D. Pulleyblank. 1986. "The Content and Structure of Phonological Representations." Unpublished manuscript, University of Arizona and University of Southern California.

Archangeli, D. 1984. "Extrametricality in Yawelmani," *The Linguistic Review* 4, 101-120.

Barker, C. 1989. "Extrametricality, the Cycle, and Turkish Word Stress." Syntax Research Center Working Paper Series SRC-89-03, University of California, Santa Cruz.

Berendsen, E. 1986. *The Phonology of Cliticization*. Dordrecht: Foris.

Bickmore, L. 1990. "Branching Nodes and Prosodic Categories." In S. Inkelas and D. Zec (eds.), *The Phonology-Syntax Connection*. CSLI Publications and the University of Chicago Press.

Booij, G. 1984. "Coordination Reduction in Complex Words: a Case for Prosodic Phonology." In H. van der Hulst and N. Smith (eds.), *Advances in Non-Linear Phonology*, 143-160. Dordrecht: Foris.

Booij, G. and J. Rubach. 1984. "Domains in Lexical Phonology." *Phonology Yearbook* **1**, 1-27.

Booij, G. and J. Rubach. 1987. "Postcyclic versus Postlexical rules in Lexical Phonology." *Linguistic Inquiry* 18, 1-44.

Borowsky, T. 1986. *Topics in the Lexical Phonology of English*. Doctoral dissertation, University of Massachusetts.

Bromberger, S. and M. Halle. 1989. "Conceptual Issues in Morphology." Unpublished manuscript, Massachusetts Institute of Technology.

Broselow, E. and J. McCarthy. 1983. "A theory of Internal Reduplication." *The Linguistic Review* 3, 25-88.

Browne, W. 1974. "On the Problem of Enclitic Placement in Serbo-Croatian." In R. Brecht and C. Chvany (eds.), *Slavic Transformational Syntax*, no. 10 in Michigan Slavic Materials. Department of Slavic Languages and Literatures, University of Michigan, Ann Arbor.

Chen, M. 1990. "What Must Phonology Know About Syntax?" In S. Inkelas and D. Zec (eds.), *The Phonology-Syntax Connection*. CSLI Publications and the University of Chicago Press.

Cho, Y.-m. 1990. "Syntax and Phrasing in Korean." In S. Inkelas and D. Zec (eds), *The Phonology-Syntax Connection*. CSLI Publications and the University of Chicago Press.

Chomsky, N. and M. Halle. 1968. *The Sound Pattern of English*. Harper and Row.

Cohn, A. 1989. "Stress in Indonesian and Bracketing Paradoxes." *Natural Language and Linguistic Theory* 7:2, 167-216.

Cole, J. and L. Uyechi. 1988. "Extraprosodicity in Mende Tonal Phonology." Unpublished manuscript, Stanford University.

Comrie, B. 1976. "Irregular Stress in Polish and Macedonian." *International Review of Slavic Linguistics* 2, 227-240.

Condoravdi, C. 1988. "Sandhi Rules of Greek and Prosodic Theory." Proceedings of NELS 19.

Condoravdi, C. 1990. "Sandhi Rules of Greek and Prosodic Theory." In S. Inkelas and D. Zec (eds.), *The Phonology-Syntax Connection*. CSLI Publications and the University of Chicago Press.

Cowper, E. and K. Rice. 1987. "Are Phonosyntactic Rules Necessary?" *Phonology Yearbook 4*, 185-194.

Dogil, G. 1979. "Metrical Stress in Polish." *International Review of Slavic Linguistics* 4, 49-71.

Fabian, E., G. Fabian, and C. Peck. 1971. "The Morphophonemics of Nabak." *Kivung* 4,147-160.

Franks, S. 1985. "Extrametricality and Stress in Polish." *Linguistic Inquiry* 16, 144-151.

Goldsmith, J. 1976. *Autosegmental Phonology*. Doctoral dissertation, Massachusetts Institute of Technology.

Hale, K. and A. Lacayo Blanco. 1988. *Vocabulario preliminar del ULWA (sumu meridional)*. Centro de investigaciones y documentacion de la Costa Atlantica, Karawala, Zelaya Sur, Nicaragua, and Center for Cognitive Science, Massachusetts Institute of Technology.

Halle, M. 1978. "Formal vs. Functional Considerations in Phonology." In B. Kachru (ed.), *Linguistics in the Seventies: Directions and Prospects*. Studies in the Linguistic Sciences 8.2, Department of Linguistics, University of Illinois, Urbana.

Halle, M. and K.P. Mohanan. 1985. "Segmental Phonology of Modern English." *Linguistic Inquiry* 16, 57-116.

Halle, M. and J.-R. Vergnaud. 1987. *An Essay on Stress*. MIT Press.

Han, E. 1988. "Glide Formation in Korean." Unpublished manuscript, Stanford University.

Hargus, S. 1985. *The Lexical Phonology of Sekani*. Doctoral dissertation, University of California at Los Angeles.

Harris, J. 1983. *Syllable Structure and Stress in Spanish*. MIT Press.

Hayes, B. 1979. "Extrametricality." In K. Safir (ed.), *MIT Working Papers in Linguistics*, Vol. 1, 77-87. 1.

Hayes, B. 1981. *A Metrical Theory of Stress Rules*. Doctoral dissertation, Massachusetts Institute of Technology. Distributed by the Indiana University Linguistics Club.

Hayes, B. 1982. "Extrametricality and English Stress." *Linguistic Inquiry* 13, 227-276.

Hayes, B. 1984/1989a. "The Prosodic Hierarchy and Meter." In P. Kiparsky and G. Youmans (eds.), *Rhythm and Meter*. Academic Press: Orlando.

Hayes, B. 1987. "A Revised Parametric Metrical Theory." *Proceedings of NELS 17*, vol. 1, 274-289. University of Massachusetts.

Hayes, B. 1989b. "Compensatory Lengthening in Moraic Phonology." Unpublished manuscript, University of California at Los Angeles.

Hoberman, R. 1988. "Emphasis Harmony in a Modern Aramaic Dialect." *Language* 64, 1-26.

van der Hulst, H. and N. Smith. 1982. "Prosodic Domains and Opaque Segments." In H. van der Hulst and N. Smith (eds.), *The Structure of Phonological Representations (Part II)*, 311-336. Dordrecht: Foris.

Hoff, B. 1968. *The Carib Language*. The Hague: Martinus Nijhoff.

Hyman, L. 1985. *A Theory of Phonological Weight*. Dordrecht: Foris.

Hyman, L. 1987. "Prosodic Domains in Kukuya." *Natural Language and Linguistic Theory*. 5.3

Hyman, L., F. Katamba and L. Walusimbi. 1987. "Luganda and the Strict Layer Hypothesis." *Phonology Yearbook 4*, 87-108.

Inkelas, S. 1987a. "Prosodic Subcategorization." Paper presented at the LSA meeting, San Francisco.

Inkelas, S. 1987b. "Yawelmani Stress Reconsidered." Unpublished manuscript, Stanford University.

Inkelas, S. 1988. "Prosodic Effects on Syntax: Hausa 'fa'." *Proceedings of the Seventh West Coast Conference on Formal Linguistics*, 375-389. Stanford Linguistics Association.

Inkelas, S., W. Leben, and M. Cobler. 1986. "The Phonology of Intonation in Hausa." *Proceedings of NELS 17* vol. 1, 327-342.

Inkelas, S. and D. Zec. 1988. "Serbo-Croatian Pitch Accent: The Interaction of Tone, Stress and Intonation." *Language* 64, 227-248.

Itô, J. 1986. *Syllable Theory in Prosodic Phonology*. Doctoral dissertation, University of Massachusetts.

Itô, J. 1988. "A Prosodic Theory of Epenthesis." Syntax Research Center Working Paper Series SRC-88-02, University of California, Santa Cruz. To appear in *Natural Language and Linguistic Theory*.

Kahn, D. 1976. *Syllable-Based Generalizations in English Phonology*. Doctoral dissertation, Massachusetts Institute of Technology. Distributed by the Indiana University Linguistics Club.

Kaisse, E. 1985. *Connected Speech: The Interaction of Syntax and Phonology*. Orlando: Academic Press.

Kaisse, E. 1990. "Toward a Typology of Postlexical Rules." In S. Inkelas and D. Zec (eds), *The Phonology-Syntax Connection*. CSLI Publications and the University of Chicago Press.

Kanerva, J. 1986. "A Cyclical Analysis of Tone in Chicheŵa Verbs." Paper presented at the 17th Conference on African Linguistics, Indiana University.

Kanerva, J. 1989. *Focus and Phrasing in Chicheŵa Phonology*. Stanford University dissertation.

Kanerva, J. 1990. "Focusing on Phonological Phrases in Chicheŵa." In S. Inkelas and D. Zec (eds), *The Phonology-Syntax Connection*. CSLI Publications and the University of Chicago Press.

Kean, M.-L. 1974. "The Strict Cycle in Phonology." *Linguistic Inquiry* 5, 179-203.

Kiparsky, P. 1982. "Lexical Morphology and Phonology." In I.-S. Yang (ed.), *Linguistics in the Morning Calm*, 3-91. Seoul: Hanshin Publishing Co.

Kiparsky, P. 1983. "Word Formation in the Lexicon." In F. Ingemann (ed.), *Proceedings of the 1982 Mid-America Linguistics Conference*, 3-29. Lawrence: University of Kansas.

Kiparsky, P. 1984. "On the Lexical Phonology of Icelandic." In C.-C. Elert et al. (eds.), *Nordic Prosody III: Papers from a Symposium*,135-162. University of Umeå.

Kiparsky, P. 1985. "Some Consequences of Lexical Phonology." *Phonology Yearbook 2*, 85-138.

Kiparsky, P. 1986. "The Phonology of Reduplication." Unpublished manuscript, Stanford University.

Kiparsky, P. 1987a. "Systematic Optionality in the Lexical Phonology of Chamorro." Unpublished manuscript, Stanford University.

Kiparsky, P. 1987b. "On the Morphology of Sanskrit Accentuation." Phonology Workshop presentation, Stanford University.

Kiparsky, P. 1988. "Vowel Harmony as Delinking." Unpublished manuscript, Stanford University.

Klavans, J. L. 1982. *Some Problems in a Theory of Clitics.* Indiana University Linguistics Club.

Klavans, J. L. 1983. "The Morphology of Cliticization", in Richardson et al. (eds.), *The Interplay of Phonology, Morphology and Syntax.* Chicago Linguistic Society.

Klavans, J. L. 1985. "The Independence of Syntax and Phonology in Cliticization." *Language* 61, 95-120.

Leben, W. 1973. *Suprasegmental Phonology.* Doctoral dissertation, Massachusetts Institute of Technology. Published in 1979 by Garland Press.

Leben, W. 1978. "The Representation of Tone." In V. Fromkin (ed.), *Tone: a Lingustic Survey.* New York: Academic Press.

Leben, W. 1980. "A Metrical Analysis of Weight." *Linguistic Inquiry* 11, 497-509.

Liberman, M. and A. Prince. 1977. "On Stress and Linguistic Rhythm." *Linguistic Inquiry* 8, 249-336.

Lieber, R. 1980. *On the Organization of the Lexicon.* Doctoral dissertation, Massachusetts Institute of Technology. Distributed by the Indiana University Linguistics Club.

Liu, Feng-hsi. 1980. "Mandarin Tone Sandhi: a Case of Interaction between Syntax and Phonology." Paper presented at the LSA summer meeting.

Mascaro, J. 1976. *Catalan Phonology and the Phonological Cycle*. Doctoral dissertation, Massachusetts Institute of Techonology. Distributed in 1978 by the Indiana University Linguistics Club.

McCarthy, J. 1979. *Formal Problems in Semitic Phonology and Morphology*. Doctoral dissertation, Massachuestts Institute of Technology. Distributed by the Indiana University Linguistics Club.

McCarthy, J. 1986. "OCP Effects: Gemination and Antigemination." *Linguistic Inquiry* 17, 207-263.

McCarthy, J. and A. Prince. 1986. "Prosodic Morphology." Unpublished manuscript, University of Massachusetts, Amherst and Brandeis University.

McCawley, J. 1968. *The Phonological Component of a Grammar of Japanese*. The Hague: Mouton.

McHugh, B. 1985. *Phrasal Tone Rules in Kirua (Vunjo) Chaga*. Master's thesis, University of California at Los Angeles.

McHugh, B. 1990 *Cyclicity in the Phrasal Phonology of Kivunjo Chaga*. Doctoral dissertation, University of California at Los Angeles.

Mohanan, K.P. 1982. *Lexical Phonology*. Doctoral dissertation, Massachusetts Institute of Technology. Distributed by the Indiana University Linguistics Club.

Mohanan, K.P. 1986. *The Theory of Lexical Phonology*. Dordrecht: Reidel.

Mohanan, K.P. and T. Mohanan. 1984. "Lexical Phonology of the Consonant System in Malayalam." *Linguistic Inquiry* 15, 575-602.

Mohanan, T. 1988. "Syllable Structure in Malayalam." Stanford University ms.

Mohanan, T. 1989. "Syllable Structure in Malayalam." *Linguistic Inquiry* 20:4, 589-626.

Moravcsik, E. 1977. *On Rules of Infixing*. Distributed by Indiana University Linguistics Club.

Myers, S. 1987. "Vowel Shortening in English." *Natural Language and Linguistic Theory* 5, 485-518.

Nanni, D. 1979. "Stressing Words in *-Ative*." *Linguistic Inquiry* 10, 753-781.

Napoli, D.J. and M. Nespor. 1979. "The syntax of word initial consonant gemination in Italian," *Language* 55, 812-841.

Neijt, A. 1984. "Clitics in Arboreal Phonology." In H van der Hulst and N. Smith (eds.), *Advances in Non-Linear Phonology*, 172-192. Dordrecht: Foris.

Nespor, M. 1984. "The Phonological Word in Italian." In H van der Hulst and N. Smith (eds.), *Advances in Non-Linear Phonology*, 193-204. Dordrecht: Foris.

Nespor, M. and I. Vogel. 1982. "Prosodic Domains of External Sandhi Rules." In H. van der Hulst and N. Smith (eds.), *The Structure of Phonological Representations (Part 1)*, 225-255. Dordrecht: Foris.

Nespor, M. and I. Vogel. 1986. *Prosodic Phonology*. Dordrecht: Foris.

Nevis, J. 1985. *Finnish Particle Clitics and General Clitic Theory*. Doctoral dissertation, The Ohio State University.

Newman, S. 1944. *The Yokuts Language of California*. The Viking Fund Publications in Anthropology: 2. New York.

Odden, D. 1987. "Kimatuumbi Phrasal Phonology." *Phonology Yearbook 4*, 13-36.

Odden, D. 1990. "Lexical Rules and Postlexical Rules in Kimatuumbi." In S. Inkelas and D. Zec (eds.), *The Phonology-Syntax Connection*. CSLI Publications and the University of Chicago Press.

Paulian, C. 1974. *Le Kukuya: langue teke du Congo*. Paris: S.E.L.A.F.

Pesetsky, D. 1979. "Russian Morphology and Lexical Theory." Unpublished manuscript, Massachusetts Institute of Technology.

Poser, W. 1984. *The Phonetics and Phonology of Tone and Intonation in Japanese*. Doctoral dissertation, Massachusetts Institute of Technology.

Poser, W. 1985a. "Cliticization to NP and Lexical Phonology." *Proceedings of the Fourth West Coast Conference on Formal Linguistics*, 218-229. Stanford Linguistics Association.

Poser, W. 1985b. "There is No Domain Size Parameter." (Abstract) *GLOW Newsletter* 14, 66-67.

Poser, W. 1986a. "Diyari Stress, Metrical Structure Assignment, and the Nature of Metrical Representation." *Proceedings of the Fifth West Coast Conference on Formal Linguistics*, 178-191. Stanford Linguistics Association.

Poser, W. 1986b. "Invisibility." *GLOW Newsletter* 16, 63-64.

Poser, W. 1988. "Features of Phonological Constituents are Features of Heads." Unpublished manuscript, Stanford University.

Poser, W. 1989. ". 1989. "The Metrical Foot in Diyari." *Phonology* 6:1, 117-148.

Poser, W. 1990a. "Evidence for Foot Structure in Japanese." *Language* 66:1, 78-105.

Poser, W. 1990b. "Word-Internal Phrase Boundary in Japanese." In S. Inkelas and D. Zec (eds.), *The Phonology-Syntax Connection*. CSLI Publications and the University of Chicago Press.

Prince, A. 1985. "Improving Tree Theory." Paper presented at the Berkeley Linguistics Society meeting.

Pulleyblank, D. 1983. *Tone in Lexical Phonology*. Doctoral dissertation, Massachusetts Institute of Technology.

Pulleyblank, D. 1986. *Tone in Lexical Phonology*. Reidel.

Pullum, G. and A. Zwicky. (forthcoming). *The Syntax-Phonology Interface*. Orlando: Academic Press.

Rice, K. 1990. "Predicting Postlexical Rule Domains." In S. Inkelas and D. Zec (eds.), *The Phonology-Syntax Connection*. CSLI Publications and the University of Chicago Press.

Rice, K. 1988. "Continuant Voicing in Slave (Northen Athapaskan): The Cyclic Application of Default Rules." In M. Hammond and M. Noonan (eds.), *Theoretical Morphology*, 371-388. San Diego: Academic Press.

Roca, I. 1986. "Secondary Stress and Metrical Rhythm." *Phonology Yearbook 3*, 341-370.

Roca, I. 1988. "Theoretical Implications of Spanish Word Stress." *Linguistic Inquiry* 19, 393-424.

Rotenberg, J. 1978. *The Syntax of Phonology*. Doctoral dissertation, Massachusetts Institute of Technology.

Rubach, J. 1984. *Cyclic and Lexical Phonology*. Dordrecht: Foris.

Rubach, J. and G. Booij. 1985. "A Grid Theory of Stress in Polish." *Lingua* 66, 281-319.

Rubach, J. and G. Booij. "Polish Syllable Structure in Lexical Phonology." Unpublished manuscript, University of Warsaw and Vrije Universiteit Amsterdam.

Selkirk, E. 1972. *The Phrase Phonology of English and French*. Doctoral dissertation, Massachusetts Institute of Technology.

Selkirk, E. 1974. "French Liaison and the X' Notation." *Linguistic Inquiry* 5, 573-590.

Selkirk, E. 1978. "On Prosodic Structure and its Relation to Syntactic Structure." Distributed by the Indiana University Linguistics Club. Published in 1980 in T. Fretheim (ed.), *Nordic Prosody II*. Trondheim: TAPIR.

Selkirk, E. 1980. "Prosodic Domains in Phonology: Sanskrit Revisited." In M. Aronoff (ed.), *Juncture*, 107-129. Saratoga: Anma Libri.

Selkirk, E. 1982. *The Syntax of Words*. Cambridge: MIT Press.

Selkirk, E. 1984. *Phonology and Syntax*. Cambridge: MIT Press.

Selkirk. E. 1986. "On Derived Domains in Sentence Phonology." *Phonology Yearbook* 3, 371-405.

Selkirk. E. and T. Shen. 1990. "Prosodic Domains in Shanghai Chinese." In S. Inkelas and D. Zec (eds.), *The Phonology-Syntax Connection*. CSLI Publications and the University of Chicago Press.

Shaw, P. 1976/1980. *Dakota Phonology and Morphology*. Doctoral dissertation, University of Toronto.

Shieber, S. 1986. *An Introduction to Unification-Based Approaches to Grammar*. CSLI Lecture Notes Series, no. 4. Stanford: CSLI Publications.

Siegel, D. 1974. *Topics in English Morphology*. Doctoral dissertation, Massachusetts Institute of Technology.

Sproat, R. 1985. *On Deriving the Lexicon*. Doctoral dissertation, Massachusetts Institute of Technology.

Sproat, R. 1986. "Malayalam Compounding: a Non-Stratum Ordered Account." *Proceedings of the Fifth West Coast Conference on Formal Linguistics*. Stanford Linguistics Association.

Stanley, R. 1967. "Redundancy Rules in Phonology." *Language* 43, 393-436.

Steriade, D. 1987. "Redundant Values." Unpublished manuscript, Massachusetts Institute of Technology.

Underhill, R. 1976. *Turkish Grammar*. Cambridge: MIT Press.

Vogel, I. and I. Kenesei. 1990. "Syntax and Semantics in Phonology." In S. Inkelas and D. Zec (eds.), *The Phonology-Syntax Connection*. CSLI Publications and the University of Chicago Press.

Wackernagel, J. 1892. Über ein Gesetz der indogermanischen Wortstellung. *Indogermanische Forschungen* 1, 33-436.

Warrier, T. 1976. *The Phonetics and Phonology of Malayalam and its Pedagogical Implications — A Generative Phonological Study*. Master's thesis, Central Institute of English and Foreign Languages, Hyderabad.

Yip, M. 1980. *The Tonal Phonology of Chinese*. Doctoral dissertation, Massachusetts Institute of Technology.

Zec, D. 1986. "Neki problemi vezani za razlikovanje klitika i afiksa." [Some problems related to distinguishing clitics and affixes.] Paper presented at *Slavisticki susreti u Vokove dane*, Belgrade, Yugoslavia.

Zec, D. 1987. "Interactions of Prosodic and Syntactic Constituency." Unpublished manuscript, Stanford University.

Zec, D. 1988a. "Bulgarian *schwa* Epenthesis: A Case for Moraic Structure." Proceedings of NELS 18, vol. 2. 553-566

Zec, D. 1988b. *Sonority Constraints on Prosodic Structure*. Doctoral dissertation, Stanford University.

Zec, D. and S. Inkelas. 1987 "Phonological Phrasing and the Reduction of Function Words." Paper presented at the LSA meeting, San Francisco.

Zec, D. and S. Inkelas. 1990. "Prosodically Constrained Syntax." In S. Inkelas and D. Zec (eds), *The Phonology-Syntax Connection*. CSLI Publications and the University of Chicago Press.

Zwicky, A. 1977. *On Clitics*. Distributed by the Indiana University Linguistics Club.

Zwicky, A. 1985. "Clitics and Particles." *Language* 61, 283-305.

Zwicky, A. and G. Pullum. 1983. "Cliticization vs. Inflection: English n't." *Language* 59, 502-513.

Zwicky, A. and G. Pullum. 1986. "The Principle of Phonology-Free Syntax: Introductory Remarks." *Ohio State University Working Papers in Linguistics* 32, 63-91.

For Product Safety Concerns and Information please contact our EU
representative GPSR@taylorandfrancis.com
Taylor & Francis Verlag GmbH, Kaufingerstraße 24, 80331 München, Germany

www.ingramcontent.com/pod-product-compliance
Lightning Source LLC
Chambersburg PA
CBHW050431240426

43661CB00055B/2348